# Introducing Practical Phonetics

# Ian R. A. MacKay, Ph.D.

Assistant Professor and Director
of the Phonetics Laboratory, Department
of Linguistics, University of Ottawa,
Ontario

# Introducing Practical Phonetics

Little, Brown and Company    Boston

For Mom and Dad
with Love

Library of Congress Catalog Card No. 78-52634

ISBN 0-316-54236-9

Printed in the United States of America

HAL

# Contents

# Part II  Basic Phonetics

# Preface

This book has been prepared for the student who will use the principles of phonetic science in some practical application. It is the result of my experience in teaching introductory phonetics to various groups of students whose main interest areas were speech pathology, deaf education, second-language teaching, and general linguistics. I believe it fills the need for a text that has no prerequisites other than general knowledge and that meets the goals of the "practical phonetician."

To this end, two principles have been incorporated into the conception of this book. The first is that theory is better accepted if a practical outcome is seen. Students of applied phonetics tend to be more practically oriented than students of linguistics, and their appreciation of the theoretical is enhanced by examples of practical applications. For this reason, the many introductory phonetics books written for the student of linguistics may not work well for the student of applied phonetics. To the student of speech pathology, for example, the matter of sentence intonation and its grammatical role in carrying meaning distinctions may remain a theoretical abstraction until that student realizes the problems created by inability to modulate the fundamental frequency (as in laryngectomees) or by inappropriate intonation (as in the second-language learner). Thus, this book focuses attention on the practical outcomes and implications of the theory it introduces. It mentions when the subject under discussion is susceptible to pathological or other aberrations, but no knowledge of speech pathology is presupposed; such references are merely interesting asides to the student specializing in another area.

The second principle is that a traditional theoretical framework is the most useful one for introducing this material to the practical phonetician. Some recent phonetics textbooks have been written within the generative theoretical framework and use a distinctive-feature matrix to classify speech sounds. However, an essential point to recognize in the distinctive-feature approach is that it tends to underemphasize the role that nondistinctive features play in the normal pronunciation of sounds. This presents no problems for phonological analysis (and indeed such a model captures generalizations that might otherwise be overlooked), but the applied (i.e., remedial or pedagogical) phonetician needs to be familiar with *all* articulatory features, distinctive as well as nondistinctive, in teaching these sounds. For example, the vowels /i/ and /ɪ/ may be distinguished in feature matrices by the feature "tenseness" (or the newer "advanced tongue root") alone, but to teach the natural-sounding pronunciation of these vowels, it is important to realize that they differ in tongue height, tongue advancement, lip posture, "tenseness" (actually, relative tongue-root position), and length. A system that satisfactorily captures phonological distinctiveness does not necessarily provide an adequate articulatory description for pedagogical or remedial ends.

The distinctive-feature approach, in conjunction with formalized rules, is very useful. The notion of rules is introduced early in this book, and features and formal rules are introduced in Part III, providing the student with the groundwork enabling him/her to read recent journal articles or take advanced courses in phonological analysis.

Chapter 4 has been included for a number of reasons. The background information is interesting to many, and it has been my experience that it helps to emphasize the separation between writing and speaking, a point missed by those students who speak of people pronouncing "letters." Also, it includes a discussion of the extent to which English spelling is alphabetic and of the reasons for differences among phonetic alphabets (a matter causing a disproportionate amount of anxiety in some students). Of course, this chapter will be of particular interest to students of linguistics and to those who intend to teach a second language to people whose first language uses a nonalphabetic writing system.

Whether or not one discusses acoustics in an introductory course depends upon many factors, including the duration of the course and the needs of the students. My experience is that the fundamentals of the acoustics of speech are useful to the applied phonetician. Further, I have found it best to discuss general acoustics first and the acoustics of vowels and consonants only after a discussion of their respective articulations. That is how this book has been set up. However, the organization is such that if the instructor decides not to discuss acoustics, or to order it differently, he may do so easily. Chapter 6 and the final sections of Chapters 7 and 8 (as well as 9) may be omitted; or, alternatively, the appropriate parts of Chapters 6, 7, and 8 may be considered together as a unit on "acoustic phonetics" after the articulations have been studied. Even if this material is not used in a first course, its inclusion allows the interested student to read in greater depth, which means that this book will remain useful to the student as he/she progresses to more advanced courses or to a course in experimental phonetics or speech science.

In general, an effort has been made to make this book complete. Certainly the instructor may find a discussion of some subjects that his students may not need. The numbered section headings make it easy for the instructor to list the topics his students are "responsible for."

I would be grateful for comments of any nature from any users of this book.

I. M.

# Acknowledgments

I owe a debt to a number of individuals who helped in various ways with the preparation of this book. First of all, Dr. Joseph Agnello trusted me as his assistant to teach his introductory phonetics course, and thus it came to my attention that an introductory textbook meeting the specific needs of students in applied areas was needed. Second, one group of those students used an earlier draft of this book as a textbook and indicated to me in various ways the strengths and weaknesses of the draft version.

Dr. Agnello made constructive criticisms of the first draft, and Dr. Joseph Foster, Dr. Ernst Franke, Dr. Richard Kretschmer, and Dr. Douglas C. Walker all made useful comments on certain sections of the manuscript. Dr. Kretschmer suggested numerous additional examples of applications of the theory presented. Of course, I alone am responsible for any errors or omissions that may remain.

My thanks go to R. D. Fournier for help in producing the spectrograms, to Paul Mercier for the Chinese examples, to Louis Kelly for the classical references, to Lucie Gagnon and Gilles Morin for the graphics, and to Esther McDonald and Rhonda Miclash for their speedy and accurate typing of two stages of the manuscript. Sarah Boardman, my editor, earns my gratitude for her assistance and support of the project. And finally, I would like to thank Diane Faissler, copyediting supervisor, for her frequent counsel and competent handling of the peculiar demands of this project.

Of course, I owe an immeasurable debt to all my teachers and to the scholars who performed the research on which this book is based.

I. M.

# Part I

## Background

# Chapter 1

## Getting the Most out of Phonetics

Most students study phonetics because it is a required course in their program. Sadly, it is often not until much later that they come to realize how practical and how basic a knowledge of phonetics is to an understanding of both normal and pathological speech for speech pathologists, audiologists, deaf educators, second-language teachers, and linguists. Like the civil engineer who applies the principles of physics to bridge-building, the practitioners of each of these professions will apply the principles of phonetics (consciously or intuitively) in day-to-day practice. For this reason, we could refer to speech pathologists, deaf educators, and second-language teachers together as "practical phoneticians."

We can make our study of a subject harder than it needs to be by our preconceived expectations, our attitudes toward the subject, and the way we approach it. It is my hope that your preconceived ideas will be examined and adjusted as you learn more about phonetics. You will discover that the science of phonetics is the fascinating study of speech sounds and the ways in which human beings use these in communicating their otherwise unshared thoughts.

Books are written in different ways and make different demands on the student. The following points explain my point of view in writing this book and outline what this book will and will not do. Understanding them will help to make your study as interesting, painless, efficient, and profitable as possible.

1. This book has been prepared particularly for the beginning student of phonetics who will use this knowledge of phonetics in the practice of another field, hence the term *practical* in the title. There exist at the present time many good books on phonetics. This one is unique in being an introduction to phonetics (demanding no previous exposure to the field) that gives the student a feeling for the practical applications through the use of examples taken from speech pathology, special education (e.g., teaching speech to the

deaf, teaching speech to children with learning disabilities), and second-language teaching. The practical examples are intended to point out the relevance of this material within these professions and to start the student thinking about ways in which the theory can be applied. They are not intended as a guide to therapy or pedagogical technique; that will come in other, more specialized courses. While every effort has been made to indicate the relevance of phonetics within these practical fields, there will doubtless be some material whose immediate practical value is not clear. It helps if one realizes that even competent graduate students and practicing clinicians encounter new situations that send them back to a review of basic phonetic concepts; they must be ever ready to apply their knowledge of phonetics in new and original ways.

2. The student of general or theoretical linguistics—and other readers not preparing to enter applied fields—can be reassured that this book does not presuppose any knowledge of speech or language pathology and that the examples are designed to be understood by persons without such knowledge. The student of linguistics may wish for a greater number of foreign-language examples than have been given and would probably like to see a fuller discussion of the functional aspects of phonetic units. However, the material in this book, along with the transcription practice, should provide the background necessary to go on to a study of phonology. The linguistics student or the general reader should not shun the examples from speech dysfunctions that are given. Speech and language pathologists realize that in order to understand deviant speech they must study normal speech; serious linguists now are giving their attention to deviant speech. Language is a system, and the ways in which a system breaks down tell us much about how it functions normally.

3. The student will find exercises in transcription in the Appendix. **Transcription** refers to writing speech in a special alphabet that records sounds more consistently than our English alphabet does. Learning to use this alphabet is an essential part of learning phonetics. The teacher may use his/her own materials or a programmed manual—with or without tapes—to supplement the exercises provided. Either way, considerable practice is invaluable; good transcription skills are as essential to the student of phonetics as typing is to a secretary. The earlier chapters of this text do not use special phonetic symbols; they are introduced in later chapters. It is expected that the student will be practicing transcription while studying this volume. Some facility with transcription before beginning this book would be helpful but is by no means necessary. However, transcription practice cannot be left entirely until after the theory has been studied. As in other fields, the theoretical and practical go hand in hand.

4. It is important to realize that transcriptions are idealized. Even skilled phoneticians consistently leave out acoustic detail and record what does not exist acoustically. This is a result of linguistic bias, a built-in inaccuracy in our phonetic transcriptions that can be minimized but not avoided entirely. Your practice in transcription should eliminate the more obvious errors in your recording of your native language, but it must be realized that nobody's transcriptions are ever perfect representations of spoken language. Rather, we agree on conventional ways of transcribing certain sounds, and by following these conventions we can be understood by others. (For example, one might want to argue about whether the word <u>fence</u> has a t-sound following the

<u>n</u>. The argument could go on indefinitely, so we simply agree that we will transcribe <u>fence</u> with a t-sound and expect that the convention will be followed.) Sometimes educated—and sometimes arbitrary—decisions must be made so that there is a consistent way of transcribing words. In the end we must realize that transcription is a skill but by no means a hard science.

In addition, there are annoying differences among the transcription systems suggested by various teachers and in certain books. Generally, the differences are minor and should not cause undue problems for the student. One system had to be chosen for this book, but others are mentioned in passing, to prepare the student for such variations. The particular system chosen is not as important as consistency in its use.

5. Phonetics is more than transcription alone, although many students feel that transcription is all there is to phonetics. Phonetics is more than that; it is the science of speech sounds. Speech pathologists, teachers of the deaf, and second-language teachers—practical phoneticians—are in the business of correcting speech. An understanding of the principles governing the phonetics of normally spoken English and phonetics in general is essential to the correction of communication disorders. The aberrations of any system can be dealt with more easily when the normal functions of the system are understood. Speech is no exception. In this book an attempt is made to clarify phonetic principles and provide practice in transcription. The practicing practical phonetician uses both the concepts and the transcription skills in the execution of his professional responsibilities. You would not be a musician just because you knew musical notation and could play scales on a piano; similarly, there is more to practical phonetics than transcription.

6. In phonetic science there are quite a number of terms, and they are not used consistently; one term may have several meanings, or several terms may have the same meaning. For example, in this book we will use the term **voiceless,** but in a text on speech pathology the author may use the term **surd** to mean exactly the same thing. On the other hand, the terms **close** and **closed,** both used in phonetics, have quite different meanings. In an introductory book, there are always two conflicting purposes. The student who is new to a field should not be burdened with so much new terminology that he feels he is doing nothing but memorizing terms. Yet, if such a book introduces too few terms, the student may be held back from reading other, more advanced books that assume a familiarity with the basics. So a compromise is made here. The new vocabulary is held to a minimum, and is of two types: those words that the student should be able to use with facility and those that he should recognize in other books. Frequently throughout this book new terms are introduced with a note that the concept is more important than the term or that the term is given in case the student runs across it in his other reading.

One word of caution: Very often the technical terms used in phonetics are common, everyday words used in a special sense. The word may have a general meaning in the common language but a very specific meaning when used by phoneticians. The word **vowel** for example, has a more restricted meaning for the phonetician than for the nonspecialist. It is important to distinguish the technical sense from the everyday sense and not to interchange them.

7. Phonetics deals with speech **sounds.** When an example is given,

pronounce it **out loud.** Listen to yourself as you pronounce the examples, and train yourself to be a critical listener of others as well as yourself. Each of us has a linguistic bias: conceptions about how we pronounce words and conceptions about how we *should* pronounce them. In Chapter 3, there are a few examples designed to show that conceptions about how words are pronounced are often inaccurate.

Also, words pronounced in isolation when you are self-conscious about pronunciation are very different from the same word pronounced in the context of a conversation when you are not thinking about your pronunciation. Without special training, we are very poor informants about how to pronounce English. Since being self-conscious affects pronunciation, we should practice catching ourselves unawares and listening to ourselves speaking in a relaxed and natural situation. Remember that first impressions about pronunciations are likely to be inaccurate.

Not only should you listen to yourself and others talk, you should watch and *examine* the act of speaking as well. With a small mirror, examine the movements of your articulators (mouth, lips, tongue). The tongue position for vowel pronunciation can be appreciated by probing with a tongue depressor or other clean, safe object, while pronouncing the sound in question. You will learn a great deal about articulatory phonetics through an examination of your own speech mechanism and how you use it.

8. There is always great variation in the pronunciation of languages, and this is true for English. In Chapter 2 we discuss dialects in some detail, but here suffice it to say that it is a normal circumstance that different people pronounce words and sentences differently. For the examples in the book, one pronunciation was chosen. This is not to say that it is the correct or best pronunciation; one was chosen simply because it is impossible to represent all pronunciations in use throughout the English-speaking world. You are not expected to start pronouncing words as they are represented in the examples (when they differ from your own pronunciation). The examples illustrate a point; they represent speech as it is used in at least some parts of English-speaking North America. If an example differs from your own pronunciation, that does not make the point illustrated invalid; the principle being illustrated is still an important principle. The examples are illustrative only; they are not ends in themselves. Do not allow yourself to be distracted from the concepts of phonetic theory by examples that are not characteristic of your own speech.

9. Many students who need phonetics for practical applications object to, or are unnecessarily confused by, foreign-language examples. These foreign examples are kept to a minimum in this book, but they cannot be entirely avoided in an introduction to phonetics. There are several reasons for this. We tend to react to examples in our own language with comments such as, ''Of course that's the way it is.'' It is hard to realize that the phonetic system of English is not the only possible phonetic system, so English examples sometimes lose their power to illustrate a principle. Also, one phonetic feature, such as pitch of the voice, can be used in different ways in different languages, and as a result there may be no English example. People with various communication disorders may use a phonetic feature differently from other speakers of English, so the foreign examples are used to free you from the bias of thinking in the English system exclusively. Another reason for foreign-language exam-

ples is that sometimes speech pathologists are called upon to correct foreign accents in speaking English, and so an understanding of the **systematic** ways in which foreigners can be expected to make errors in English is necessary. These errors are not random, idiosyncratic errors; they follow a pattern consistent with the phonetic system of the individual's native language. A few foreign examples at this stage should help you to deal with this problem when it arises. Of course, this information is essential to the second-language teacher as well.

When you come across a foreign-language example, do not skim over it and assume it is beyond your understanding. These examples are basic and straightforward, and they are taken chiefly from the Western languages that are most commonly studied in school: Spanish, French, and German. A few examples are taken from less familiar languages, but they need not intimidate you when you realize that it is not necessary to speak or understand a language in order to understand an example from that language. (I give a few examples from Chinese, yet I cannot speak or understand Chinese. Knowing something *about* a language is not the same as being able to speak it.)

In this book you will find the phrase "in English" used repeatedly. This is to remind you that the principle being discussed is true for standard English only. The situation may be quite different in a foreign language, in another dialect of English, in a foreigner's way of speaking English, or in the speech of someone with a communication disorder.

10. Students of phonetics sometimes question the value of being asked to practice pronunciation, auditory discrimination, and transcription of sounds from foreign languages. Actually, such exercises as these are used to develop skills that are essential to the student of phonetics and to the professional who uses phonetic principles. Sounds produced by those with pathological conditions of speech are not standard English sounds; otherwise they would not call attention to themselves. It is obviously not very enlightening to say that an individual "talks funny." Successful speech improvement depends in part upon the pathologist's or teacher's ability to identify the particular sound that is being produced. Correct identification of nonnormal sounds can be greatly aided by the ability to produce these sounds. Practice in pronouncing foreign sounds will help you achieve this end.

Another reason for practicing the pronunciation of foreign sounds is that it forces the pathologist or teacher to gain voluntary control over his speech articulators. Often the practical phonetician will be teaching such voluntary control to others, and it will be useful to you to have made such an effort yourself with sounds that are as hard for you as standard English sounds are for others. For example, learning to pronounce the nasalized vowels of French will give you voluntary control over your velum. When you attempt to train a person who does not control his velum well (say, someone with a reconstructed palate or a deaf speaker), your own previous experience at conscious control may prove useful. One speech sound of the Welsh language (the voiceless fricative ḻ) is very similar to a certain type of lisp (the bilateral lisp); familiarity with such a "foreign" sound as this is useful to the practical phonetician. In general, speech pathologists and language teachers will train others to control their speech mechanism consciously to produce sounds not previously within their repertoire; thus their phonetic training should include the production of sounds that are foreign to them.

11. It is also beneficial to have practice pronouncing, discriminating, and transcribing dialects of English other than your own. Besides all of the reasons brought out under point 10 above, there is an additional reason for having familiarity with other dialects of English: clients coming to speech pathologists will not always speak the same dialect as the pathologist. For example, there is great variation among English dialects in the pronunciation of syllables that end with an r-sound. Serious problems might result if the pathologist, ignorant of dialect differences, diagnosed a perfectly acceptable dialect feature as a pathological condition and tried to correct it. A child might even come out of therapy speaking in a way that was unacceptable to his peers. So if your phonetics teacher asks you to transcribe English that is different from your own, he/she is attempting to develop two necessary skills: good auditory discrimination and transcription ability and a familiarity with dialect variations.

12. Some sections of the book and some topics covered are more basic than others. The instructor may want to make certain sections optional or may give some sections as background reading without demanding detailed study. The instructor will make these decisions according to the needs of his/her students and the duration of the course. The more advanced material—even if it is not treated in detail in your first course—is included in the hope that this book will continue to be a useful resource as you take other courses, and even in your professional life after your academic training is completed.

# Chapter 2

# Speech, Language, and Dialect

## 2-1 Speech

Human beings communicate with one another primarily by speech, and speech brings human beings closer together than one might imagine. Speech sounds travel through the air at a rate of about 1,100 feet per second. By contrast, impulses travel along nerve pathways in the body at a rate of less than 200 feet per second. As a result, the time it takes for a spoken word to be heard and understood by a listener may be shorter than the time it takes for a neural message to travel from the toe to the brain. In this sense, speech brings a person closer to the mind of another than he is to parts of his own body!

In terms of biological evolution, the development of vocalizations (animal cries, the precursor to speech) was a great advancement. Vocalizations are a particularly efficient means of transmitting information. Very little energy is required to produce sounds that carry quite a distance. Sounds can be heard around obstacles and are unaffected by light or weather. The hearing apparatus can respond to a wide range of intensities and frequencies and to minute amounts of energy. For example, a 15-watt light bulb is rather dim, but a 15-watt amplifier, using the same amount of energy, will produce a very loud sound, as any stereo enthusiast knows.

In human evolution, animal cries have given way to speech as intellectual development made language possible. The greater complexity of the sound signal has meant that we have lost some range of transmission as compared to some lower animals, but this is counterbalanced by the greater flexibility in meanings that we can express. In short, it is hard to imagine biological evolution having arrived at a more efficient signal system.

Human beings communicate primarily by means of speech. Writing is also important to us, particularly in contributing to the advance of civilized cultures. However, our own society is unusual in the stress it places on writing and literacy. Often, our ideas about correctness in speech come from the written form, as we shall see in Chapter 3.

9

For most of the time that man has been on this earth, writing was unknown. Only in very recent years have large populations been able to read and write. Many countries still have a high rate of illiteracy, and, surprisingly, even now only one country in the world, Iceland, claims 100% literacy among its normal adult population. In the world today, there are as many as 5,000 languages spoken, but only a few hundred have literate speakers or even a writing system.

Plainly, writing is not our primary or our most natural means of communication. Still, writing and the relationship between speech and writing are interesting topics. Chapter 4 will briefly examine systems for writing down the spoken word. The interested student may go on to study the difficulties some children have in learning to read and write.

A casual examination of our own habits tells us a great deal about the relative roles of speech and writing. Most people find writing quite difficult, even a short term paper or a short letter. Few of us, though, are often at a loss for words. That letter home that did not get beyond the first paragraph turns into a long telephone conversation. Talking comes naturally to us, and our thoughts are expressed more easily and more clearly in speech than in writing.

Not only is speech a more natural way of expressing thoughts than writing, it is also the chief means by which information is received from others. For example, current events: how much knowledge comes from hearing reports on the radio and television and through discussion with others? How much comes through reading newspapers and newsmagazines? For most, the comparison is quite one-sided, for this as well as other topics, and in addition to radio, television, and conversation, we are "spoken to" through records, tapes, videotapes, and public address systems in homes, cars, offices, places of work, elevators, and elsewhere. Few people are ever very far from the voice of another human being.

Speech is often easier to understand than the written word, and speech and writing may complement one another. In university courses, one listens to lectures and reads textbooks. The lectures, ideally, are intended to help in understanding the textbook, as well as complementing the material found in it. It is a common experience to discover that after you have heard an author speak on a topic, his books or articles are easier to read. In short, speech is the primary means of communication, whether for art or commerce, education or entertainment.

The extreme importance of speech means that the individual who is handicapped in speech is at a great disadvantage in society. Speech is taken for granted to such a degree by most people that there is a tendency to treat verbally handicapped people as if they were, at best, a little stupid, and at worst, freaks. This is prejudice of the worst and most unwarranted kind, of course, but it exists. Each person can do his best to fight prejudice in himself and others, but the speech pathologist, teacher of the deaf, and second-language teacher can take more constructive measures: he/she can attempt to bring deviant speech up to the standard of the general population.

There are many varied approaches to the topic of speech. The linguist takes the point of view that speech is the most basic way that a person's knowledge of language is **realized,** or manifested; he proceeds to analyze what is systematic about language. The next section deals briefly with this approach.

The phonetician analyzes the sounds that make up speech; most of this book is devoted to such an analysis.

## 2-2 Language

Speech is made up of speech sounds, and this book will consider those speech sounds and the principles governing them. However, it is important not to forget that speech is only one aspect of language. If that seems an obvious remark, let us stop and think about what that means. What is language? It is easy to think of instances of languages; there are English, French, Spanish, German, Blackfoot, and Basque, for example, but what is **language,** the quality common to all those languages named, and several thousand others besides?

Asked what language is, most of us will reply that it is a means by which we can express our thoughts, ideas, and feelings. But if you consider this definition carefully, you will find it does not explain very much.

In fact, we will not attempt to define language. Rather, we will give a few statements about language that might be part of a definition. One of the most important and fundamental aspects to consider in trying to define language is that an analysis of language reveals the presence of a **system.** This system influences linguistic structure, that is, the way we form sentences and the way we form words from smaller meaningful units (the addition of plurals, prefixes, and suffixes), and it influences the way human beings learn their own native language at their mother's knee.

Linguists call their statements of the workings of this system **rules,** and they go on to demonstrate to us that our knowledge of our native language is governed by these rules, which are internal. These **rules** are not like the rules learned in elementary school, admonitions such as "Don't say ain't." They are not rules that one is usually conscious of; they are internal and unknown. They are rules such as the one that governs the way word order is changed in certain types of questions or the one that tells the speaker to add the word do to most negative sentences. You do not have to stop and consciously think about why you add the word "do" when you give the negative of the sentence "I like cheese" as "I do not like cheese." But there is an internal (mental) rule that tells you to construct the sentence that way. There are thousands of such rules that form your every sentence. Taken together, these rules are everything you know about your native language. The sum total of these rules is called a **grammar** by linguists. This is not the same kind of grammar you may have thought of as a dull subject you studied in school. It is the grammar (or knowledge) of English that you have in your head, made up of many individual rules that tell you how to form the plural, how to form the past tense, what individual words mean, and how they all fit together to form sentences.

In this sense, grammar is like gravity; it simply *exists.* It exists in the head of all people who can speak any language, whether they have studied it formally or not. Grammar existed long before there were grammarians. The "rules" of grammar, as we are using the term, are like the "laws" of gravity discovered by physicists. Laws of physics simply state what gravity has always done (and what gravity will continue to do whether or not anyone is interested in analyzing it). Thus, these grammar rules are purely **descriptive.** But the term grammar often suggests another type of rule: the grammarian's edict or the schoolteacher's admonition mentioned above ("Don't say <u>ain't</u>"). Such rules are termed **prescriptive,** since they tell one what he **should** do (of course, there is no analogy to the prescriptive rule in physics; no physicist tells gravity what it ought to do!). The prescriptive sense of the term grammar rule is not used in this book.

Any individual who speaks a language has a grammar—that is, a set of rules—in his head that is infinitely more complex and detailed than the written grammar found in any book. (Probably the most complete written grammar of English is that written by Otto Jespersen [1949], a Dane. It fills seven volumes, yet it is far from complete.)

There are a number of kinds of evidence that this highly complex unconscious internal grammar exists. First, there is an infinite number of different English sentences. Throughout your life you produce, read, and hear millions of sentences, almost none of them ever used before or again, yet you understand them. If language were not systematic and rule-governed, there would be no way of explaining this fantastic ability to create and comprehend millions of novel sentences.

A second kind of evidence for the existence of rules is that they come to our conscious attention when we study a foreign language. When we try to talk or write in a foreign language, we realize just how complicated a simple sentence is. Of course, an English sentence is no less complicated than a French or a Spanish sentence; it is just that the rules of the English sentence are unconscious to us. For example, you will agree that the sentence "I have five big round red rubber balls" is a good English sentence while "I have big red five rubber round balls" is not. Though there are one hundred twenty different possible sequences of the five adjectives, only one way strikes us as being correct. (Try the other one hundred nineteen sequences to convince yourself.) When an English noun is preceded by more than one adjective, a very complex set of rules determines their order. This poses serious problems to the foreigner learning English, but the native speaker never needs to think about it at all when he speaks or writes. To him, the rules are internal and he is not conscious of them. To the person learning a second language, the rules are explicit and conscious, and for this reason they seem complex and difficult.

One's internal grammar also includes rules of phonetics (pronunciation). For example, your grammar tells how to pronounce a t-sound, how much variation is permissible in pronouncing it, and how speakers of other dialects might be expected to pronounce it. A rule of your grammar also tells you that t-sounds contrast with d-sounds. Another group of rules tells you how to interpret meaning from intonation patterns, and so on.

In fact, though you probably have not studied it formally, *you have a highly sophisticated knowledge of the rules of English phonetics in your head.* You learned about English phonetics as a child, when you learned most of the rest of your English grammar (any grammar course you may have taken subsequently is only the frosting on the cake—most of what we learned of the grammar of our native language was learned before we set foot in a schoolroom). We will look formally at various aspects of English phonetics throughout this book; in the process, we will be making some of your unconscious knowledge of English phonetics conscious. You will probably be surprised at the complexity of your unconscious knowledge.

The exact nature of the rules in an individual's grammar depend on his native language, naturally enough, but also on the regional variant (dialect) he speaks, and there is even some variation from person to person. It is certainly true that some individuals with a speech or language dysfunction have a rule-system that is significantly different from that of the rest of us.

In this sense, "ungrammatical" speech or language does not exist (at least, it is extremely rare). If a person speaks a particular regional or social dialect in which it is normal to say "I ain't got none" and "You shoulda saw it," it cannot be said that this person speaks ungrammatically. His double negative or nonstandard past participle represent regular, systematic usages in his speech; they are not idiosyncratic errors. His speech follows rules just as the prescribed standard language does; his rules differ in some specific details, accounting for the differences between his speech and standard speech. But while this individual's speech may be different from the norm, it is regular and rule-governed, and thus can be described by a grammar; it is therefore grammatical. When someone's speech or written language differs from the norm, we tend to say that his speech is "ungrammatical"; but it *does not lack grammatical structure*, its grammatical structure just differs from the prescribed norm or standard. (However, as Chapter 3 will emphasize, there is good reason to be prescriptive and to attempt to conform to the standard.)

This way of viewing language—deviant as well as standard—as a rule-governed phenomenon is not just a theoretical abstraction that is useful only to linguists. It has very real practical benefits to the person practicing language or speech remediation. This kind of approach is useful both in analyzing the individual's problem area and in planning a program of therapy. Of course, the foregoing remarks apply equally to second-language teaching. This is an area not to be underestimated, since most speech therapists are called upon from time to time to help with the correction of foreign accents. The same approach to analyzing the individual's speech can be made with the foreign speaker, though of course the pathologist is less likely to be on the lookout for organic disorders when dealing with foreign accents.

The job of the practical phonetician is twofold. First he/she has to analyze the rule-system (or grammar) of his client or student: how is that individual's rule-system the same as that of standard English? how is it different? in other words, which specific rules are deviant? Then one must plan a remedial program tailored to the specific aspects of the individual's deviant grammar. How does his/her speech differ from the norm? Precisely what are the differences? What consistency is there to his/her errors? Is it possible that three or four seemingly unrelated errors are the product of one rule that is deviant? Answers to these questions bring one closer to a strategy for improving the individual's speech.

## 2-2.1 Speech and Language

The word **language** is normally used to describe a particular symbolic system used by a people, as in the English language or in the Spanish language. In the preceding section, we emphasized the more abstract meaning: language is a systematic way of relating symbols to things or concepts symbolized, and such a system is common to all the peoples in the world. We noted that a particular language (such as English) can be described by a grammar, which is made up of a set of rules. These rules make explicit every aspect of a language, including the syntax (the way words go together to form sentences), the morphology (the way words are formed), the semantics (meaning), and the phonetics. However, just as a map is not the territory but only a representation of it, a set of rules is no more than an attempt to represent the grammar of a particular language.

All human beings have in their heads a grammar of their native language, which they learned unconsciously and naturally as children. When they speak, they are putting that knowledge of grammar to work and are producing English sentences. This is the sense in which we stated that speech is a **realization** of language. To **realize** can mean 'to make real' or 'to manifest,' and when we speak, we are making real our knowledge of English. Language can be realized in other ways. At the moment, in creating English sentences with a pencil and paper, I am realizing language in writing. A deaf person may use gestural **signs** to realize his internal knowledge of language (though in a culture having no writing or gestural system, the deaf may not develop any knowledge of language).

So, while every language may be realized in **speech,** many are realized in no other way. All languages are first and foremost spoken; that they may be written is a secondary fact. You may think of the example of computer "languages," which are written but not spoken. However, these are not languages in the same sense as human languages; they are more akin to codes. When we talk of computer languages, we are speaking in metaphor. In the same way, we may speak metaphorically about the language of the birds, though we know that their communication systems bear very little resemblance to human language.

In summary, speech and language are not synonymous. Speech is the most basic way that we realize language. We cannot study language by opening up the head and looking in, so our understanding of language must come from its overt realizations, namely, speech and writing. We study these overt human productions in order to gain an understanding of the grammar of particular languages and an understanding of language in the more abstract sense.

## 2-3  Dialect

The word **dialect** is often misused and abused, so we will make a brief attempt to clarify the concept. To many, the word is emotionally loaded, having strong positive or negative connotations. However, those of us who deal professionally with language—normal or deviant, from a clinical or pedagogical point of view—must have a more comprehensive and objective understanding of the concept of dialect.

All languages that are spoken on a daily basis by a group of people change over time. **Speech community** is a loose term for a group of people speaking the same language. In one sense, the whole English-speaking world is one community; in another sense, the upper and lower classes in the same city may really be separate speech communities if there is little verbal interaction between them. No living language resists change (though some languages change more rapidly than others). If you were shown a document written in

Old English of a thousand years ago, it is unlikely that you would recognize it as English, much less be able to read even a single word.

So-called dead languages do not show the same pattern of change, since they are no longer anyone's native language. As soon as there is no one growing up speaking a language, that language becomes "dead." Usually such a language simply disappears, especially if there are no written records. If there are written records, or some religious or ritualistic reason for preserving the language, it may remain unchanged for many years. Latin has been preserved in this manner, mainly through the influence of the Roman Catholic Church and the abundance of written records.

A living language continues to change. Vulgar Latin, the everyday language of the Roman people, was taken throughout Europe during Roman conquests (classical Latin was a somewhat artificial creation used as the language of scholarship and oratory). Vulgar Latin developed through slow change into such modern languages as French, Spanish, Portuguese, Italian, and Romanian. Note the divergent direction of language change: Roman troops took virtually the same language to Spain and France, but because of the subsequent isolation of the groups, modern Spanish and French are not mutually intelligible; that is, speakers of Spanish and French cannot understand each other.

The force producing language change is an irresistible one, as has been shown, but it is influenced by various social factors. Periods of great social change and the mixing of cultural groups lead to faster language change (as in Britain during the past thousand years). Social stability and isolation lead to slower language change (as in Iceland during the same period; a modern schoolchild in Iceland can read a thousand-year-old document with little difficulty). The migration of a group of people to a new location leads to greater language change in the group that moved than in the one that stayed home, though either group may preserve words or expressions no longer used by the other.

The English language was brought to North America from England by people who initially spoke like those who stayed behind. In other words, the English of England and the English of North America were very similar 250 years ago. But all of us are aware that today North Americans do not speak the same as the British. To give a few examples, the word whilst was used at one time in both North America and Britain. The British continue to use the word whilst but North Americans do not. The word lieutenant was once pronounced "left-tenant" on both sides of the Atlantic; George Washington would have referred to his officers this way. This pronunciation continues to be current in Britain and Canada but has changed in the United States. The vocabulary of the automobile is not the same in Britain as in North America because the automobile was invented after the separation of the two speech communities. (Lorry corresponds to truck, boot to trunk, wing to fender, fascia to dashboard, and so on.)

In fact, the speech habits of *both* speech communities have changed over the years since the British colonized the North American continent. But the direction of change has been somewhat divergent, and the rate of change has varied. For the most part, mutual intelligibility is retained, so we speak of dialects of the English language.

A **dialect** is an identifiable variant of a language, and *every* identifiable form is called a dialect. Dialects vary in vocabulary, pronunciation, and syntax. Of course, in this book we are interested primarily in the phonetic differences, which include the pronunciation of individual sounds, the intonation, and the stress.

Languages differ from one another in the same ways as dialects do. It is a matter of degree, and sometimes of politics, whether we talk of dialects or languages. For example, Danish is mutually intelligible with Norwegian. But the two are called different languages for political reasons. By contrast, the so-called dialects of Chinese are not mutually intelligible in many cases; in fact, some of these "dialects" are no more similar to one another than English is to German. (There is, however, one common writing system for all dialects of Chinese. Chinese who speak different dialects are known to use pencil and paper, or to "write" characters in the air with their finger, to aid their conversations.)

The separation leading to the creation and perpetuation of dialect differences may result from a number of causes. Geographical separation is the most obvious factor creating dialect differences, which may ultimately become language differences. Economics can keep people apart: wealthy people may only talk to other wealthy people, poor people to other poor people. In countries where class barriers exist, such barriers are another reason for keeping speech communities separate despite geographical proximity. People in the same vocation or milieu tend to stay together and to develop particular means of expression; for example, the argot (slang) of the underworld is often difficult for the rest of us to understand. Groups stay separate for many reasons, and these groups may be identified by such diverse criteria as age, race, or ethnic background. Even religion can keep groups isolated from one another.

As a child learns his native language in his parents' home and with his playmates, he is acquiring the rule-system of the grammar of the language he hears. Any child of normal intelligence develops a rule-system almost identical to that of his parents and peers; his development of language is determined by the language spoken around him. Thus, a child acquires the dialect of those with whom he interacts; racial and ethnic differences in dialect are determined not because the infant belongs biologically to such and such a race but because, being of normal intelligence, he performs a uniquely human achievement: he learns exactly the form of language spoken around him.

A common misunderstanding with respect to dialects is the belief that the word **dialect** means a degenerate form of a language. There is often a strong emotional attachment to one's own form of expression. Such a feeling is understandable and is not bad in itself; however, the habit of using emotionally charged epithets, such as degenerate or snobbish, to characterize the dialects of others shows both pettiness and ignorance. Degenerate forms of languages do not exist, since all dialects serve their respective speakers' communicative needs equally well. Similarly, no dialect is intrinsically snobbish; a person cannot be accused of snobbishness simply for speaking the dialect he learned as a child (though it is true that pretentious use of a dialect other than one's own is a common affectation).

The term **dialect** is not reserved only for other people's mode of expression; *every* identifiable form of a language is a dialect. As a result, we may use the term very precisely or very loosely. For example, in discussing the

English-speaking world, we may want to identify very broad dialect categories: British English, Australian English, Scottish English, Canadian English, American English, and so on. In considering just the United States, the category American English is too broad, so we identify Northern, New England, Midwestern, and Southern dialects of American English. In considering New England, however, since there is not one homogeneous speech form but many, we must further subdivide into more restricted dialects. We may find characteristics peculiar to one city, such as Boston or New York, and even to particular neighborhoods. This process can go on ad infinitum. In the end, we realize that each individual has his own particular way of speaking, which we would call his **idiolect,** although this is usually not a very useful concept. What is important is to realize that the word *dialect* implies no judgment, that every form of a language is a dialect, and that the term may be used in a broad or a restricted sense. Keeping these facts in mind should reduce the misunderstandings often generated in discussions of dialects.

We have said that dialect differences arise because speech communities are separated from one another. But it is not correct to think that there was once a perfect and homogeneous English language that has somehow been divided up into dialects. One runs into the chicken and egg problem: which came first? Clearly, neither English nor any other language was ever completely homogeneous; all languages at all times have had variations.

So, for example, the English that was taken to the early British colonies was not a single form but many. Particular areas may have been settled by groups predominantly of one British dialect area, and this fact may explain some of the local character of the speech. A very clear case is Australia, which was originally a penal colony having a disproportionately large number of speakers of the Cockney dialect (a London working-class dialect). The present-day speech of Australia shows the results of this fact.

In summary, we have seen that dialects develop through normal language change and that the direction of this change is divergent when speech communities do not interact with one another. We have seen that dialect diversity is perpetuated by children learning faithfully and accurately the language of their parents and peers; we have further seen that dialect variation does not reflect the degeneration of an ideal that has been lost.

It *is,* however, true that some dialects are held in higher regard by the society than others, and society exerts a pressure toward conforming: finding a job or receiving some other reward from society may come only to those speaking a certain way. While any dialect is as good as any other from a linguistic or communicative point of view, this might not be so from the social point of view. It is clear that the pathologist or language teacher will have to make a choice from time to time as to which of several different forms to teach. When they differ, should you teach the form of *your* dialect, your client's dialect, or the "standard" dialect? This is an important issue, one you will certainly face. Your decision in these cases should be based on objective knowledge of the nature of dialects.

Students of phonetics should sensitize themselves to dialect variations; they may be asked to transcribe or pronounce distinctions not made in their own dialect. This is good practice, not only to develop a perception of speech sounds but to have a familiarity with dialect variation. More than once, children have had dialect features diagnosed as pathological conditions; the psychological effects of this upon the client could be serious.

## Questions for Discussion

1. In what ways other than speaking and writing do people communicate?
2. What advantages does speech have over writing as a means of communication? and vice versa?
3. What differences would you expect to find between your unconscious grammar of English and that of someone who cannot hear or speak but can read and write?
4. What problems with dialect do you expect the speech therapist, teacher of the deaf, or second-language teacher to run into?
5. What dialect features do you think might be diagnosed as errors?
6. What kinds of attitudes do you expect that verbally handicapped people (those with speech dysfunctions, the congenitally deaf, the foreigner) will have to face in society?

## Questions for Further Study

1. What are some nonvocal ways that animals communicate?
2. Psychologists have investigated the effects of a person's having no verbal interaction with others. Locate and report some of these findings.
3. How do linguists state their rules of grammar?
4. Describe in detail a dialect of English. How does it differ from standard English?
5. Speech was once the only form of language known to most people. In this century, the written word has been stressed. Now, some people believe that the written word is becoming less important as television takes over much of the burden of entertaining and even educating. Locate some of the arguments emphasizing the spoken word over the written word in the television age.

## Annotated Bibliography

For reading in greater depth on some of the topics brought up in this chapter, suggestions are made below under the appropriate topic headings; the bibliographies of these authors give additional sources. The complete reference information will be found in the References section at the end of the book.

Speech and Language

Two of the best introductions to the study of language and speech, written in the traditional structuralist style, go under the same title: *Language*. One is by Sapir [1949], the other by Bloomfield [1961]. The Sapir book emphasizes speech more than does the Bloomfield volume.

A more recent volume, which looks at language in the theoretical framework outlined in this chapter, is Fromkin and Rodman's *An Introduction to Language* [1974]. We will refer to this volume again under other topic headings. This volume is easier reading than most.

The anthology *Communication, Language, and Meaning*, edited by Miller [1973], gives a series of excellent articles on speech and language from the psychological viewpoint. Howell and Vetter's *Language in Behavior* [1976] is an examination of language from a social science viewpoint.

Langacker's *Language and Its Structure* [1968] and Wardhaugh's *Introduction to Linguistics* [1972] both provide an introduction to the way the linguist analyzes language.

## Animal "Languages"

The essential difference between human language and animal communication systems is a question with linguistic, philosophical, and theological implications. An overview of this question can be found in three of the above-named volumes: those by Langacker [1968], Miller [1973], and Fromkin and Rodman [1974].

Recently, the "linguistic" accomplishments of chimpanzees have gained considerable attention, partly because they challenge some of the linguist's differentiations between human and animal communications. Indeed, some linguists have revised their definition of language since the chimp experiments began. One book on this subject, describing several chimps' accomplishments and discussing the scientific, philosophical, and linguistic implications, is Linden's *Apes, Men and Language* [1976]. The book is written from a journalistic point of view, and many of the author's interpretations and conclusions in the linguistic, scientific, and philosophical domains may be disputed. However, it makes an interesting point of departure for a discussion of some of the issues. Some articles on this topic are: Brown [1972], Premack [1971], and Branowski and Bellugi [1970]. Allen and Underwood [1971] and Bau [1975] have written nontechnical articles discussing the linguistic accomplishments of several chimps; these have been published in popular magazines.

## Dialect

General discussions giving a good introduction to dialect may be found in the Sapir [1949], Bloomfield [1961], Langacker [1968], and Fromkin and Rodman [1974] books cited above. Most introductory books on the subject of language will discuss dialect.

The American dialect of English is described, and its origins examined, in Marckwardt's *American English* [1958] and Mencken's *The American Language* [1936].

An excellent anthology of articles concerning dialects of American English can be found in *Readings in American Dialectology*, edited by Allen and Underwood [1971]. *Americanisms*, edited by Mathews [1966], is a dictionary of words and expressions originating in the United States.

A thorough and nontechnical description of the Canadian dialect of English can be found in Orkin's *Speaking Canadian English* [1970].

## Language Acquisition

On the question of how children learn their native language, there is a vast number of recent articles and books. A concise introduction can be found in Fromkin and Rodman's *An Introduction to Language* [1974]. A very long and detailed study of language acquisition can be found in Brown's *A First Language: The Early Stages* [1973].

## Foreign Accents in English

Wise's *Applied Phonetics* [1957] describes in detail the ways in which speakers of several foreign languages can be expected to pronounce English. It may be a useful reference when correcting foreign accents. This volume also describes American and British dialects of English.

# Chapter 3

## Speech Training, Correctness, and Phonetics

### 3-1 Historical Perspectives of Speech Training

#### 3-1.1 Speech Pathology

Speech pathology as a separate profession has its background in two disciplines, elocution and clinical psychology. Elocutionists (or voice and diction teachers) aim their efforts mainly toward actors, announcers, public speakers, and others who want to improve their speaking and acting voices. Elocution training stresses clarity, projection, and protection of the voice. At one time, society was less tolerant of variations in speech, and one task of the elocution teacher was to eliminate regional or social dialect features from a person's speech. (This theme is treated excellently in George Bernard Shaw's play *Pygmalion*, which was adapted into the Broadway musical and Hollywood film *My Fair Lady*.) Although they were not properly trained for this task, elocutionists were further called upon to help those with various articulation and other speech problems, since there were no other professionals with speech training.

The psychologist trained in clinical techniques was called upon to provide therapy for individuals with speech dysfunctions when these were believed to be psychological in origin. The results were not always as satisfactory as one might wish, since in most cases the clinical psychologist's training did not include speech. (In fact, psychology, until relatively recently, ignored speech and language, whether normal or deviant. Even into the 1950s and 1960s, most ventures by psychologists into the realm of speech and language were rather naive. Recent works, however, have reversed this trend; psycholinguistics has become a serious field of scientific inquiry.)

In the mid-1920s a need was recognized for a profession to serve all disorders of speech. Thus, in the 1920s and 1930s academic training programs in speech pathology were begun. These early programs still showed a strong association with elocution, since they were situated in English departments or theater departments. By now, speech training for actors, announcers, and public speakers has tended to become specialized and separate, as has the practice of speech pathology.

While speech pathology has broken away from the mold of elocution, some traditions have remained, as we shall see in the next section. While old associations have been broken, new ones have grown up. The modern speech pathologist calls upon the physician for consultation concerning organic sources of speech problems and upon the clinical psychologists when it is believed that serious psychological problems prevent successful symptomatic treatment of the disorder. The speech pathologist's training comes not only from other speech pathologists but from speech scientists, phoneticians, physiologists, linguists, educators, and others. Speech pathology is truly an interdisciplinary study.

## 3-1.2 Special Education

As with speech therapy, special education as a separate discipline grew out of other disciplines, and the modern schools of thought reflect this development. Education of those with learning disabilities, those with emotional disorders, and the mentally retarded grew out of the discipline of psychology, with its emphasis on the cognitive and affective domains of human performance. As a result, language as a separate entity has always been underplayed within special education. The content of messages has been stressed at the expense of the medium; thus, questions of linguistic importance have been ignored. Children with obvious cases of speech impairment have been referred to speech therapists, while little attention has been paid to other linguistic aberrations.

Education of the deaf grew out of the discipline of speech and hearing. Thus, the emphasis has traditionally been on audiological considerations and on communication skills (speech reading and signing); language has not been treated as a subject worthy of separate consideration. The teaching of speech to the deaf has emphasized an analytical rather than a synthetic approach; that is to say, speech has been reduced to individual sounds that it is believed can be recombined into sentences, but later chapters will show that normal-sounding speech is not merely the simple combination of individual speech sounds.

## 3-1.3 Second-language Teaching

Language teachers often have little or no training. Many second-language teachers have no more qualification than that they are native speakers of the language they are teaching. Others are qualified only by the fact of having studied the literature of a particular language and perhaps by having a teaching degree, but general courses in education often overlook the specific requirements of language teaching. Of course, the ability to speak a language more or less correctly does not necessarily mean that one is able to teach that language or its pronunciation (though some individuals with a natural flair succeed at this task without formal training).

The field of applied linguistics grew out of linguistics and education to answer the needs of those requiring training in second-language teaching as well as other applied areas. Most aspects of linguistic theory find practical application in language teaching, and the teaching of pronunciation, specifically, is aided by a study of phonetic theory.

This brief historical overview of speech therapy, special education, and second-language teaching is not intended to disparage but rather to point up some areas in which a new emphasis could pay practical dividends. This book stresses the view that an understanding of phonetic theory, as part of a greater linguistic system, can aid the speech pathologist, special educator, or language teacher in the execution of his/her professional duties.

## 3-2  Correctness

The pathologist or teacher of speech and language is a professional who corrects and trains others. Implicit in this statement is the assumption that the professional knows what is correct and what the goal of therapy is. Presumably he sets up a model of correctness in his head and aims at that model. It is well to ask ourselves *how* we know what is correct.

Standard notions of correctness in speech and language are based in part on outmoded beliefs, some of which can be traced to the roots of modern speech pathology in the disciplines of elocution, English, and theater. Grammarians have in the past tended to be extremely conservative and even didactic. They saw as their role not only describing language but deciding what was correct and even preventing the slow change that is the natural evolution of languages.[1] Grammarians have succeeded in greatly influencing the language because of their educational influence. For example, most of us have been taught in school to distinguish who and whom and have been reprimanded for using like where we should use as. In both these instances, the language changed to allow the formerly incorrect usages and the grammar books did not keep up with the change. In these cases, "correctness"—as stated in the grammar books—was determined by what was done in the past and in some cases by the arbitrary preferences of grammarians themselves.

Correctness is also influenced by the notion of a **standard dialect.** The normal diversity of regional and social dialects is not without its problems. For purposes of studying language, teaching language, and having a common literature, a choice must be made among a number of equally good dialects. For these reasons, the idea of a literary standard dialect has grown up. The dialect chosen is usually that of a region with social prestige, resulting from political and economic power. This is the dialect that is taught in schools and is most commonly found in print. Publishing houses and the educational system are the greatest forces preserving this dialect. The effect is that throughout the English-speaking world the written form of the language is much the same, though there is great variation in the spoken form.

---

[1] Linguists, by contrast, take a more objective approach in their study of language. Generally, they do not see their role as one of influencing languages but rather of describing and analyzing what they find, whether or not it agrees with their personal preferences. Of course, linguists are human and let their biases—linguistic and otherwise—show from time to time! (Bloomfield [1961] has some interesting observations on the rising influence of grammarians in his final chapter.)

Besides the literary standard, each country has a spoken standard dialect, which is generally maintained by educational systems and broadcasting networks. (One can often observe that radio and television announcers vary less in their speech habits from region to region than do their audiences.) The spoken standard may be closer to some regional dialects than to others. In the United States, the standard spoken dialect is nearest to the Midwestern dialect. In Britain, the standard dialect approximates a class dialect more than any regional one. And in Canada, spoken English varies little among the regions (with the notable exception of Newfoundland), and thus the standard is not markedly different from the speech habits of any speakers.

The standard dialect serves several useful functions in a diverse society. First, books are not limited in their audience; the same printed material can be read by speakers of various dialects. Second, the standard spoken dialect has a unifying effect; mutual intelligibility could be lost if the spoken forms were too divergent. Indeed, speakers of certain dialects in the United States cannot talk to one another easily; however, these individuals watch and understand the same television programs. A similar situation exists in Britain.

The written form of the language serves a different purpose from the spoken form. Greater precision and economy of words is possible in writing; in speech, gestures and tone of voice carry information that cannot be conveyed in writing. Since these forms are different, it is not useful to suggest that the written form be the model for correct speech, though many have promoted this notion.

These facts, taken as a whole, make one question traditional standards of correctness. Those standards are not necessarily to be rejected, or replaced by purely personal preferences, but one should know on whose authority decisions about correctness are made and decide whether or not that authority should be followed.

## 3-2.1 Spelling Pronunciations

One aspect of the appeal to correctness that deserves special mention is the belief that spelling provides the answer to questions of pronunciation. Simply stated, a **spelling pronunciation** is a pronunciation based on the spelling of a word. It may be a purely idiosyncratic or erroneous pronunciation, or it may be general and affect the standard pronunciation of a word after the passage of time.

If someone pronounced the final s of Arkansas, this would be a case of spelling pronunciation that was purely erroneous and unlikely to affect the name as pronounced by the residents. The Canadian province of Newfoundland is often mispronounced with the stress on found, immediately identifying the speaker as an outsider. The river Thames in England and in Canada is pronounced "temz" (/tɛmz/), but the river of the same name in the United States is pronounced as the word is spelled; the spelling pronunciation has displaced the original pronunciation there. The United States towns of Cairo and Lima are likewise pronounced according to their spelling.

Current North American pronunciations of ate (to rhyme with "fate") and often (with a "t") are spelling pronunciations which have become accepted and standard, as is the British pronunciation of lieutenant mentioned in Chapter 2 (apparently this resulted from the fact that the letters u and v used to be written alike).

Spelling pronunciations that are purely erroneous pose no particular problem; standard pronunciations can be verified in a reputable dictionary. Spelling pronunciations that have displaced earlier pronunciations, such as "ate" (no longer rhyming with "bet" in North America), similarly pose no problems, since the new pronunciations are standard and accepted. The matter does become problematical when a person (particularly the practical phonetician correcting the speech of others) uses the spelling of a word as the authority for pronunciation in the belief that the way a word is spelled indicates how it "should" be pronounced. This belief persists despite the obvious irregularities in English spelling. It has been suggested that this tendency, which is particularly strong in the United States, can be traced in part to the prescriptivist attitude of early grammarians and lexicographers (dictionary compilers) such as Noah Webster. Webster's "spelling" book—which contained advice on pronunciation and points of grammar—sold an incredible 40 million copies,[2] at a time when Americans were asserting their political and cultural independence and, as part of the effort to shake off the trappings of colonial status, looked to authorities on correctness in linguistic and other matters. This book undoubtedly had an important influence on the pronunciation of English in the United States.

As was pointed out in Chapter 2, language is constantly changing, and pronunciation changes along with other aspects of language. And since English spelling was mostly standardized at an early time, before certain important sound changes occurred, and was often preserved in the form preferred by certain individual printers, and since we often borrow foreign words in their original spellings, there is little reason to believe that spelling is a valid authority for pronunciation.

However, there are many people who believe that the word often should be pronounced with a t-sound because the word is spelled that way. They insist that the word either should, on the authority of the spelling, be pronounced with the vowel of "die" and not that of "see." Widespread U.S. pronunciations of such words as creek, roil, and sumach are judged to be improper for the same reason. Many also promote the careful distinction of pairs of words such as which and witch on the same grounds and insist that interest must be pronounced with three syllables. One may wonder just how we "ought" to pronounce lamb, hiccough, or colonel, if spelling is taken to be the authority![3]

[2] Laird [1970] has an interesting chapter on Webster, whom he calls "the preeminent cracker-barrel lexicographer." As Laird describes him, "[he] knew all the answers. More a hack of all intellectual trades than a scholar, he was passably schooled but not learned, not even in the subject for which he is now best known. He was intelligent, but he had neither wit nor profundity, and he probably never felt the lack of either quality. He was alert, devout, industrious, patriotic, persistent, public-spirited, conceited, and perverse. Ignorance never dampened his fire, nor did a sense of humor temper his finality" (p. 263). It is obvious that Webster had strong opinions about correctness, and since he wrote a best-selling schoolbook on pronunciation, it is apparent that some now-standard American pronunciations can be traced to his whims and preferences.

[3] The opposite tendency, to reform spelling to conform to pronunciation, is also strong. Much energy has been devoted to this question, just as a great deal of energy is spent on learning spellings judged correct, no matter how illogical. The student is encouraged to read further in this interesting topic, but it is beyond the scope of this book. We will, however, examine briefly in Chapter 4 the ways in which our spelling is not alphabetic.

Related to the matter of spelling pronunciations is the question of pronunciations that are judged or perceived to be "better" or "more correct" despite common custom to the contrary. We often find in North America certain teachers trying to impose the "broad a" in words such as <u>half</u> and <u>dance</u>, despite the overwhelming predominance of the "flat a" pronunciations of these words in North America. This misguided effort becomes truly ludicrous when this attempt at "correction" extends to words such as <u>hat</u>, which have the flat a in all dialects. (For these and other interesting examples, see McDavid [1971].) One must again ask on whose authority the broad a pronunciation is judged to be superior.

In summary: (1) There is considerable value in stressing a standard form of the language, for purposes of mutual intelligibility, but this should not be forced upon students in the face of differing regional customs. (2) Care should be taken not to teach a pronunciation that is purely personal, erroneous, or representative of an isolated local custom; choose, rather, a regional or national standard. (3) In order to determine the correct or acceptable pronunciation for a word, use the authority of regional custom or an up-to-date dictionary from a reputable publisher in your own country. Do not use the spelling of the word as an authority.

## 3-2.2 The Maintenance of Linguistic Standards

In Chapter 2, we stressed the primacy of speech, as opposed to writing. We then went on to say that dialect variations represent neither degeneration of language nor intellectual differences on the part of their respective speakers. In this chapter, we mentioned the origins of the appeal to authority but rejected the notion that there is a final authority of correctness.

There is a distinct danger that these facts will be interpreted as "anything goes." Some individuals use these points as arguments for abandoning *all* standards of speech or writing. We must therefore stress again the positive effects of a standard dialect, not as the one dialect we must all learn to speak all the time but as a model that we do not stray too far away from. Mutual intelligibility remains the chief argument for the maintenance of a standard dialect. Therefore, while we must not accept unquestioningly every edict issued by grammarians and dictionary-writers, by the same token we must not abandon all linguistic standards. Since the second-language teacher and speech therapist are shaping people's speech habits, these issues must be regarded as important. Serious thought should be given to these issues before facing them in a clinical or classroom situation.

## 3-3 Intuitions About Speech Sounds

There is much to be learned about the way English is structured even for a native speaker of English. Intuitions are frequently incorrect, particularly with respect to the sounds of the language. Teaching the sounds of English requires the ability to analyze those sounds; that in turn requires humility in admitting that one's own intuitions are not always correct. A few examples:

1. What is the difference in the pronunciation of these two sentences, when they are spoken in a normal conversational manner?

> I can't do that.
> I can do that.

Most would point to the t-sound in the first sentence as the difference between the two; however, in normal speech, the t is usually not pronounced at all. It is the **vowel** of the word can that is different in the two sentences. In the first sentence, the word can is pronounced with the vowel of the word "bat"; in the second sentence, this word has the vowel of the first sound in the word "about." Also, the n of the word can is usually prolonged slightly in the first sentence. (At this point, it might be useful to remember that when words or sentences are pronounced self-consciously in isolation, they are likely to be pronounced in an unnatural way.)

2. What is the final sound in the words dogs and cats? Is it the same in each word? While they are both spelled with the letter s, the final sound is pronounced like the z of "buzz" in the word dogs, and like the s of "bus" in cats.

3. How is the word miss pronounced? Do people realize that usually it is pronounced "mish" in the sentence "I miss you"?

4. What is the sound of the letter n in the word think? Is it pronounced like all other n's? In this case, the n is pronounced like the final sound of the word sing, not like the final sound of the word sin.

5. Is the h of the word his always pronounced? When the sentence, "He's got his books" is said in a normal conversational way, is the h pronounced? Most people do not pronounce it.

These examples are intended to point out the fact that the sounds we think we hear at first casual observation are not necessarily the sounds that are really there. Our intuitions about the sounds of our native language are wrong often enough that a formal study of speech sounds is a prerequisite to teaching or correcting these sounds.

## 3-4 Phonetics

It has been shown that before teaching or correcting the speech of others, one should make a formal study of the speech sounds of the language being taught and of the universal principles governing the speech sounds of all languages. This is the science of phonetics.

**Phonetics** is the scientific study of speech sounds and the "laws" that describe their patterning. The scope and goals of this field can be best appreciated by looking at the subdivisions of phonetics.

**Articulatory phonetics** is the study of the human speech production mechanism. **Acoustic phonetics** is the study of the physical properties of the speech sounds: their frequencies, timing features, and so on. **Auditory phonetics** is concerned with hearing, perception, and "processing" of speech by the brain. **Experimental phonetics** is an umbrella term for an experimental approach to the three areas mentioned. **Historical phonetics** examines changes in sounds that occur over time in all languages of the world. No language stays constant, and this field looks at the principles and regularities of sound changes.

Closely allied to phonetics, and using its findings and principles, is **phonology** (sometimes called **linguistic phonetics**). Phonologists study the functioning of phonetic units in language.

This book is primarily concerned with articulation of speech sounds, their classification, and their functioning in language. It also provides examples from the realm of clinical and pedagogical applications.

Who is interested in phonetics? It is generally considered to be a branch of linguistics, but the principles of phonetics are of interest to people in many fields. Linguists are interested in phonetics because sounds are the basic units of spoken language. The ways in which phonetic changes occur have an influence upon the ways in which languages change. Sound changes thus affect vocabulary, syntax, and sometimes even meaning, making this a profitable field of study for the linguist.

Communications engineers—for example, those who design electronic equipment for transmission of the speech signal—are interested in phonetic principles because they are concerned with making verbal transmissions intelligible. To take one example, the cost of telephone service can be reduced by making one wire serve to carry more than one message, but this involves some loss of the original signal. The communications engineer needs to know what phonetic components of the speech signal can be cut out without loss of intelligibility. With telephones, this is a matter of convenience and cost. In the case of an airport control tower and an airplane pilot, it can be seen that understanding what parts of the speech signal are essential to communication is a matter of life and limb. With respect to this point, Professor John W. Black of the Ohio State University tells of an experience during World War II. He was involved in studies of intelligibility, and was systematically studying how intelligible verbal messages remained when they were garbled or distorted in various ways. This was critical for the war effort, since the object of the research was to improve the intelligibility of radio transmissions between controllers and pilots and of intercom communications between pilots and gunners in fighting planes. Miniaturized electronic parts were not of good quality, and in the extremely noisy surroundings of the aircraft there were often serious misunderstandings among crew members. In one instance, on a training run, the pilot told a gunner at the rear of the craft, "Get your brass out," referring to ammunition. The next moment, the gunner was parachuting to earth. Such an error would have been very serious on a real bombing run.

The previously mentioned areas of phonetics might be put under the general heading of **descriptive phonetics,** since speech sounds are studied with a view to recording, describing, analyzing, and categorizing them. The practice of changing a person's speech habits can be called **normative** or **remedial** phonetics since it involves making a change toward a norm or standard. It is clear that being a good remedial phonetician presupposes a familiarity with the principles of descriptive phonetics.

Phonetic remediation is the prime concern of the speech pathologist, deaf educator, or second-language teacher. A study of general phonetics is basic to the practice of correcting phonetically imperfect speech, chiefly because speech is usually defective in ways that are consistent with phonetic theory. By way of corollary, phonetic principles provide the clinician with a systematic approach to practical problems of therapy.

These facts provide us with a way of describing the practical phonetics referred to in the title of this book. **Practical phonetics** involves an understanding of general phonetics, of course, but beyond that it involves an attitude toward applying known principles in original ways to solve clinical problems. The need for originality in applying theory must be stressed; articulatory irregularities are too numerous and too varied to memorize a simple therapeutic approach to each clinical or pedagogical problem encountered. The scope of this discussion permits only examples of applications to be presented; by the end of one's formal study of phonetics, only the individual's imagination will limit him/her in the application of this knowledge.

## Questions for Discussion

1. Phonetics is the scientific study of the sounds of language. What does the word **scientific** mean in this definition?
2. Find some examples in addition to those given in the chapter about which your initial intuition about speech sounds is not accurate.
3. How will you decide what is the correct form to teach? How will you decide whether your student's or client's pronunciation is wrong?
4. Find examples of spelling pronunciations other than the ones given. What are some spelling pronunciations children use? One person is supposed to have remarked that the word <u>facetious</u> only occurred in speech but never in writing and that the word "fack-a-tye-us" occurred in writing but never in speech. Has a similar situation occurred with you? With what word(s)? Were you ever confused about the pronunciation of <u>misled</u>?
5. Find additional examples of spelling pronunciations (a) that have become standard and acceptable and (b) that are common but are still considered errors.

## Annotated Bibliography

Speech Pathology

Since many students using this text will be studying speech pathology, it will not be useful to provide a long list of books in that field; other courses provide reading lists. A student who is not studying speech pathology and would like an overview of that field will find that the best place to start is probably Van Riper's *Speech Correction* [1972]. This book is a classic in its field; its reference lists will provide further sources.

History of the English Language

We have briefly mentioned the rise of a standard dialect from regional dialects, and the fact that regional dialects in North America have their roots to some extent in the dialects of Britain. Baugh's *A History of the English Language* [1957] provides a long and interesting account of the English language from its first beginnings to the present day.

SPELLING PRONUNCIATIONS. Further examples and discussion of spelling pronunciations can be found in Fromkin and Rodman's *An Introduction to Language* [1974] and Bloomfield's *Language* [1961], as well as in most other general introductions to the study of language.

CORRECTNESS. Correctness is discussed in Langacker's *Language and Its Structure* [1968]. An almost limitless number of articles and books appear on this topic; a selection has been included in the References: Barzun [1967], Fowler [1965], Hill [1967], Hook and Mathews [1968], Lloyd [1967], Lloyd [1951], and Pooley [1968].

# Chapter 4

## Writing Systems

### 4-1 Introduction

The development of a system of writing was of untold importance. It allowed people to record what they had discovered, and what their ideas and feelings were. No longer did successive generations have to rediscover what was already known or have to rely on the imperfect memory of the older people in the society.

A detailed history of writing systems is far beyond the scope of this book, but it is well to look briefly at alternatives to the alphabet, and to compare phonetic and nonphonetic writing systems. The interested student is encouraged to investigate the history of writing in greater detail.

Writing systems can be divided into the pictographic, ideographic, rebus, syllabic, alphabetic, and hybrid types. The operating principle of each type is quite distinct, and the names have a clear association with the operating principles. Each of these systems has been (or is) in use, and each contrasts sharply with the phonetic transcription system (itself an alphabetic system).

### 4-2 Pictographic Writing

It is said that a picture is worth a thousand words. The principle of pictographic writing is to use a picture instead of words. This means of communication was used to some extent by American Indians before and after the arrival of Europeans.

In this system, a single picture, or occasionally several pictures, are used to represent a message or short narrative. There is not a one-to-one correspondence between the number of items in the picture and words: in fact the content of the picture could be expressed many different ways in words. Study the sample pictograph in Figure 4.1.

Note that there is a close correspondence between the objects repre-

**Figure 4.1.** A Pictograph. This Indian "letter" has been adapted from Henry R. Schoolcraft, *Information Respecting the History, Condition, and Prospects of the Indian Tribes of the United States* (Philadelphia: 1853, Vol. I, pp. 418–419). An interpretation of the pictograph is also given. Compare the interpretation with the drawing to discover the conventions the "writer" used. How is each of the following concepts expressed in the pictograph?

An agreement of opinion _____
An offering of friendship _____
The rank of chief (vs. mere warrior) _____
The rank of a more important chief _____
A settled or civilized way of life _____
The location of the writer's home _____
The totem-group to which the Indians belong _____

**Interpretation:** A chief of the eagle totem, four of his warrior-kinsmen, a fifth warrior (of the catfish totem), and another chief, who is more powerful than the first leader, are all agreed in their views. They extend friendship to the president of the United States in the White House. The eagle chief intends to settle at a location on a river, and his kinsmen will occupy houses, thus adopting the white man's culture. It is hoped the president will understand the offer of friendship and return it.

(From *Problems in the Origins and Development of the English Language*, Second Edition by John Algeo © 1966, 1972, by Harcourt Brace Jovanovich, Inc., and reprinted with their permission.)

sented in the picture and the content of the message, with little latitude for abstract representations. But there will be cultural conventions; the pictograph is not completely international. For example, we use a form of pictographic writing in wordless cartoons. In these cartoons we sometimes see a light bulb in a little balloon above a person's head. This indicates to us that the person has had an idea. It is doubtful, though, whether the symbol would have any meaning to an Australian Bushman. The use of lightning bolts to indicate anger is similarly culturally bound. A picture of a man with a spear in his hand chasing a small animal, however, would likely have the same meaning to both the Australian Bushman and to us. Besides our use of cartoons, we can find pictographic communication in our culture in traffic signs, signs in airports, and in some advertising. For example, a photograph of a smiling person holding a distinctively shaped bottle of soft drink on a hot summer day would carry a clear meaning.

The advantages of pictographs are that it is easy to learn the system and make broad interpretations, and that the sender and receiver of the message do not need to speak the same language (this latter reason explains their use by the Indians, who spoke a large number of mutually unintelligible languages). The disadvantages are that the meaning is vague and open to question and misunderstanding, abstract ideas are hard to represent, and some artistic ability is needed. To a phonetician, the greatest disadvantage is that neither words nor sounds are represented at all.

## 4-3 Ideographic Writing

In **ideographic** writing (also called **logographic**), each symbol represents a word.[1] The symbol may look like the object it represents, or may be totally unrelated in form. Sentences are made up of a string of symbols, or **characters.** In contrast with pictographic writing, everyone familiar with a particular ideographic system will read the same message, *word for word*, from a written string.

In English, the numerals 1, 2, 3, . . . are ideographic symbols. They each represent one whole word, or one concept, but they are not spelled out as we spell other words. We use many other ideographic symbols, among them %, &, $, ¢, @, and #.

Chinese writing is probably the best example of this system in use today, although it is by no means a purely ideographic system. Indeed, it would probably be impossible to find an example of a purely ideographic writing system. In practice, Chinese characters are frequently made to serve double functions through the use of the rebus principle (section 4.4), but here we will concentrate on those aspects that are purely ideographic.

The operating principle of the ideographic system is that each character has a meaning, unrelated to the pronunciation of the word it represents. Thus, the characters are combined according to meaning and not to sound. For example, Figure 4.2 gives some examples of Chinese characters. Here we see the character for 'tree.' Written once, it is pronounced "mù"[2] and means 'tree.' Written twice, it is pronounced "lín" and means 'woods.' Written three times in a triangular format, it is pronounced "sēn" and means 'forest.' Notice that while the written element stays constant, the pronunciation changes. Just as in English the words <u>tree</u>, <u>bush</u>, and <u>forest</u> are unrelated in pronunciation, though we would have to agree that there is some small connection in meaning among them. These ideographs are based on units of meaning, not units of sound of the spoken word. But there is an exact correspondence between symbols and spoken words. The symbol for "sēn" ('forest') can only be read "sēn" and no other way. A synonym such as "a group of trees" cannot be correctly substituted in reading; as in English, "a group of trees" is written and spoken differently from "forest."

Another common feature of ideographic systems is the use of characters that have meaning but no equivalent in pronunciation. In Figure 4.3, for example, we see the Chinese characters for 'bird,' 'eagle,' 'pigeon,' and 'duck.'

[1] We are using the term **word** rather loosely. Linguists might use the term **morpheme.** For our purposes, we can think of each character as representing an idea or word: a single unit of meaning.
[2] These words are written according to the standard Pinyin system, and not in the International Phonetic Alphabet. The tones are marked; these are discussed in Chapter 13.

mù
'tree'

lín
'woods'

sēn
'forest'

**Figure 4.2.** Chinese ideographic characters are combined according to meaning and not according to sound. Thus 'forest' is represented in writing with three 'trees,' but the spoken word forest (sēn) bears no relation to the spoken word tree (mù).

These are pronounced "nǐao," "yīng," "gē," and "yā," respectively, and it can be seen that, as in English, the pronunciations of the words have nothing in common. However, as illustrated in Figure 4.3, the written name of each of these kinds of bird has the (unpronounced) character for 'bird' as part of it: while the Chinese normally *say* their equivalent for 'eagle,' 'pigeon,' and 'duck,' they always *write* eagle-bird, pigeon-bird, and duck-bird.

      If this seems terribly complex, it might help to realize that in limited circumstances we do something similar in English. The word pairs one and first, and two and second, have members that are unrelated in sound though related in meaning. But we write 1 and 1st, and 2 and 2nd. The 2 of 2nd does not represent the same sound as the 2 written alone, but it does represent the

nǐao
'bird'

yīng
'eagle'

gē
'pigeon'

yā
'duck'

**Figure 4.3.** The Chinese ideographic characters for 'eagle,' 'pigeon,' and 'duck' each contain the character for 'bird,' though the spoken word for each does not contain the word "nǐao."

same meaning. So the meaning 'two' is conveyed by an ideographic character whose form stays constant even when the pronunciation changes.

In an ideographic system, compound words are written just as one might expect (see Figure 4.4). For example, the word for 'automobile' is "qì chē" (literally 'steam cart'), which is written as <u>steam</u> plus <u>cart</u>. Similarly, the word for 'bus' ('public automobile') is written as <u>public</u> (i.e., 'nonprivate, collective') plus <u>steam</u> plus <u>cart</u>.

The main advantage of the ideographic system is that, since there is no sound recorded, people who speak different languages can use the same system. In fact, people who speak certain dialects of Chinese cannot talk to one another, although they can write to one another, which is one reason the Chinese have resisted changing to the Roman alphabet. The Japanese, whose

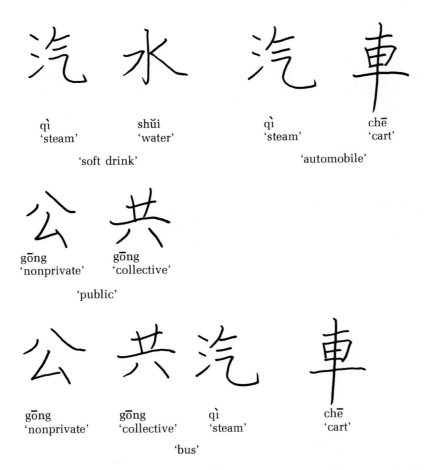

| qì | shŭi | qì | chē |
| 'steam' | 'water' | 'steam' | 'cart' |
| 'soft drink' | | 'automobile' | |

| gōng | gōng |
| 'nonprivate' | 'collective' |
| 'public' | |

| gōng | gōng | qì | chē |
| 'nonprivate' | 'collective' | 'steam' | 'cart' |
| 'bus' | | | |

**Figure 4.4.** In the Chinese characters for compound words, the characters for the individual parts are combined as one would expect. The spoken word for 'car' or 'automobile,' for example, is "qì chē," meaning literally 'steam cart' (something like the earlier English expression "horseless carriage"), and is written with the characters for 'steam' and 'cart.' The spoken word for 'public' is a compound made up of parts meaning 'nonprivate' and 'collective,' which happen to be homophonous. The usual spoken word for 'bus' is 'public automobile' (literally, 'nonprivate collective steam cart'); both the spoken word and the character are four-part compounds.

spoken language is unrelated to Chinese, successfully use Chinese characters in writing (although, as we shall see a little later, they also use a syllabic writing system for some words). In a similar way, our numerals are international. A Swede might do half a multiplication problem and, even if you could not speak to him, you could finish the written problem for him. But the alphabetic writing of Swedish does not help the nonspeaker to understand written Swedish.

The main disadvantage of the ideographic system rests in the greater number of symbols a person must learn in order to be literate. This causes problems in typing and typesetting. The fact that sound is not represented gives the ideographic system international potential but is a disadvantage to the phonetician.

## 4-4 Rebus Writing

In ideographic writing, there is the problem of the vast number of symbols needed, as well as difficulty in finding symbols for such abstract concepts as 'beauty' and 'justice.' Through the rebus principle, the use of each character can be extended. It is easiest to demonstrate this by example; we will first look at a hypothetical example, and then at an example from Chinese.

Imagine that we used the ideographic character _____ for 'plain.' We could write "Wheat grows best in the _____." Extending the use of the symbol by the rebus principle, we could then write "That is the _____ truth" ('plain') or even "The carpenter smooths the wood with a ———" ('plane').

Imagine that we had another character □ that meant 'air.' We could write "Fresh □ is better than smog." By the rebus principle, we could extend the use of this symbol to another word that sounds the same and write "He is □ to a great fortune" ('heir').

Then we could combine these symbols and write "□ ———" for 'airplane.'

By the rebus principle, an ideographic symbol has a phonetic or sound value as well being used to represent homophones[3] whose meaning is unrelated. One character would thus do for sun and son, brake and break, etc. These units are combined, as we demonstrated with airplane above. Similarly, the characters for bee and leaf could be combined to represent belief.

In English, we are using the rebus principle when we write "4 sale" meaning 'for sale.'

Let us look at examples from Chinese. In Chinese the words meaning 'empress' and 'after' are homophones, both pronounced "hòu." As can be seen in Figure 4.5, the same character is used for both, originally that for empress. The words meaning 'elephant' and 'compared to' are both pronounced "xiǎng"—the character for 'elephant' is used for both.

---

[3] Homophones: words that are pronounced alike but are different in meaning and history, such as son and sun; mail and male; tied and tide; I'll, aisle, and isle. Whether or not two words are homophones is not dependent upon spelling. Well (satisfactorily) and well (a hole dug for the purpose of finding water or oil) are homophones that happen to be spelled alike; their meanings and origins are quite separate. Passed and past are not true homophones, though they are pronounced identically. They are actually two specialized senses of the same word, as judged on historical and semantic grounds.

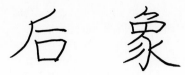

**Figure 4.5.** The rebus principle is illustrated in these Chinese characters. Originally, the character on the left meant only 'empress,' pronounced "hòu." Now it is also used to represent the homophonous word meaning 'after.' The character on the right originally meant 'elephant'; now it is used in that meaning and for 'compared to.' These words are homophonous, both being pronounced "xiăng."

A slightly modified rebus principle is also used in Chinese. The word <u>eagle</u> is almost homophonous with the verb <u>must</u> (only the tone is different). The character for <u>eagle</u> (Figure 4.3) is the character for <u>must</u> plus <u>bird</u>. The character for <u>must</u> gives the approximate pronunciation, and the unpronounced character for <u>bird</u> gives the sense and thus suggests the exact pronunciation.[4] In Chinese writing, we say that the character for <u>eagle</u> consists of a *phonetic element* (the character for <u>must</u>) and an unpronounced *radical* (<u>bird</u>) that suggests the sense.

As you can see, the ideographic system, when its characters are extended through the rebus principle, becomes rather unwieldy in practice, mostly because of the shifts in operating principle. A character may be used for any of three reasons: (a) it *looks* like what it represents (e.g., the numeral 1 in English), (b) it has an arbitrary relationship to what it represents (e.g., the numeral 5), or (c) it represents another word that *sounds* like the word in question (e.g., "4 sale"). While it is successfully used in Chinese, a language with a great deal of homophony, it would work less well for a language such as English, in which there is little homophony and many words are long (how would you represent <u>arbitrary</u> by the rebus principle?).

## 4-5 Syllabic Writing

The pictographic and ideographic systems do not represent sound at all. Rebus writing is based on homophony (sounding alike) but does not divide words into consistent units of sound. Syllabic writing is the first system we will examine that consistently links written symbols with units of sound of the spoken language.

A language that uses a syllabic writing system has a group of symbols, roughly corresponding to our alphabet, called a **syllabary.** There is one symbol for each different syllable possible in that language. The number of symbols is usually greater than in our alphabet, but many fewer than in the ideographic system.

The phonetic structure of a language needs to be well suited to a syllabic writing system; there should not be too great a number of different syllables. Japanese is a language with a simple syllable structure, and a limited number of different syllables.

[4] In speech it is not likely that there will be any confusion, since context supplies some information; for example, the sentence, "I have money in the bank" does not confuse you, even though you know that the word <u>bank</u> can also mean 'the side of a river.'

|     | a | i | u | e | o |
|-----|---|---|---|---|---|
| —   | ア | イ | ウ | エ | オ |
| k   | カ | キ | ク | ケ | コ |
| s   | サ | シ [1] | ス | セ | ソ |
| t   | タ | チ [2] | ツ [3] | テ | ト |
| n   | ナ | ニ | ヌ | ネ | ノ |
| h   | ハ | ヒ | フ [4] | ヘ | ホ |
| m   | マ | ミ | ム | メ | モ |
| y   | ヤ |   | ユ |   | ヨ |
| r   | ラ [5] | リ [6] | ル [6] | レ [6] | ロ [6] |
| w   | ワ |   |   |   | ヲ [7] |
| n   | ン |   |   |   |   |
| g   | ガ | ギ | グ | ゲ | ゴ |
| z   | ザ | ジ [8] | ズ [9] | ゼ | ゾ |
| d   | ダ | ヂ [8] | ヅ [9] | デ | ド |
| b   | バ | ビ | ブ | ベ | ボ |
| p   | パ | ピ | プ | ペ | ポ |

**Figure 4.6.** The Japanese Katakana Syllabary, in which each symbol represents an entire syllable consisting of a vowel or a consonant followed by a vowel. For example, the symbols in the first column represent the syllables a, ka, sa, ta, na, ha, etc. The second n is not the syllable na but a syllable consisting of the sound "n" alone; this sound can stand alone as a syllable in Japanese. The last five rows of symbols are modified versions of other symbols. The consonants are pronounced more or less as would be expected, but note that the vowel symbols heading the five columns have their International Phonetic Alphabet pronunciations. Thus a is pronounced as in "father"; i as in "machine"; u as in "super"; e as in "hey"; and o as in "tote." The symbols having numbers beside them are pronounced not as expected but as follows: (1) shi, (2) chi, (3) tsu, (4) fu, (5) r-like consonant, (6) l-like consonant, (7) o, (8) zhi (/ži/), (9) zu. See the examples of words written in the syllabary in Figure 4.7.

English, on the other hand, has a great many different syllables. While we will look at the English syllable in some detail in Chapter 12, for the moment you can appreciate its complexity by trying to think of all the different-sounding one-syllable words in English. The number is very large (and there are many syllables found only in polysyllabic words—such as the second syllable of **language**). An English syllable can have 0, 1, 2, or 3 consonants before the vowel, and from 0 to 4 consonants following the vowel. This creates enormous possibilities for combinations. By contrast, the Japanese syllable consists of either just a vowel, or a consonant followed by a vowel (such as **ko**).

While Japanese is mostly written in borrowed Chinese ideographic characters, there is need for a phonetically based way of writing certain words

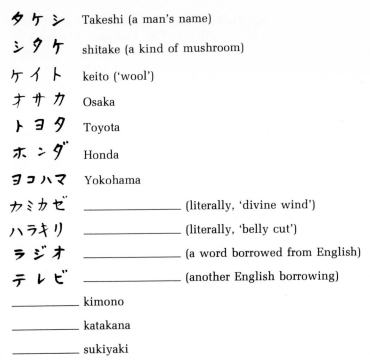

タケシ    Takeshi (a man's name)

シタケ    shitake (a kind of mushroom)

ケイト    keito ('wool')

ナサカ    Osaka

トヨタ    Toyota

ホンダ    Honda

ヨコハマ   Yokohama

カミカゼ   _____ (literally, 'divine wind')

ハラキリ   _____ (literally, 'belly cut')

ラジオ    _____ (a word borrowed from English)

テレビ    _____ (another English borrowing)

_____ kimono

_____ katakana

_____ sukiyaki

**Figure 4.7.** Examples of the Use of the Katakana Syllabary. Examine the first seven examples by comparing them with the complete Katakana in Figure 4.6. Then write the next four words in the Roman alphabet. Two are Japanese words that are probably familiar, and two are English words borrowed into Japanese. Try writing a few words in the Katakana using the models in Figure 4.6:

(these include foreign and onomatopoeic[5] words, as well as words that have no Chinese equivalent[6]).

Japanese makes use of two syllabaries; Figures 4.6 and 4.7 illustrate one of these, called the *Katakana*. Study the examples given; these will clarify the use of the syllabic principle, in which each different syllable has a distinct symbol. The second syllabary, called the *Hiragana*, has an emphatic effect, somewhat like our use of italics.

Eskimo is also written in a syllabary that was developed by missionaries. The symbols are based on geometric shapes and give a pleasing appearance on the page. (An alphabetic system is also employed.) In 1821, Sequoya, a Cherokee Indian, developed a syllabary for his native language, a particularly remarkable feat, since he was completely illiterate and therefore had to discover the very principle of writing as well as to develop a system specific to his own language. To this day, whenever Cherokee is written, it is written in syllabary, not in the Roman alphabet.

[5] Onomatopoeic words are also sometimes called **imitative**. They sound somewhat like the noises they are representing. Words such as "quack," "bark," "squeak," "woof," and "cuckoo" are imitative.
[6] The grammar of the two languages is totally different since the languages are unrelated. Japanese has many inflections and function words unlike anything found in Chinese. Thus, Chinese ideographic characters cannot represent every word of spoken Japanese.

The main advantage of a syllabary is that if the language is well suited to one, there is great economy of writing. The Japanese place name *Yokohama* is written in just four symbols, corresponding to the four syllables of the word. If a language is not well suited to a syllabary, it is not economical at all. The Japanese have borrowed many English words, and for many the way they must be written in the syllabary is very complex, simply because of the complex syllable structure of English.

The most important difference between the syllabary and the other systems we have examined is that it is phonetic, and therefore allows for a way to write new words that come into the language. Also, onomatopoeic words are easier to represent than in an ideographic system.

In English we sometimes use the equivalent of a syllabic system in riddles and advertising. When a company advertises a product as being "E-Z" to use, each symbol represents a syllable. The first syllable has just one sound, like the ee-sound of "meet," while the second syllable is a z-sound followed by the ee-sound. So the letter z is not being used as in an alphabet but as if it were part of a syllabary. It represents a whole syllable, in this case made up of two speech sounds. Similarly, if we write "I C U" for "I see you" or "I O U" for "I owe you," we are using these symbols in a syllabic way.

## 4-6 Alphabetic Writing

In an **alphabetic** writing system, each distinctly[7] different sound of the spoken language is represented by a separate symbol, and each symbol represents only one sound. The written symbols are called **letters,** and they go together to make up an **alphabet** (named for **alpha** and **beta,** the first two letters of the Greek alphabet).

The alphabetic principle is used in most Western languages and many others besides. The principle of one sound to one symbol is followed quite closely in some cases (such as Spanish or Russian) and quite poorly in other cases (such as English or French).

### 4-6.1 A Brief History of the Alphabet

The Sumerians, who had a flourishing culture in Mesopotamia around 3000 B.C., are generally credited with having the first system of writing, an ideographic system. It was developed to serve the needs of a rather advanced commercial trade. A later stage in the development of this system is called **cuneiform** ('wedge-shaped') in reference to the stylized form of the characters in clay tablets. At the same time, the Egyptians were using a similar system, called **hieroglyphics.** It is likely that the hieroglyphics were an adaptation of the Sumerian script; and certainly the development of the hieroglyphics was influenced by the cuneiform writing.

Both the hieroglyphic and cuneiform systems appear to have undergone a process of **phonetization;** that is, while they started out purely ideographic, they became, at later stages, at least partially phonetic. Apparently, the first step in this process was the phonetic use of ideographic symbols through

---

[7] We will give the notion of *distinctly* different speech sounds a more precise definition in Chapter 11.

the rebus principle. Some symbols remained purely ideographic, while others came to represent whole syllables; these were combined, much as we combined □ and ——— to represent 'airplane.' As a result of this process, many symbols lost their ideographic value, and were interpreted as having purely a sound value. By this means, a syllabary was born. At their most advanced stages, both the cuneiform and hieroglyphic systems remained a mixture of ideographic and syllabic principles.

But a purely syllabic form of the hieroglyphic symbols was borrowed by the Phoenicians, a Semitic people who traded on the Mediterranean Sea. The *West Semitic Syllabary,* consisting of twenty-two syllabic symbols, had evolved by 1500 B.C.

This syllabary was different from the syllabaries we have examined in one important respect: the symbols did not indicate the vowels, only the consonants. It may appear that such a system should not properly be called a syllabary, but rather an incomplete alphabet. But because of the phonetic structure of the West Semitic language, such a system accurately represented the sounds of the words. Also, each symbol represented one consonant followed by one vowel—though the particular vowel was not always specified—and may thus be called a syllabary.[8]

Words in the West Semitic language were made up of alternate consonant and vowel sounds, and normally began with a consonant. Also, the number of different vowels was fewer than in English, and the particular vowel in a word was at least partially determined by the consonant preceding it. Thus, it is evident that this syllabary would have served well to write the language for which it was developed.

This West Semitic syllabary was borrowed by the Greeks in the tenth century B.C. Like English—and in contrast to the Semitic languages—the Greek language had clusters of consonants together without vowels in between, and thus the Semitic syllabic characters could not represent spoken Greek very well. Unmodified use of the syllabic characters would have resulted in only the consonants being represented, presenting considerable ambiguity to the reader.

The Greeks overcame this difficulty by a simple modification. They used the Semitic symbols to represent only the consonants without the accompanying vowels. Since Greek had fewer consonants than were represented in the syllabary, there were symbols left over to represent the vowels alone, without the Semitic consonant. For example, the West Semitic syllabic character, <u>aleph</u>, the ancestor of our letter <u>A</u>, represented the syllable '<u>a</u> in West Semitic. The apostrophe represents the **glottal stop** (written in the International Phonetic Alphabet as ʔ—see Chapter 8). This consonant appears in the English expression <u>uh-uh</u> (meaning 'no') between the two vowel sounds. The Greeks had no such consonant in their language, so it was a simple matter to let this letter represent the vowel <u>a</u> instead of the syllable '<u>a</u> (or ʔa). In its most fully developed form, the Greek alphabet had added five letters that did not correspond to any symbols of the Semitic syllabary.

While the Greeks used the first true alphabet, it is not so much their single-handed invention as it was a minor modification of the Semitic sylla-

---

[8] The limited evidence available regarding the transition from ideographic to syllabic to alphabetic symbol systems is interpreted differently by various authorities. For example, some of the sources cited in the Annotated Bibliography differ on this issue.

bary, one small step in the transition from pictographic to alphabetic writing. The modern Greek alphabet is a direct descendant of this first alphabet. Saint Cyril brought Christianity to Slavic peoples, and many Slavic languages, such as Russian and Ukrainian, use the Cyrillic alphabet, also a direct descendant of the Greek alphabet.

The Etruscans, who lived in part of what is now called Italy, borrowed the alphabet from the Greeks and in turn passed it along to the Romans. The Romans adapted the alphabet to the particular phonetic structure of their language, and as they increased their military, political, and cultural influence over Europe, the alphabet went with them.


## 4-6.2 The Roman Alphabet

The Roman alphabet was well suited to the Roman language, Latin. For the most part there was a one-to-one correspondence between sounds of the spoken language and letters of the alphabet; however, the sound-system of Latin was different from that of the modern languages that presently use the Roman alphabet, and so this alphabet is well adapted to these modern languages. Some of the peculiarities of the spelling of English and other languages can be attributed to the attempt to make the Roman alphabet serve languages for which it was not developed.

In the alphabet as used by the Romans, there was only one letter corresponding to our U, V, and W (inscriptions where a letter V is used for both U and V are not uncommon). Similarly, I and J were not distinguished, and Y was used only to represent the vowel sound of certain words borrowed directly from Greek. These facts partly explain why these letters are used to represent different sounds in various languages. To take one example, the letter j is used to represent the sound of our letter y (as in "you") in quite a number of European languages (as well as in the International Phonetic Alphabet).

The letter C provides the most confused picture in the original Roman alphabet. It variously represented sounds corresponding to our letters k (as in "keep"), g (as in "good"), and s (as in "set"). The letter G was introduced to reduce the confusion of having one letter represent more than one distinct sound: it was originally a letter C with an added crossbar (note the resemblance in the forms of the capital C and the capital G). The fact that the one letter C represented both the k-sound and the s-sound, as it still does in the English words "camp" and "cent," is the result of a sound change that occurred in Latin. The k-sounds preceding the vowels i and e came to be pronounced as s-sounds. This fact makes the spelling of Latin seem more regular, but it does not help the situation in modern English.

These examples are provided to demonstrate that some of the peculiarities of spelling in English (and other European languages) can be traced either to the peculiarities of Latin itself, or to the ways in which the Roman alphabet has been adapted to languages whose sound-systems are very different from Latin.

The Latin language had fewer speech sounds than many languages that use its alphabet; there are not enough letters in the Roman alphabet to go around. For example, Latin had only five vowels corresponding to the five letters a, e, i, o, and u (plus y in Greek loan words). Most dialects of English have about 13 vowels (and several diphthongs besides) that must be represented by these five symbols (the use of the letter y̱ in English does not help, since y̱ is not consistently distinguished from i̱). While the lack of consonant symbols is less serious, it is true that Latin had fewer consonant contrasts than English does.

This problem has been solved with varying degrees of success for the various languages using the Roman alphabet. One way around the problem is to add symbols not found in the Roman alphabet. English and several other languages make extensive use of the letter ḵ; in the Roman alphabet the use of ḵ was very restricted. But we would need to add about eleven more symbols, and use each letter that we have in a distinctive way, in order to have enough for every sound of English.

In German, the letter β has been added to represent the s-sound. Danish has added the vowel letter æ to its alphabet. But for the most part, languages using the Roman alphabet have been quite conservative and have not developed new symbols to supplement the old. Indeed, several non-Roman letters were used in the alphabet of Old English, but these have been abandoned.

Another way to extend the use of a limited number of symbols to a larger number of sounds is through the use of **diacritics,** or "accents." French, German, Spanish, Portuguese, Czechoslovakian, and the Scandinavian languages use various kinds of diacritics to modify letters. Some examples are: é, è, ô, ö, ü, ä, ñ, ç, ø, č, and å.[9] English does not make use of diacritics to extend its alphabet.

Another way to extend the alphabet is by the use of **digraphs**. A digraph is a combination of two letters representing one sound. For example, the p̱ẖ of telep̱ẖone represents one sound, as does the ṯẖ of ṯẖrough, the ea of dean, the s̱ẖ of s̱ẖore, the o̱o̱ of mo̱o̱n, and so on. Digraphs are used commonly in English and other European languages.

## 4-6.3 Why English Spelling Is Not Alphabetic

A true alphabetic system uses a one-to-one correspondence between distinctive speech sounds and letters of an alphabet. English spelling violates the principle in several ways.

1. One sound is often represented by more than one spelling. The first vowel sound in te̱a̱, te̱e̱, pe̱o̱ple, ski̱, and fe̱tus (also spelled fo̱e̱tus) are examples, as are the underlined consonants in f̱ellow, telep̱ẖone, and toug̱ẖ.
2. The same letter often represents several different sounds. For example the o̱ in wo̱men, wo̱man, bo̱ne, co̱t, lo̱ve, and po̱rt. These problems led George Bernard Shaw, the great playwright and advocate of spelling reform, to suggest that the word f̱i̱s̱ẖ could be written "ghoti," using the g̱ẖ of enoug̱ẖ, the o̱ of wo̱men, and the ṯi̱ of naṯi̱on. Clearly, English spelling is not *that* bad, but it presents a number of difficulties, more of which are discussed below.
3. A third problem with English spelling is that it uses digraphs, a practice that

[9] The use of diacritics is not restricted to European languages. Notice that the last five rows of characters in the Japanese Katakana syllabary (Figure 4.6) are previously used characters with diacritic marks added.

violates the basic alphabetic principle of one letter to one sound. Used consistently, digraphs do not cause serious problems, but they can cause confusion in compound words. For example, you might argue that the digraph ee is used quite consistently in English to represent one single vowel sound. But note that when two e's come together in a compound word such as re-enter, the double e does not represent the same sound as in meet. Of course, the hyphen indicates this fact, but the hyphen itself must be inconsistently used because of the use of digraphs in our spelling. We must use a hyphen to separate the two e's of re-enter, since the digraph ee has its own value, but the hyphen is not needed in a word like recopy or redupli-cate, since letters that can form digraphs are not brought together in these compounds. Even this is not a consistent guide, however, since the words reenter and reestablish may be spelled with or without a hyphen. Zoology is never spelled with a hyphen, though the digraph oo normally is pronounced as a single vowel; similarly, the words mishap, pothook, and sweetheart lack hyphens.

4. English spelling is not alphabetic because we sometimes use letters that represent no sound at all. These so-called silent letters certainly cause problems for those learning to spell English. We can find examples in such words as debt, island, right, plate, psychic, pneumatic, and castle.

5. There are sounds that are not represented in the spelling of English words. The word use, for example, begins with a y-sound, just as the word you does. This same y-sound is also left out of the spelling of the word mute, and other, similar words.

## 4-6.4 Spelling Is Not Pronunciation

Considering the extent to which English spelling is not alphabetic, it is hard to imagine that anyone would think it the authority for pronunciation or would assume that pronunciation is consistently represented by the written word. Yet Chapter 3 has already shown that the phenomenon of spelling pronunciation has changed the pronunciation of many words.

Though it may seem obvious, it should perhaps be emphasized that there is a great difference between spelling and sounds. We hear people talk of pronouncing "letters," but it is of course not *letters*, rather *speech sounds*, that one pronounces. These may or may not be well represented by letters in writing.

Digraphs deserve special mention. I have heard teachers of English as a second language tell their students that to pronounce the th-sound of a word like "thought," they should try to pronounce a t-sound and an h-sound together! This is of course completely ridiculous; the th-sound is a *single* sound, no matter how it is represented in writing. There is no reason to assume that the combination of *letters* corresponds to a combination of *sounds*. (This sound is spelled th because of traditions begun by French-speaking scribes who were unfamiliar with the single letter that was used to represent this sound in Old English.)

A similar case is the word "better," which does not have two t-sounds. English pronunciation does not have double consonants such as exist in some languages. Double consonant *letters* are irregularly used in English spelling to represent other phonetic qualities, such as vowel quality or stress placement. The difference in the vowel of "catty" and "cater" is not *because* one word is spelled with two t's and the other with one; rather the doubling of the consonant letter *indicates* the vowel quality. Only in spelling does "catty" have two t's. Similarly, in the words "material" and "matter" the single or double letter indicates the stress pattern. Once again, a spelling convention (such as a double t) is used to indicate something *unrelated* in the pronunciation of the word (such as vowel quality or stress).

The sound usually spelled sh in English is not an s-sound plus an h-sound. Nor does the word "back" contain a c-sound and a k-sound; rather, this combination of letters is used after certain vowel sounds to represent a *single* consonant sound.

The spelling of words tends to mislead us about pronunciation in another way: we may think that words spelled differently are pronounced differently, even when this is not the case. Most of us pronounce "prints" and "prince" similarly in speech, but the effect of spelling is so strong that we tend to feel that the two words are pronounced differently. Our reaction when told that the two are pronounced alike may be, "But 'prints' has a t in it." The presence or absence of the *letter* t in the spelling of the words has nothing to do with whether or not there is a t-sound in the *pronunciation* of them.

In summary, be careful not to let your knowledge of spelling distort your perception of speech *sounds*.


## 4-7 Hybrid Writing Systems

A hybrid in the world of plants has mixed parentage: it is a cross between two strains. A hybrid writing system is one that mixes two or more principles. We have already noted that the Japanese have a hybrid system: they use Chinese ideographs, plus two syllabaries. The hieroglyphics were a hybrid system: some symbols had a purely ideographic content, and some had a phonetic content through the rebus principle. *All* rebus systems are hybrid, since there must be ideographic symbols before these can be modified to represent a phonetic content.

Some languages, such as Hebrew, have an alphabetic system that transcribes just the consonants, but not the vowels. In modern Hebrew, diacritics have been added to show the vowels.

When we are writing English quickly, we tend to use special symbols to represent whole words, following an ideographic principle. Other words we write out in full. In fact all abbreviations short-circuit the alphabetic principle and give a hybrid result.

While the alphabetic principle may be used in reading to "sound out" a new word, or to recognize less common words, reading is accomplished, to some extent, by ideographic means. In reading, one does not usually scan each letter of each word; rather, each word is recognized as a whole unit (a *Gestalt*, in psychological terms) having a certain meaning. An example will show that this is so. If you were to see the word nea written, it would likely take you quite a while to realize that what was meant was the joint in the middle of the leg. It is easy to "sound out" this misspelling, but when you simply read it, it makes no sense. The k of knee, while it plays no role in the pronunciation, helps one to recognize the word in writing. This shows that we read to a certain extent by ideographic, rather than alphabetic, means.

To take another example, look at the underlined words in these phrases:

"A <u>uniformed</u> guard stood at the door."

"It is a waste of time for <u>uninformed</u> people to try to have a debate."

One has no difficulty in reading these sentences, even though the letter <u>u</u> at the beginning of each similar underlined word represents a totally different sound (the vowel of "c<u>u</u>t" in the first case, and the consonant-vowel combination of "<u>u</u>se" in the second). The only difference in the spelling of the two words is the fourth letter, <u>n</u>, of "uninformed"—and certainly there is no regular pattern in English spelling by which the pronunciation of the letter <u>u</u> is changed by a letter <u>n</u> three letters later in the word. This example shows that we do not read familiar words by "sounding them out," but rather by recognizing them as whole units. Even in an almost perfectly alphabetic language like Spanish, a reader will recognize common words as a unit, but will make use of the alphabetic principle for reading less common words.

## 4-8 The International Phonetic Alphabet

By the nineteenth century, Europeans had colonized much of the world: North America, Africa, Asia, the South Pacific. In the process of expansion, many hundreds of groups of peoples were discovered, speaking many hundreds of different languages. The Europeans needed to learn these languages, at least the rudiments of them, for purposes of trade, living side by side in peace, conversion to Christianity, exploitation, and so on. Written records were necessary for the benefit of subsequent travelers in the region. Thus, a hodgepodge of different scripts was developed to transcribe these languages, usually depending upon the native language and even upon the whims of the person who was recording the language. For this reason, and for the benefit of the study of philology (word and language history) that was flourishing at the time, some form of standard writing system was needed. The International Phonetic Association was founded in 1886 by the French phonetician Paul Passy, and the Association developed the International Phonetic Alphabet (IPA).

The IPA was intended for use in transcribing the sounds of any language that had been discovered or might be discovered in the future. This would allow anyone familiar with the system, no matter what his native language, to have a very good idea of how to pronounce it.

The original attempt was very nearly as successful as we could expect, for very few modifications to the system have been made over the years. A few refinements have been added, but other than that, the system is essentially as it was. It should not be expected to be perfect, however, since there are always minor phonetic differences that cannot be recorded. For example, speakers of French, English, and Italian do not produce exactly the same kind of ee-sound, and while the IPA can record some of this difference, it cannot record all of it.

### 4-8.1 Differences in Phonetic Alphabets

Since the IPA was designed for the purpose of writing down the sounds of any language, it would seem that it could handle English in a simple and consistent way, and so it may come as a surprise to see that different books use slightly different sets of symbols for the same sounds.

The reasons for this are quite straightforward. The IPA is by its very nature a compromise: since it can record with reasonable accuracy the sounds of any language, it is not perfectly suited to any one language. The concern of this book is mostly with English, although other languages are mentioned from time to time to illustrate a point. The IPA is not well suited to some of the peculiarities of English, particularly the vowels, so different authors have adapted it to English in slightly different ways. There is another reason for these differences in ways of using the phonetic alphabet: it depends on just how specific a representation is desired. For example, perhaps a system that will record just the gross phonetic form of English words is needed. Perhaps a system that will show dialect differences is needed. This can require a very specific system in some situations, such as if we wish to record the slight differences in the vowels of Martha's Vineyard (a small island off the coast of Massachusetts) as compared to those of mainland Massachusetts. The demands of a phonetic alphabet would be again slightly different if it was being used to show a foreigner how to pronounce English. Many readers of this book will use it to record misarticulations and mispronunciations, so that other pathologists can see how a particular client pronounced a word on a particular occasion. This is a purpose for which the IPA was not developed, so some modifications are needed to make it suitable.

There is still another reason for differences in phonetic alphabets, particularly in North America. Many of the classic letters of the IPA are different in shape from any of the letters available on most typewriters. Common usage has substituted other symbols that can be written more easily without special equipment. For example, the first sound of the word show is written in the IPA as [ʃ], but North American phoneticians have most frequently substituted the symbol [š] (borrowed from the Czechoslovakian alphabet), since it is easier to write.

In this book the various possibilities will be indicated. Preferences in instruction and laboratory materials may differ, however, so remember that other forms are in use. Since they may be encountered in other books, it is well to have a passing familiarity with the symbols even though they may not be the preferred usage in this book.

Table 4.1 summarizes the International Phonetic Alphabet. You will not need to know all its symbols; many are reserved for exotic languages with uncommon speech sounds. The specific symbols we need in our study are introduced in Chapters 7 through 10.

**Table 4.1.** The International Phonetic Alphabet
Revised to 1951

**CONSONANTS**

| | Bi-labial | Labio-dental | Dental and Alveolar | Retroflex | Palato-alveolar | Alveolo-palatal | Palatal | Velar | Uvular | Pharyngal | Glottal |
|---|---|---|---|---|---|---|---|---|---|---|---|
| Plosive | p b | | t d | ʈ ɖ | | | c ɟ | k g | q ɢ | | ʔ |
| Nasal | m | ɱ | n | ɳ | | | ɲ | ŋ | ɴ | | |
| Lateral Fricative | | | ɬ ɮ | | | | | | | | |
| Lateral Non-fricative | | | l | ɭ | | | ʎ | | | | |
| Rolled | | | r | | | | | | ʀ | | |
| Flapped | | | ɾ | ɽ | | | | | ʀ | | |
| Fricative | ɸ β | f v | θ ð \| s z \| ɹ | ʂ ʐ | ʃ ʒ | ɕ ʑ | ç j | x ɣ | χ ʁ | ħ ʕ | h ɦ |
| Frictionless Continuants and Semi-vowels | w ɥ | ʋ | ɹ | | | | j (ɥ) | (w) | ʁ | | |

**VOWELS**

| | Bi-labial | | Front | Central | Back |
|---|---|---|---|---|---|
| Close | (y ʉ u) | | i y | ɨ ʉ | ɯ u |
| Half-close | (ø o) | | e ø | | ɤ o |
| Half-open | (œ ɔ) | | ɛ œ | ɜ ɞ | ʌ ɔ |
| Open | (ɒ) | | a | æ ɐ | ɑ ɒ |

(Secondary articulations are shown by symbols in brackets.)

OTHER SOUNDS.—Palatalized consonants : ƫ, ԁ, 'etc.; palatalized ʃ, ʒ : ɕ, ʑ. Velarized or pharyngalized consonants : ɫ, đ, ᵶ, etc. Ejective consonants (with simultaneous glottal stop) : p', t', etc. Implosive voiced consonants : ɓ, ɗ, etc. ʀ fricative trill. σ, ǫ (labialized θ, ð, or s, z). ᶅ, ᶎ (labialized ʃ, ʒ). ɿ, ƈ, ɕ, ʚ (clicks, Zulu c, q, x). ʟ (a sound between r and l). ŋ Japanese syllabic nasal. ʄ (combination of x and ʃ). ʍ (voiceless w). ʟ, ʏ, ɷ (lowered varieties of i, y, u). ɞ (a variety of ǝ). ɵ (a vowel between ø and o).

Affricates are normally represented by groups of two consonants (ts, tʃ, dʒ, etc.), but, when necessary, ligatures are used (ʦ, ʧ, ʤ, etc.), or the marks ‿ or ⁀ (t͡s or t͡s, etc.). ‿ also denote synchronic articulation (m͡ŋ = simultaneous m and ŋ). c, ɟ may occasionally be used in place of tʃ, dʒ, and ȝ, ƍ for ts, dz. Aspirated plosives : ph, th, etc. r-coloured vowels : eɹ, aɹ, ɔɹ, etc., or eʴ, aʴ, ɔʴ, etc., or ę, ą, ǫ, etc.; r-coloured ǝ : əɹ or əʴ or ɹ or ə, or ɚ.

LENGTH, STRESS, PITCH.— : (full length). · (half length). ' (stress, placed at beginning of the stressed syllable). ˌ (secondary stress). ˉ (high level pitch); ˍ (low level); ′ (high rising); ʽ (low rising); ˎ (high falling); ˏ (low falling); ˆ (rise-fall); ˇ (fall-rise).

MODIFIERS.— ˜ nasality. ◦ breath (ḷ = breathed l). ˒ voice (ş = z). ʻ slight aspiration following p, t, etc. ˳ labialization (n̫ = labialized n). ˏ dental articulation (ṭ = dental t). ˋ palatalization (ż = ʒ). ˳ specially close vowel (ę̣ = a very close e). ˒ specially open vowel (ę̢ = a rather open e). ˔ tongue raised (e˔ or ę̣ = e̝). ˕ tongue lowered (e˕ or ę̣ = e̞). ˖ tongue advanced (u˖ or u̟ = an advanced u, ṱ = t̟). ˗ or ˔ tongue retracted (i˗ or i̠ = ɨ˖, ṯ = alveolar t). ˒ lips more rounded. ˓ lips more spread. ˎ consonantal vowel. ˳ syllabic consonant. ˳ consonantal vowel. ꞈ variety of ʃ resembling s, etc. Central vowels : ï(= ɨ), ü(= ʉ), ë(= ə˔), ö(= ɵ), ɛ̈, ö̈. ˳ (e.g. ṋ) syllabic consonant.

SOURCE.—International Phonetic Association. Reprinted by permission.

## Questions for Discussion

1. Some people claim that writing was a discovery rather than an invention. Which term is more appropriate?

2. Give some examples from your experience of ways in which our culture uses the various types of writing systems. Choose examples other than those given in the chapter.

3. Why did the developers of the IPA choose an alphabetic rather than a syllabic system?

4. Summarize the relative merits and disadvantages of the various writing systems. For each type, try to think of a situation where it would be the best means of written communication.

5. What regularities are there in English spelling? For example, what sounds does the letter g represent in such words as "go," "gin," "right"? What rules govern the sound-symbol correspondence? What exceptions are there (such as "margarine")? Examine other letters and digraphs in the same way.

6. In section 4-6.4 we discussed how certain spelling conventions represent quite unrelated phenomena; for example, consonant letters are doubled not because the consonant sound is doubled but rather to indicate vowel quality or stress placement. Find and discuss other examples of such conventions.


## Annotated Bibliography

Short articles on writing systems can be found in Fromkin and Rodman's *An Introduction to Language* [1974] and in Langacker's *Language and Its Structure* [1968].

Exercises in transliteration (changing from one script to another) can be found in Algeo's *Problems in the Origins and Development of the English Language* [1972].

There is a good number of short books on the history of writing that give more detail than this chapter. For example, Moorhouse's *The Triumph of the Alphabet* [1953] includes an interesting section on deciphering unknown scripts.

An excellent chapter on the development of scripts and the relationships among them can be found in Pedersen's *The Discovery of Language* [1967].

# Part II

# Basic Phonetics

# Chapter 5

## Physiological Phonetics: The Anatomy of Speech

### 5-1 The Organs of Speech

This chapter will deal with the physiological structures that are used in the production of speech. Our overview of these structures will necessarily be very brief; we will, for the most part, be naming the organs in order to provide a vocabulary for use in subsequent chapters. Students of speech pathology will of course study anatomy and physiology in considerable detail during their training. Other students of phonetics are advised to read further in the anatomy and physiology of the speech mechanism; suggested sources are given in the Annotated Bibliography for this chapter.

It has been said that speaking is an overlaid function, that every organ used in speech has another primary function. Lungs, larynx, tongue, teeth, and lips are all found in lower animals, which do not have speech, of course, and which produce a less varied repertoire of vocalizations. While it may be accurate to say that speech is overlaid on the vocal organs, this view overlooks the high degree of cerebral specialization unique to human beings.[1] This specialization of the higher brain centers is incredible in its complexity, permitting a retention of the rules of grammar and the vocabulary of language, but beyond that, permitting the fine control and minute synchronization of the various muscles brought into play in speaking.

---

[1] Indeed, one author, Lieberman [1975], goes so far as to suggest that the evolution of not only the brain but the other "organs of speech" was influenced by adaptations that increased the ability to speak, at the expense of more "basic" functions. Using a Darwinian argument, Lieberman points convincingly to the right-angle bend in the human vocal tract and the low placement of the larynx in man as compared to our closest relative, the chimpanzee. Our vocal tracts are not as well adapted for breathing, biting, chewing, or swallowing (there is a greater chance of asphyxiation from choking), despite the fact that these functions would seem to have primary survival value.

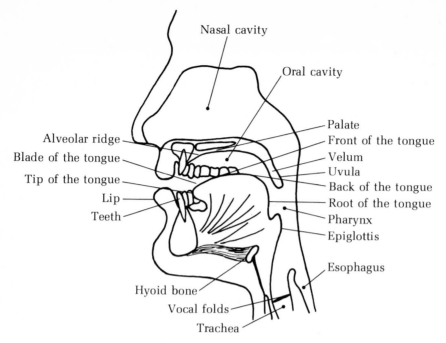

**Figure 5.1.** A cross section of the head showing the articulators important in the production of speech.

## 5-2 The Supraglottal Organs

The supraglottal organs (those above the larynx), as well as the vocal folds, are the speech organs that will be mentioned most frequently throughout this book. Figure 5.1 gives a schematized cross section of the head, with the important articulatory organs identified.

We will examine each of these organs in turn. In each case, the organ is given its usual name, many of which are usually derived from the Latin, and the adjective form of the name is mentioned as well. These adjectives will be important for referring to speech sounds; for example, a speech sound made with the **lips** is a **labial** sound.

The organs of speech are only catalogued here; the movements of these organs will be the subject of Chapters 7 and 8.

THE LIPS. The lips are used to close the oral cavity in the production of some consonants. They may be rounded in the production of certain vowels. The adjective form of this word is **labial** (L. *labia*, 'lips')[2]; when both lips are involved, we speak of a **bilabial** sound.

THE TEETH. Sounds involving the teeth are referred to as **dental** sounds (L. *dentes*, 'teeth'). The upper teeth more often than the lower ones are involved in speech production.

[2] All Greek references are from H. G. Liddell and R. Scott, *A Greek-English Lexicon*, Oxford: Clarendon Press, 1973. All Latin references are from C. T. Lewis and C. Short, *A Latin Dictionary*, Oxford: Clarendon Press, 1969.

THE TONGUE. The tongue is the most agile organ of speech; in fact, the word **tongue** means 'language,' not only in English, but in many other languages as well (the word **language** is derived from the Latin word *lingua*, for 'tongue'). Many gestures of the tongue are used in speech, and the tongue contacts many of the other speech organs. The tongue is divided into five regions: the **tip,** the **blade,** the **front,** the **back,** and the **root;** these are indicated in Figure 5.1. The adjective form of **tongue** is **lingual,** of **tip** is **apical** (L. *apex*), and of **blade** is **laminal** (L. *lamina*).

THE ALVEOLAR RIDGE (L. *alveus,* 'trough,' 'tray'). Also called the **gumridge,** this is the ridge directly behind the upper front teeth. The adjective form is **alveolar.**

THE PALATE (L. *palatum,* 'palate'). The term **palate** is somewhat confusing, since the velum is often called the "soft palate." Generally, when the term **palate** is used without modification, it is the hard palate that is being referred to. This latter usage is observed throughout this book.

The palate is the hard, bony part of the roof of the mouth, which extends from the alveolar ridge to the velum. The adjective form is **palatal.**

THE VELUM (L. *velum* [*palati*], 'veil [of the palate]'). The velum is the soft part of the roof of the mouth without bony support. It is sometimes called the "soft palate," but in order to prevent confusion, the term **velum** will be used exclusively in this book. The velum has two functions in speech; i.e., the tongue may be arched upward to contact it, and here we speak of a **velar** sound, and second, the velum itself may be raised or lowered, closing or opening, respectively, the passage to the nasal cavity. The latter function is of great importance in speech production, since many sounds require oral pressure which cannot be built up if the velum is not blocking off the nasal cavity from the oral cavity. In reference to this valve function, a different adjective form of the word is used; here we speak of **velic** opening and closing. In summary, tongue contact with the velum results in a **velar** sound. Contact of the velum against the back wall of the oral cavity results in **velic** closure.

THE ORAL CAVITY (L. *os/oralis,* 'mouth,' 'oral'). This cavity is a resonating chamber of primary importance to speech, since its size and shape can be modified so greatly. Its internal volume can be changed by modification in tongue and jaw position.

THE NASAL CAVITY (L. *nasus,* 'nose'). Velic action allows the nasal cavity to be either open or closed with respect to the rest of the vocal tract. This on-off function affects the quality of the sounds produced.

THE PHARYNX (Gk. *pharynx,* 'throat'). The pharynx is the space behind the root of the tongue. In some languages, its shape is modified in order to affect the quality of speech sounds produced. It has been traditionally assumed that this does not occur in English, so we do not have a class of **pharyngeal** sounds as there is, for example, in Arabic. (Recent research, however, suggests that there is modification of the pharyngeal cavity which is not dependent upon other articulatory movements; see Chapter 7.)

THE TRACHEA (Gk. *trachea*, 'neck'; 'place to grab someone to strangle him'). The trachea is the air passage leading to the bronchi and then to the lungs. The function of the **epiglottis** (Gk. *epiglottis*, 'on top of the glottis') is to cover the entrance of the trachea during swallowing, and to guide food into the **esophagus** (Gk. *aesophagos*, 'eating food'), the passage leading to the stomach.

## 5-3 The Larynx

The **larynx** (Gk. *larynx*, 'upper part of the windpipe')[3] is a complex structure situated at the upper end of the trachea, below the pharynx. The hard cartilage in front of the larynx can be felt by placing the hand on the throat. Most commonly in men, part of this cartilage (the "Adam's apple") protrudes conspicuously from the throat; however, a self-examination will demonstrate that the cartilage extends upward beyond this protrusion. Of course, the structures are similar in men and women; only the size differs.

Within the larynx is a pair of muscular bands, so situated that they may block the passage of air through the larynx on its way to and from the lungs. These are the **vocal folds** (sometimes called the vocal cords or vocal bands).

The larynx serves two functions besides speech. (1) During swallowing, the epiglottis covers the larynx and the vocal folds close. This is to prevent food or liquid from entering the trachea. In the event that something "goes down the wrong way," the vocal folds enter into the cough mechanism to eject the foreign substance. (2) The larynx also aids the upper part of the body in strenuous muscular activity. Many of the muscles of the upper body are anchored to the rib cage. As one uses these muscles, they press against the rib cage for support. In the absence of the vocal folds, this pressure would force the air out of the lungs. The partially collapsed rib cage would not provide a suitable anchor for the muscles, and one's strength would be reduced. To prevent collapse of the rib cage, the vocal folds are brought tightly together in a reflex action as one strains the muscles of the upper body. (You can demonstrate this to yourself by trying to speak while lifting a heavy object.) In the case of many weight lifters and some other athletes, so much pressure is placed on the vocal folds that calluses are formed on them and a gravelly voice quality results.

The vocal folds are muscular bands at either side of the air passage. The term **vocal cords,** now less commonly used than previously, suggests falsely that they are situated like the strings of a musical instrument. Rather, they are bands of muscular tissue protruding from the sides of the air passage. Figure 5.2 gives a cross-sectional view of the vocal folds.

The front ends of the vocal folds are anchored to the **thyroid cartilage,** which is the cartilage one feels at the front of the throat. The back ends are attached to the **arytenoid cartilages,** each of which acts as a lever in that it swivels and stretches the vocal folds. The arytenoid cartilages are controlled by muscles attached to them, including the vocal folds themselves.

The relative muscular tension of the vocal folds and the other mus-

---

[3] Aristotle defined *larynx* as 'the part of the vocal apparatus used in sounding vowels.' In Biblical Greek, *larynx* meant 'speech.'

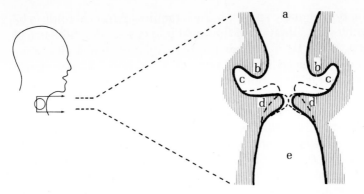

**Figure 5.2.** The vocal folds as seen in cross section from behind. The dotted outlines show the vibration of the vocal folds during phonation. a, the pharynx; b, the false vocal folds (ventricular folds); c, the ventricles of Morgagni; d, the vocal folds; e, the trachea (windpipe).

cles acting on the arytenoids serves to position the vocal folds according to their function. For normal respiration (A), the vocal folds are separated at their posterior (back) end. For heavy respiration (B), the vocal folds are separated even further. For whispering (C), the vocal folds are brought together along almost their entire length; a small space near the arytenoids allows the noisy passage of air. For phonation (speech) (D), the folds are **approximated** (brought into light contact) along their entire length. During physical exertion (E), they are brought together along their entire length, but under much greater tension than for phonation (Figure 5.3).

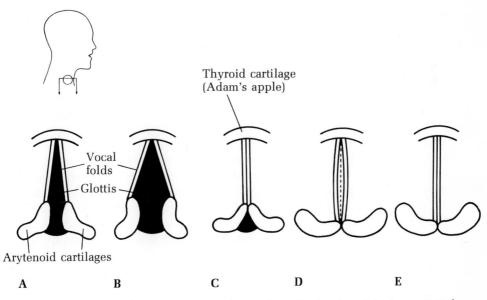

**Figure 5.3.** The vocal folds as seen from above. A. Normal respiration (vocal folds apart). B. heavy respiration (wide apart). C. Whispering (restricted, noisy air flow through small opening). D. Phonation (vibrating, as indicated by dotted line). E. Physical exertion (pressed tightly together providing airtight seal).

The production of many speech sounds requires the vocal folds to be **phonating.** This involves the vibration of the vocal folds under the influence of air passing over them. When their tension and position are suitable, the pressure of the air from the lungs will force them apart. Because of their elastic nature and the operation of the Bernoulli effect,[4] they close again after opening. This cycle is repeated many times per second, producing a buzzing noise. The vibration can be felt if one places the hand on the throat while saying "ah."

The speed with which the vocal folds vibrate, called the **fundamental frequency,** is to some extent controlled by such factors as the age, sex, and size of the individual, and it is to some extent under the voluntary control of the speaker. One can say "ah" on a higher or lower note than normal; singing is accomplished by adjusting the fundamental frequency of vocal fold vibration to follow the melody.

Those speech sounds that are produced while the vocal folds are vibrating are known as **voiced** sounds. Those that are produced while the vocal folds are apart are known as **voiceless** sounds.

When the vocal folds are apart, either for respiration or during the phonation cycle, there is a roughly triangular space between them. This space is known as the **glottis** (Gk. *glottis,* 'mouthpiece of pipe in which reed is inserted'; 'mouthpiece of trumpet'; metaphorically, 'mouth of windpipe'); like the hole in a doughnut, it is nothing in itself but is defined by what surrounds it.

## 5-4 The Subglottal Organs and Airstream Mechanisms

Below the glottis, the trachea descends into the chest, where it branches into the two **bronchi** (Gk. *bronchos,* 'trachea'; 'bronchial tube'), which lead to the two lungs. Air flow into and out of the lungs is controlled by the **diaphragm** (Gk. *diaphragma,* 'barrier') and the **intercostal muscles** (L. *inter costas,* 'between the ribs'). The diaphragm is a wall of muscle separating the abdominal cavity from the chest cavity. The intercostal muscles control the rib cage.

For speech, there must be a movement of air, which may be impeded momentarily to build up pressure. This movement of air may be either incoming (ingressive) or outgoing (egressive). In English, as in most languages, an egressive breathstream is normally used for speech, though some languages use an ingressive airstream for certain speech sounds. An ingressive airstream in English is usually restricted to speech produced during strenuous exercise— particularly running—or to talking excitedly while out of breath; under these circumstances, one may talk on both an ingressive and egressive airstream.

There may also be variation in the mechanism by which air is caused to flow.

The **lungs** draw air in and expel it. An airstream initiated by the

[4] The Bernoulli effect serves to reduce the pressure of a gas as it passes through a constriction. In the case of the larynx, the constriction is situated between the vocal folds. Pressure of the air from the lungs forces the vocal folds apart. As soon as the air flows out, its pressure drops according to the operation of the Bernoulli effect. This reduced pressure is not sufficient to keep the vocal folds apart, and they shut once more. Pressure builds up once more, and the cycle is repeated many times per second.

lungs is known as a **pulmonic** airstream (L. *pulmones*, 'lungs'). All languages use pulmonic air for speech sounds (vowels are pulmonic in all languages), but some languages use other airstream mechanisms besides.

The **pharyngeal**, or **glottalic**, airstream mechanism uses the larynx as the moving force or initiator. The larynx can be raised and lowered in the throat by muscles which are attached to it; this occurs involuntarily in swallowing (if you place your hand on your throat and swallow, you can feel the entire larynx moving up and down). The vertical movement of the larynx can be brought under voluntary control, though it may need to be learned at a young age for successful mastery. If the vocal folds are brought tightly together, and the larynx is raised or lowered in the throat, air will be pushed ahead of it, or pulled behind it. By means of this pharyngeal (glottalic) airstream mechanism, sufficient air pressure can be developed for the production of consonants, both ingressive and egressive. Numerous languages, among them some African and some AmerIndian languages, use the pharyngeal airstream mechanism.

The **velaric**, or **oral**, airstream mechanism uses the tongue as an initiator. The back of the tongue is arched upward to contact the velum, much as in the production of a k-sound. While forming a seal along the top and sides, the tongue is pushed forward (for egressive sounds) or pulled back (for ingressive sounds). The tip of the tongue may contact the palate or alveolar ridge, just as it might for consonant sounds produced with the pulmonic mechanism. The egressive velaric airstream is not used to produce speech sounds in any known language, but the ingressive velaric airstream is used to produce a class of speech sounds known as **clicks**. The interjection represented in writing as "tut-tut" or "tsk-tsk" is a click, as is a sound horseback riders sometimes make ("gee-up"). Clicks are speech sounds in such languages as Zulu and Hottentot.

In summary, there are six possible airstreams for speech, namely the ingressive and egressive varieties of the **pulmonic, pharyngeal,** and **velaric** mechanisms. The pulmonic egressive airstream is used in all languages, and is the only one used in English (with the exception of some interjections, and speech produced while crying or running). Among the languages of the world, the pulmonic ingressive airstream is rare, and the velaric egressive mechanism is unknown (though the latter is used by laryngectomees).

Only the pulmonic mechanism can be prolonged so as to produce a continuous chain of speech sounds; this fact explains why it is used in all languages. The other mechanisms allow the production of one or two speech sounds only, before the supply of air must be renewed. Phonation may accompany the pulmonic or velaric mechanisms, but not the pharyngeal mechanism, since this mechanism demands the complete closure of the vocal folds, which prevents their vibrating.

These varieties of airstream mechanisms have interest not only for the student of exotic languages. The speech pathologist may deal with individuals who are unable to produce speech by the normal means, and exotic airstream mechanisms are sometimes brought to bear. Some otherwise normal children develop velaric mechanisms for consonant production, as do children with certain organically based speech disorders. And some deaf, as well as normally hearing, children talk on an ingressive pulmonic airstream. Therapy or counseling may be required in these cases.

## 5-4.1 The Laryngectomee and Airstream Mechanisms

The **laryngectomee** is an individual who has undergone surgical removal of the larynx, usually as a result of cancer or injury. In such an individual, the normal pulmonic airstream mechanism cannot be used.

Since there would be no way to prevent food and liquid from entering the trachea in the absence of the epiglottis and vocal folds, the trachea is connected to a permanent incision in the front of the throat called the **stoma.** The laryngectomee breathes through the stoma; there is no connection between the mouth and the lungs.

Not only is the pulmonic airstream missing in the laryngectomee; the source of vibration, the vocal folds, is missing as well. One of several types of prosthetics may compensate for their loss, or the laryngectomee may use another airstream mechanism in producing **esophageal speech.** Esophageal speech results from normal articulatory movements during a controlled and prolonged belch. During a belch, tissue at the top of the esophagus vibrates noisily and thus can substitute for the vocal fold vibration. Air for the purpose of speech may be taken into the esophagus by swallowing or by the so-called glossopharyngeal press. The latter is a modified **ingressive velaric** air mechanism used to inject air into the esophagus. An accomplished esophageal speaker may produce six or more words per injection of air.

An **egressive velaric** speech is used by some laryngectomees. Called "buccal speech" (Vulgar Latin *bucca,* 'mouth') or "pharyngeal speech" by therapists,[5] this mechanism is highly unsatisfactory in that the mechanism for producing an airstream interferes with the articulation of speech sounds.

Of course, the **pharyngeal** airstream mechanism is not used by laryngectomees because it is dependent upon a normal and complete larynx.

The Annotated Bibliography for this chapter cites a number of studies on the clinical applications of various airstream mechanisms. Table 5.1 summarizes the airstream mechanisms; Figure 5.4 diagrams the operation of the various airstream mechanisms.

## 5-5 Anatomical Anomalies Affecting Speech Production

In this section we will introduce some common anatomical anomalies, due to birth defect, disease, aging, or surgery, that can affect speech production. The exact nature of the effects will be better understood once Chapters 7 and 8 have been studied, since it is in these chapters that the articulation of speech sounds is described in detail.

We have already outlined the drastic effects on speech of surgical removal of the **larynx.** Other anomalies of the larynx caused by injury, disease, or abuse of the voice can prevent the normal vibration of the vocal folds.

**Cleft palate** is a surprisingly common congenital defect in which the nasal and oral cavities are connected through a cleft or split in the palate. Unrepaired, the effects upon speech are serious, not only in giving a nasal quality to the speech and preventing normal production of many consonants,

---

[5] **Pharyngeal speech** is an unfortunate term since it is the result of the velaric and *not* of the pharyngeal airstream mechanism.

but also in preventing the child from learning normal velic movements. Since the oral and nasal cavities are connected no matter how the velum is placed, the child does not learn to control it.

**Cleft lip** is a congenital split in the upper lip which may be surgically corrected at an early age. It is commonly referred to as **harelip.**

Abnormalities of the **velum** and its musculature may prevent the proper closure of the nasal cavity from the oral cavity. Such abnormalities may accompany cleft palate; an unrepaired cleft palate will aggravate any velic deficiency for the reasons stated above.

Removal of the **tongue** and supporting structures severely disrupts

**Table 5.1.** Airstream Mechanisms

|  | Pulmonic (Lungs initiate) | Pharyngeal (Glottalic) (Larynx initiates) | Velaric (Oral) (Tongue initiates) | Esophageal |
|---|---|---|---|---|
| **Egressive** Usage | Universal; all languages have pulmonic sounds. With rare exceptions, it is the only airstream mechanism used in English and other European languages. | Rare. Some consonants in some African and AmerIndian languages. | Used by some laryngectomees, but not known in any natural language. Called "buccal" or "pharyngeal" speech by speech therapists. | Used by most laryngectomees, but not in any natural language. |
| Mechanism | Air is forced out of the lungs by diaphragm and intercostal muscles. Voicing possible. Cannot be used by laryngectomee. | Air is forced out of the pharynx by raising of the larynx with closed vocal folds. No voicing possible. Cannot be used by the laryngectomee. | Air is forced out of oral cavity by action of tongue against velum. Voicing is theoretically possible with normal larynx, but this mechanism is not used by anyone with a normal larynx. | Air (under pressure due to elasticity of esophageal walls) is allowed to escape slowly from esophagus. Constant pseudovoicing. |
| **Ingressive** Usage | Rare. Usually a variant of the egressive pulmonic airstream, used when speaking excitedly while out of breath. Sometimes used by deaf (and some normally hearing) children. | Rare, though more common than egressive pharyngeal. Some consonants (called "pharyngealized" or "glottalized") in some African and AmerIndian languages. | Used in some languages (e.g., Zulu, Hottentot) for sounds called clicks (English "tsk-tsk" is a click). Modified form used by laryngectomees to inject air into esophagus: glossopharyngeal press. | Unknown for speech of any kind. |
| Mechanism | Air is brought into lungs by diaphragm and intercostal muscles. Voicing is possible. Cannot be used by laryngectomees. | Air is sucked into oral and pharyngeal cavities by lowering larynx with closed vocal folds. No voicing is possible. Cannot be used by laryngectomee. | Clicks: Air is sucked into oral cavity by action of tongue back. Glossopharyngeal press: Air is forced into the esophagus by action of the tongue back. | (Air is injected by swallowing or by velaric ingressive mechanism.) |

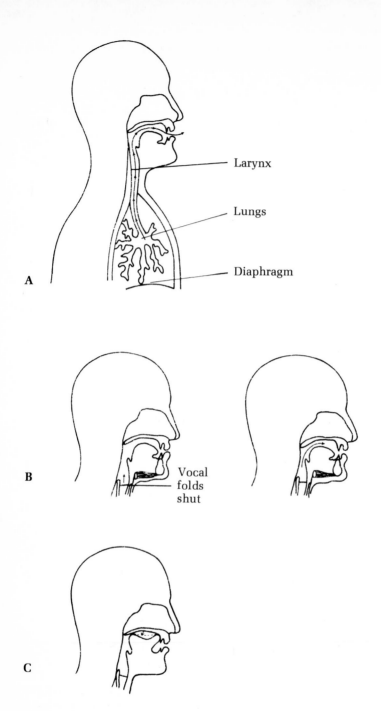

**Figure 5.4.** Airstream Mechanisms. A. Pulmonic. Air is forced out of or drawn into the lungs by the action of the diaphragm and the intercostal muscles. B. Pharyngeal or glottalic. The larynx is raised or lowered with the vocal folds closed. Air is forced out or drawn in. In the illustration, the larynx is raised, and air is forced out. C. Velaric. The tongue touches the roof of the mouth in two places. The back of the tongue is retracted, reducing air pressure between the two points. The front of the tongue is then lowered suddenly, and air rushes in producing a "click."

speech production; therapy for the **glossectomee**[6] is a neglected area of speech therapy. Through the use of compensatory movements of the remaining structures—notably the lips and the floor of the mouth—many glossectomees produce intelligible speech. While much less common than the laryngectomy, the glossectomy is more devastating to speech production.

Temporary **physical states** that interfere with speech production are as prevalent as the common cold. The nasal passages may be blocked; there may be abnormal amounts of mucus; or inflammation within the larynx may prevent normal phonation.

Normal **hearing** is essential not only for the development of speech in the child, but for the maintenance of speech in adults. Our reliance upon self-monitoring is demonstrated by the deterioration in the speech of individuals who become deaf as adults. Therapy may be used to reduce this deterioration.

Injury to the **brain,** often the result of a stroke, may result in an impairment known as **aphasia (dysphasia** in less serious forms). The aphasic individual generally has difficulty both in producing and in comprehending spoken and written language. For this reason, it may be better termed a language pathology than a speech pathology, since there is usually no direct damage to the speech articulators. However, aphasia is often accompanied by **apraxia** (or **dyspraxia**), which is a complete (or partial) inability to make a voluntary movement, usually a result of brain injury also, which may affect the speech articulators as well as other parts of the body. If the individual retains some voluntary control over the speech articulators, compensatory gestures may be learned.

## Questions for Review

This chapter has introduced many new terms, most of which will be used in subsequent chapters for describing the articulation of speech sounds. The following outline is given for the purpose of reviewing these terms:

1. Name the structure referred to by each adjective:

    labial        ———————————
    dental        ———————————
    lingual       ———————————
    apical        ———————————
    laminal       ———————————
    alveolar      ———————————
    palatal       ———————————
    velar         ———————————
    velic         ———————————
    pharyngeal    ———————————
    glottal       ———————————
    laryngeal     ———————————

2. The five divisions of the tongue, front to back, are: ———————————, ———————————, ———————————, ———————————, and ———————————.

[6] -*ectomy* is a suffix referring to the surgical removal of an organ. The suffix -*ectomee* refers to an individual who has undergone such an operation. Thus, a **glossectomy** is the surgical removal of the tongue; a **glossectomee** is a person whose tongue has been removed. The same convention is used for **laryngectomy** and **laryngectomee**.

3. Describe briefly how each of these airstream mechanisms works:
   a. Pulmonary.
   b. Pharyngeal (glottalic).
   c. Velic (oral).


## Annotated Bibliography

A most thorough study of the anatomy and physiology of the speech mechanism can be found in Zemlin's *Speech and Hearing Science* [1968].

The organs of speech are described and illustrated in considerable detail in Gray and Wise's *The Bases of Speech* [1959]. Detailed but clear sketches of anatomical structures, and particularly the muscles involved in speech, can be found in Shearer's *Illustrated Speech Anatomy* [1963].

A film illustrating speech production through x-ray films and animation is Bell Telephone Laboratories' *The Speech Chain* [1963] (this film also describes the hearing mechanism). The companion volume, also entitled *The Speech Chain*, by Denes and Pinson [1973], gives descriptions of the speech and hearing mechanisms.

Ladefoged's *Three Areas of Experimental Phonetics* [1967] includes a report on studies of the particular muscles involved in producing an airstream for speech. The airstream mechanisms are described in greater detail in Abercrombie's *Elements of General Phonetics* [1967], and in Brosnahan and Malmberg's *Introduction to Phonetics* [1970].

Moore's *Organic Voice Disorders* [1971] has an excellent detailed section on the structure of the larynx, and the action of the vocal folds.

Van den Berg's article "Myoelastic-Aerodynamic Theory of Voice Production" [1958] discusses in some detail theoretical views on the mechanism by which the vocal folds vibrate.

The following journal articles report clinical experiences with various airstream mechanisms used by esophageal speakers: Palmer [1970], Weinberg and Westerhouse [1973], Peterson [1973], Zwitman and Calcaterra [1973], and Marshall [1972]. Van Riper's *Speech Correction* [1972] provides a good introduction to the various pathological conditions of the speech mechanism mentioned in this chapter.

Lieberman's *On the Origins of Language* [1975], mentioned at the beginning of this chapter, is fascinating reading. Lieberman discusses his theory of the evolution of linguistic ability and even such matters as the likely phonetic repertoire of Neanderthal and other early men.

# Chapter 6

## Acoustic Phonetics: The Physics of Sound

### 6-1  Sound

This chapter deals with the basic unit of which speech consists: sound. Many speech pathology and audiology programs require a separate course in this subject. For this reason, we will reduce our examination of the topic to a minimum; in any case, we need only the fundamentals of the physics of sound in order to pursue our study of human speech sounds.

Sound is the passage of a disturbance through the air; it advances by causing vibratory motion of individual air molecules. It travels through the air at a rate of about 1,100 feet per second, and considerably faster through denser materials such as water or steel. It needs a medium through which to travel; sound cannot pass through a vacuum.

Sound travels by a wave motion, in a pulsating fashion. The analogy is often made that sounds travel in air as ripples do in a pond. This analogy is a useful one for introducing the behavior of waves, since we have all experienced water waves. There are some differences between surface waves on the water and sound waves in the air, but these differences will be considered after we have examined the points of commonality.

### 6-2  Wave Motion

If we throw a pebble into a still pond, we note that a series of ripples fans out in all directions from the source of the disturbance. These ripples or waves move onward, while individual water molecules return to their original location after the wave has passed. Let us look at how this works.

In Figure 6.1, a stone has just been thrown into a body of water, and ripples are beginning to move away from the source of the disturbance. Indi-

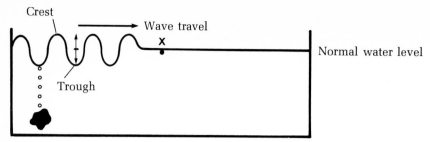

**Figure 6.1.** A surface wave on water. As the wavefront advances, individual spots on the water surface rise and fall.

vidual molecules of water move up and down as a result of the disturbance. The high points are called **crests;** the low points, **troughs.** Let us look at one particular drop of water on the surface, say the point X in Figure 6.1. It may help to visualize a cork riding on the surface of the water. What happens to this cork (or drop) as the wave approaches? As the crest approaches, it rides *up* to its highest point. As the crest passes, it rides *down* to its original position, and it continues riding down to a low point in the trough of the wave. As the next crest approaches, it rides up past its starting position, and back to the peak of the next crest. This continues as long as there are waves passing the spot. Note that this individual drop of water has ridden up and down, up and down, but has *not moved forward or backward.* The same drop of water is part of each successive wave that passes.

It is essential to recognize the fact that while the wave moves continuously forward, the individual particles of the material through which it travels (in this case, water) do *not* move a great distance; they just oscillate around one average, or rest, position.

## 6-2.1 Dimensions of Waves

Since waves can vary in a number of ways, it is useful to have a vocabulary to describe their dimensions. First, a term is needed to indicate one single unit of a wave. One **cycle** refers to one complete wave, that is, one complete crest and trough. One cycle can be measured from crest to crest, but it is more usual to indicate one cycle as starting at the baseline, rising above it, falling below it, and rising back up to it again (Figure 6.2). The word **cycle** does not have any dimension; it simply means one complete wave. Cycle implies something repetitive, and indeed, we expect one cycle to be followed by another that is just like it.

Waves can vary both in their physical dimensions (their size), and in their temporal dimensions (their timing).

## 6-2.2 Physical Dimensions of Waves

Waves have physical size. They can be bigger or smaller, longer or shorter. Special terms are used for these dimensions.

One physical dimension of waves is how high the crests are and how

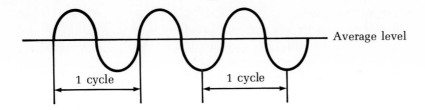

**Figure 6.2.** The cycle of a wave.

deep the troughs are. (This is related to the amount of energy that is behind the wave.) It is called the **amplitude.** The greater the amplitude, the higher the crests of the waves.

The second physical dimension is the length of one cycle: how far is it from one crest to the next? This dimension is called the **wavelength,** logically enough. This can be measured in any unit of length: inches, feet, centimeters, meters, etc. (the use of metric units is more common here, as in other scientific measures). Figure 6.3 illustrates amplitude and wavelength.

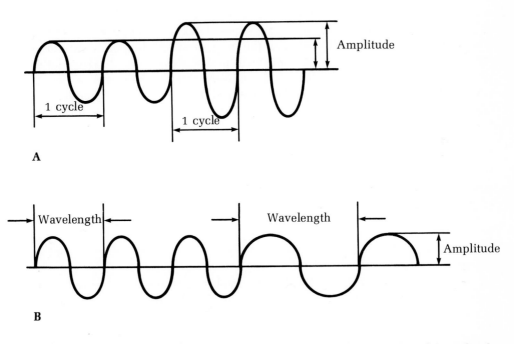

**Figure 6.3.** Amplitude and wavelength. A. Same wavelength, different amplitudes. The amplitude refers to the height of the wavecrests. B. Same amplitude, different wavelengths. The wavelength is the physical length of one cycle (in inches, feet, meters, or other unit of length).

## 6-2.3 Temporal Dimensions of Waves

If we were to decide on a particular constant period of time, say 1 minute, and count the number of cycles (that is, the number of complete waves) that occurred during that period of time, we would have a measure of how often or how frequently the wave cycle repeats itself. This measure is descriptively called the **frequency** of a wave. The 1-minute time period would probably be useful for counting waves on the ocean, but in dealing with sound, the time period of 1 second is found to be most useful. Thus, the standard unit of frequency is **cycles per second** (cps), or the number of complete wave cycles that occur each second. The term cycles per second is being replaced by the less descriptive term **hertz** (Hz), but the new term has the same meaning as the old.

The **speed of propagation** of a wave refers to the speed at which it propagates ('travels') through a medium. In the case of ripples on a pond, this speed is easily measurable. A stopwatch will measure the time it takes for the wavefront to cross the pond. Knowing the distance across the pond allows us to calculate the speed. In the case of sound in air, the speed of propagation is a little less than 1,100 feet per second (330 meters per second).

The speed of propagation—or speed of travel—is not related to frequency. This fact will be important to the discussion of sound, since high-frequency (high-pitched) sounds travel at the same speed as low-frequency (low-pitched) sounds.

The **period** is the other temporal dimension of waves, although it is less important for our purposes than the frequency. Frequency answers the question, how many cycles occur in one standard time period? **Period** answers the complementary question, how long does it take to complete one cycle? There is a direct relationship between the frequency and the period: the more cycles there are per second, the shorter time each cycle must take. Mathematically, one can state the relationship between the two measures as a reciprocal function. For example, what is the period in a measured frequency of 10 cycles per second? If there are 10 cycles in 1 second, then each cycle must take 1/10 of a second. If the frequency were 150 Hz, the period would be 1/150 of a second, and so on.

In summary, we have introduced two physical dimensions of waves, the amplitude and the wavelength, and three temporal ones, the frequency, the speed of propagation, and the period. The rest of this chapter will build on these basic concepts.

## 6-2.4 Periodicity

Every statement made above implied a rhythmical type of wave motion in which each cycle is exactly like the preceding and following cycle. Such a wave motion is called **periodic**, like the wave shown in Figure 6.4A.

Some types of wave motion that occur naturally are not rhythmical; each cycle is unlike the others. Such a wave is termed **aperiodic** since it has no regular period. The wave in Figure 6.4B is aperiodic. Because the cycles are not occurring at regular intervals, one cannot speak of the frequency of such a wave motion, and while it might be possible to measure the wavelength or period of a single cycle, these terms are usually reserved for periodic waves.

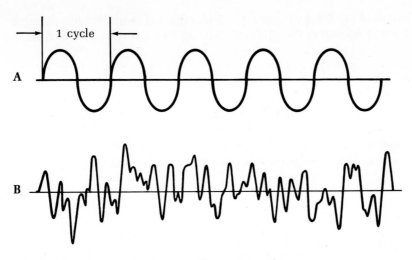

**Figure 6.4.** Periodicity. A. A periodic wave. B. An aperiodic wave.

## 6-3 The Wave Motion of Sound

We have looked at the behavior of waves in general and at water waves in particular. This has allowed us to become familiar with the basic dimensions of waves. If we wish to understand the wave motion of sound in air, however, we must realize that the water wave analogy has its limitations; there are some important differences between the two kinds of waves.

The first difference between the two kinds of waves results from the differences in the media through which they travel. Air is a gas, and like all gases, it completely fills the space that contains it, distributing itself equally throughout. Air is elastic, and can be compressed and rarefied. Water, on the other hand, is a liquid. It cannot be compressed or rarefied; it will take up the same space whether it is placed in a large container or a small one. It is not elastic in the same way air is.

The second way in which sound is different from ripples on a pond is that waves on the water are **surface** waves; they result from a rise and fall in the surface of the water. Waves in the air, by contrast, are actually *in* the medium. Sound does not travel along the surface of the air (there is no surface of the atmosphere like the surface of a lake); it travels *through* the air.

There is a toy that is generally called a "Slinky." It is a long, springy coil several inches in diameter, like a big soft spring. Children like it because it will "walk" down stairs and seems to be animate. Imagine a long Slinky lying on the top of a table, stretched and held at both ends. If one end is quickly pushed and pulled back to its original position, the shock so generated will travel the length of the Slinky. In fact, if the far end is securely held, the shock may bounce off and travel back to the starting point.[1] The way that the shock

[1] This demonstration, however, would work best on a surface of ice or with the Slinky suspended horizontally along its length by strings from the ceiling to reduce the friction of rubbing the tabletop.

travels the length of the Slinky is very much like the way sound travels through the air. Notice that no part of the Slinky moves up and down like the surface of the water.

This brings us to the third difference: in the surface waves on the water, the surface of the water is moving up and down while the wavefront is moving forward, at right angles. In the Slinky, each individual spot oscillates back and forth about its resting place. This back-and-forth movement is along the same path as the travel of the wave. In this respect, the motion of the Slinky is like that of air molecules disturbed by the passage of sound. Each molecule of air is displaced back and forth on the path the sound travels (Figure 6.5).

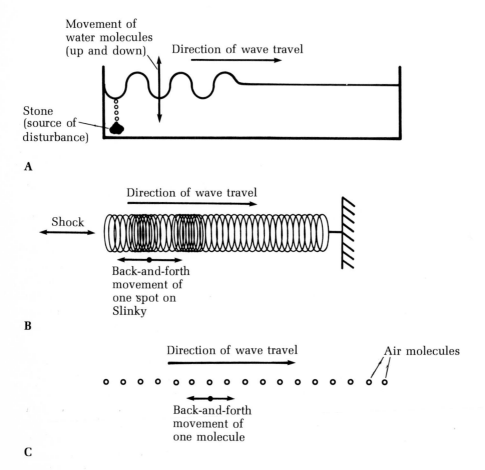

**Figure 6.5.** Wave motion on water, in a Slinky, and through the air. In each case, the wave travels in a single direction (though it may reflect back later), whereas a particular molecule or "spot" moves back and forth about a single place. A. Waves on water, showing that the wave travel is perpendicular to the direction of travel of water molecules. B. A shock wave traveling through a Slinky, showing that wave travel is parallel to the direction of travel of a spot on the Slinky. C. As a sound wave passes through the air, each molecule of air moves back and forth on the same path that the wave travels.

What is happening at a particular point in space that is being bombarded by sound? There is a rhythmical rise and fall in air pressure as a result of the passage of the disturbance. Suppose some disturbance originates a sound wave. This disturbance compresses nearby air molecules, or forces them more tightly together, creating a period of higher-than-average air pressure. Being elastic, the group of molecules springs back to its normal spacing. This springing brings the air pressure back to normal, but the molecules, in springing apart, continue past their starting point and end up further apart than they began. This results in a lower-than-normal air pressure. They return to normal spacing, and therefore normal pressure, after the passage of the disturbance. Also, in springing apart so far, the group of molecules disturbs the next group of molecules, compressing them in turn. By this means the disturbance is passed from molecule to molecule (Figure 6.6). The nature of sound at any one place is an alternate rise and fall in air pressure. In other words, there is an alternate compression and rarefaction of the air molecules.

Figure 6.7 shows a periodic sound wave. This looks like the earlier diagram of a water wave, but there is an important difference. In the water wave, the rise and fall of the tracing in the graph represented a rise and fall in the surface of the water. In Figure 6.7, the rise and fall of the tracing does *not* represent an up-and-down motion of air particles. Rather, it represents a rise and fall in air pressure.

The movement of sound waves in air is three-dimensional; that is, sound radiates in all directions from a source. This is indicated in Figure 6.8, in which the solid lines represent points of high pressure, or crests; the spaces between the lines represent points of low pressure, or troughs.

## 6-4 The Dimensions of Sound Waves

We will see in this section how the various dimensions of waves apply in the specific case of sound waves.

### 6-4.1 Periodic and Aperiodic Waves

A periodic wave will be perceived as having a musical or tonal quality, as does a single note from a musical instrument. An aperiodic sound will be perceived as being "noisy," like a hiss. A prolonged vowel sound, such as "ah," is predominantly periodic; a consonant sound such as "s" or "sh" is aperiodic.

### 6-4.2 Frequency

The frequency of sounds that we hear is much greater than that of waves on the water. A very good, young human ear can hear sounds between a low of 20 Hz and a high of 16,000 to 18,000 Hz (abbreviated 16 to 18 kHz, where k stands for *kilo*, meaning 'thousand'). Sounds whose frequency is below 20 Hz may be felt as vibration or heard as a series of individual clicks, and sounds whose frequency is above 18 kHz are not perceived at all, though many animals (e.g.,

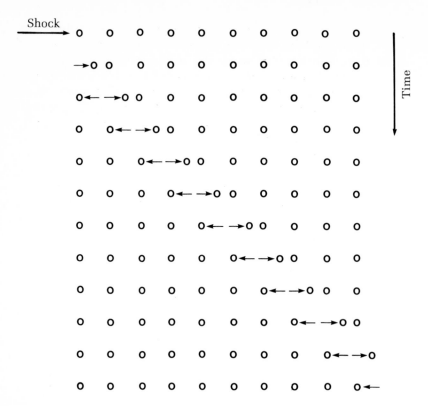

**Figure 6.6.** Passage of a shock wave through the air. The circles represent individual air molecules. Each successive row down is a moment later in time. The oscillation of individual air molecules is passed from molecule to molecule. By this means, the shock moves along the row, but the individual molecules return to their original places. If there were a continuous sound rather than a single shock, the cycle would repeat itself many times per second.

dogs and bats) can hear sounds of higher frequencies than man can. It is a universal fact that age reduces our range of hearing, as well as the acuity throughout the range that we do have.

Sounds of a high frequency are perceived as being high-pitched; low-frequency sounds are low-pitched. To give an idea of what particular frequencies sound like, these examples may be useful. If you turn up the volume control on a record-player amplifier without playing a record, you hear a humming sound. The frequency of this sound is 60 Hz because the amplifier operates from 60-cycle alternating current. Middle C on the musical scale is 256 Hz. The octave scale in music is based on a doubling of frequency: C above middle C is 512 Hz, C above that C is 1024 Hz, and so on.

## 6-4.3 Amplitude

The amplitude of sound waves corresponds to the amount of compression and rarefaction that occurs. A bigger original disturbance will cause air molecules to be displaced further; this causes a greater rise and fall in air pressure. In turn,

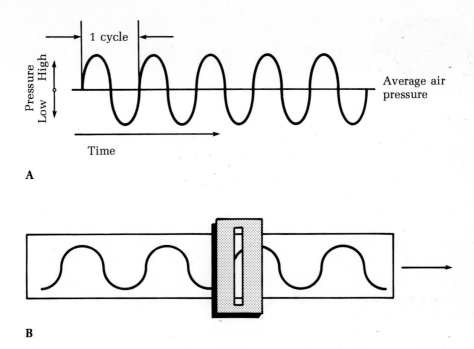

**Figure 6.7.** The Rise and Fall of Pressure in a Sound Wave. Periodic sound wave. A. The up and down of the curved line does not correspond to any up-and-down movement of the wave. Rather, the portion of the curve above the baseline indicates higher-than-normal air pressure; the portion below represents lower-than-normal pressure. Time is represented along the baseline; this is not a static "picture" of a sound wave. To understand this sketch, trace along the curve. *At a single point in space*, the pressure rises above normal, then falls, then rises, and so on. B. A good demonstration of the nature of the sound wave can be made from a strip of paper with a wave drawn on it and passing it behind a piece of cardboard with a slit in it. You will see the up-and-down motion of the pressure at a *stationary point* in space as the wave passes.

**Figure 6.8.** Sound waves moving away from a point source. The solid lines represent points of high pressure, or crests; the spaces between the lines represent points of low pressure, or troughs.

this causes the eardrums to move a greater distance back and forth. Greater amplitude is perceived as increased loudness.[2]

Our ears respond to a remarkable variation in amplitude. The minimum amplitude that can be perceived corresponds to the slight pressure needed to displace the eardrums by about the diameter of a hydrogen molecule. The maximum sound amplitude that can be endured without pain corresponds to a pressure about one million times as great as the minimum amplitude that can be perceived.

Amplitude and frequency are independent of one another; one dimension can be varied without affecting the other. This means that a high-pitched or low-pitched sound can be loud or soft; frequency is not determined by amplitude, and vice versa.

6-4.4 Wavelength

When dealing with sound, we do not usually discuss wavelengths, since information about frequency and amplitude accounts for most of the variation in sounds that we hear. However, wavelengths for sounds can easily be calculated if we know the speed at which sound travels and the particular frequency involved. The speed of sound through air is about 1,086 feet per second at sea level and normal barometric pressure (barometric pressure will affect the speed of sound slightly).

A simple multiplication of the velocity of sound by the period of a particular wave will give its wavelength, as shown in the following examples. (In using this formula, it is important to keep the unit of time constant in both velocity and period; here the unit is 1 second. Writing the units out clearly, as

___

[2] The terms **frequency** and **amplitude** refer to physical dimensions that can be measured objectively. The corresponding terms **pitch** and **loudness** refer to perceptual or psychological dimensions that can only be measured through subjective reports. Special scales are used for the perceptual dimensions. The term **volume** is often used interchangeably with **loudness** in everyday conversation. Actually, **volume** is properly used for another perceptual dimension of sound, namely the extent to which a sound seems to fill a room.

has been done in the examples, will help prevent confusion about the meaning of the answer, since the time unit can be seen to cancel out.)

$$20 \text{ Hz:} \quad \frac{1086 \text{ feet}}{1 \text{ second}} \times \frac{1 \text{ second}}{20 \text{ cycles}} \quad = 54.3 \text{ feet (per cycle)}$$

$$18 \text{ kHz:} \quad \frac{1086 \text{ feet}}{1 \text{ second}} \times \frac{1 \text{ second}}{18,000 \text{ cycles}} = 0.060 \text{ foot}$$

$$256 \text{ Hz:} \quad \frac{1086 \text{ feet}}{1 \text{ second}} \times \frac{1 \text{ second}}{256 \text{ cycles}} \quad = 4.24 \text{ feet}$$

The lowest pitch human beings can hear—20 Hz—corresponds to the longest wavelength, over 54 feet. The shortest wavelength corresponding to a sound human beings can hear—18,000 Hz—is 0.060 foot, or about three-quarters of an inch. The wavelength of middle C is about 4¼ feet.

It is apparent that, for certain frequency ranges, human beings make use of wavelength in localizing sound (that is, in determining from which direction a sound originates); since our ears are several inches apart, we can perceive whether or not the waves reaching the two ears are in the same phase of their cycle. Indeed, the greatest problem for those individuals suffering from a unilateral (one-sided) hearing loss is that they have difficulty localizing. Fortunately, phase is not the only cue for localizing, so such individuals retain some of this ability.

Wavelength is dependent upon the speed of travel of the sound. For example, sound travels through a steel bar at about 16 times the speed it travels through air. So the wavelengths would be about 16 times as long for the same frequency.

## 6-5 Harmonics and Resonance

### 6-5.1 Harmonics

If a sound source is producing a periodic tone of a certain frequency, there will usually be additional tones, called **harmonics,** which are whole-number multiples of the basic or **fundamental frequency.** For example, if a sound source is producing a tone whose fundamental frequency is 100 Hz, there will usually be tones of 200 Hz, 300 Hz, 400 Hz, etc. These are called the second, third, and fourth harmonics, respectively. (There will also be a fifth, sixth, and seventh harmonic, and so on ad infinitum, but these higher-order harmonics are usually very weak.)

The relative amplitudes of the various harmonics may differ, depending upon the sound source, but typically, the second harmonic is the strongest one (however, weaker than the fundamental), the third a little weaker, the fourth weaker still, etc. In the case of musical instruments, the pattern of harmonics (or **overtones,** as they are called in music) is usually more complex. For example, in a certain instrument, the fourth harmonic might be the strongest, followed by the second, and so on. The relative amplitude of the various harmonics thus accounts for the differences in sound quality when the "same" note is played on different musical instruments.

The fundamental frequency of the voice, as produced by the vibrating vocal folds, will similarly have harmonics. The function of these in speech production will be discussed later in this chapter.

## 6-5.2 Resonance

Resonance is the property of many objects to vibrate at a "preferred" frequency. For example, a tuning fork or a guitar string will vibrate at a certain frequency if an external force supplies an appropriate "push." Unless the physical properties of the object change (as happens in fingering a guitar), there is no change in the particular frequency of vibration, called the **resonant frequency.**

In these examples, the external force that starts the vibration is a light impact (in the case of the tuning fork) or plucking (in the case of the guitar), but sound, too, can give the "push" that will start sympathetic resonant vibration. This can be demonstrated by standing next to a piano and shouting: the piano strings will audibly vibrate as a result of the force supplied by your voice. *The fact that sound can be the energy source for resonance is of basic importance to speech.*

Another aspect of resonance which is important to speech is the fact that it has a way of reinforcing sounds, thereby increasing their loudness. To demonstrate this fact, take an ordinary wristwatch (the type that ticks, not an electronic or quartz watch) and hold it in your hand at arm's length from your head. Listen for the ticking. Now place it on the hard surface of a desk or counter. The ticking will normally be much louder, since the rigid desk top resonates.

The cause of this reinforcing effect can be best understood through an analogy. A children's playground swing moves back and forth in a way analogous to wave motion. We can talk about the cycle (one movement back and forth), the amplitude, and the frequency of the swing's motion; similar physical laws apply in this case as in the case of waves. A particular swing with a particular child on it will have one certain frequency at which it "prefers" to swing; this is its resonant frequency. If this child is given a series of gentle pushes, he will swing quite far with very little energy exerted; the amplitude of the child's swinging will be much greater than the amplitude of the push, but the pushes have to be timed just right: a gentle push at the right moment will increase the amplitude of the swing, but even a very hard push will not help if it is made at the wrong moment. The frequency of the pushes must match the resonant frequency of the swing in order for them to be effective; the frequency of the swinging motion *cannot* be changed by changing the frequency of the pushes.

By an analogous means, resonance generates loud sounds through the reinforcement of correctly timed external waves.

The foregoing discussion dealt with solid objects resonating: swings and tuning forks. There is another type of resonator that is basic to speech—the air space. Any enclosed or partially enclosed air space will have particular frequencies at which it will reinforce sound waves, and other frequencies at which it will damp (reduce) these waves.

Let us take a familiar example of an air-space resonator. Most of us have discovered how it is possible to produce a whistling sound by blowing across the mouth of a soft-drink bottle. What is happening to produce this sound? Clearly, the whistling sound does not come from the neck of the bottle. If the neck is cut off the bottle and one blows across its mouth, the sound produced will be the sound of rushing air, an aperiodic "whooshing" noise. (The word **noise** is generally reserved for sound that is aperiodic or non-melodic.) When one blows across the mouth of an intact bottle, it is not this low-amplitude noise that is heard predominantly but a high-amplitude periodic tone.

The air space inside the bottle has its own resonant frequency. The noise at the neck of the bottle is analogous to many people giving random pushes to the child on the swing. The pushes that are correctly timed will reinforce the swinging; the poorly timed pushes will simply be dissipated energy. In an analogous way, the noise at the neck of the bottle supplies the energy (the "pushes") necessary to make the air space resonate loudly at its preferred frequency. Some of the cycles of the aperiodic noise will be timed correctly and have the right period to reinforce the resonance; others will not, and will dissipate. We say that the external noise source *excites* the resonance.

The resonance of an air-space resonator normally involves a band of frequencies rather than a single frequency, and there may be one, two, three, or more of these resonant bands. For example, the bottle may have a resonant frequency of 1300 Hz, but this does not mean that the note heard will be a pure 1300 Hz tone. If the bottle has a narrow frequency band, the tone produced may be a mixture of frequencies from 1290 Hz to 1310 Hz; such a sound would strike us as being quite pure, or musical. On the other hand, the bottle might have a wide frequency band, in which case the tone might be a mixture of frequencies from 1250 to 1350 Hz; this would strike one as being fuzzier and less musical. Thus, the width of the resonant **band** corresponds to the range of excitable resonant frequencies.

An air-space resonator may have two or even more resonant frequencies. So, continuing the same example, the bottle might have one resonant band centered at 1300 Hz and another resonant band centered at 2200 Hz. These two bands may have different widths: the 1300-Hz band may have a bandwidth of 60 Hz (from 1270 to 1330 Hz), and the 2200-Hz band may have a bandwidth of 100 Hz (from 2150 to 2250 Hz). Figure 6.9 shows what a spectrogram of the sound produced by this bottle would look like.

Air-space resonators may vary in the following ways: (1) the resonant frequencies may vary (higher or lower), (2) the width of the resonant band may vary (wider or narrower), (3) there may be one, two, or more resonant bands. The resonating qualities of a particular resonator are determined by the configuration of the resonator. Continuing the same example, the tone of the soft-drink bottle could be changed in several ways. If the **size** of the bottle were changed, say to an 8-ounce bottle instead of a 12-ounce bottle, the tone would change. Or if the **shape** of the bottle were changed—by taking bottles of two different brands of soft drink with distinctively different shapes—the tone would change. Both size and shape are changed by partially filling a bottle with water. If the material of the bottle were changed, there would be a change in the resonating qualities of the bottle. (This theoretical change would actually be

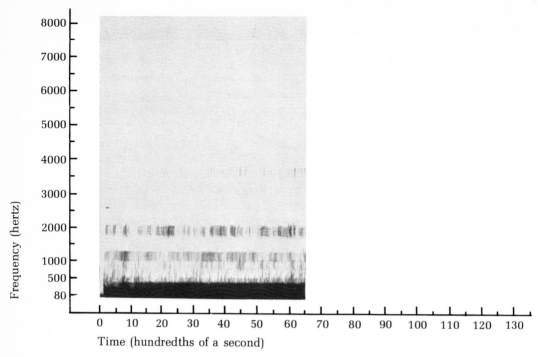

**Figure 6.9.** A spectrogram of the sound produced by a soft-drink bottle resonator. A spectrogram is an acoustic analysis of a sound; that is, the sound is divided into its component parts. Time is shown on the horizontal axis (this sound sample is 65/100, or about two-thirds, of a second in length), amplitude is shown by darkness of shading, and frequency is indicated along the vertical axis. This spectrogram was made of the sound produced by blowing across the mouth of a soft-drink bottle. There is a strong component of the sound across the frequencies 80 to 500 Hz. There are peaks centered at about 1300 Hz and 2200 Hz.

very small. For demonstration purposes, the bottom could be cut out of the bottle and replaced with a stretched rubber membrane in order for the effect to be noticeable.)

In summary, an enclosed air-space resonator: (1) needs an external source of sound to excite the resonance, (2) will emphasize certain frequencies and damp others, (3) increases loudness through reinforcement, and (4) has characteristic resonant frequencies that are independent of the external source of sound; they depend on: the size of the resonator, its shape, and the material it is made of.

## 6-6 Addition of Waves

In the previous section we discussed two situations in which one sound source produces periodic sound waves of several frequencies at once: (1) In the case of most sources of sound waves, there are harmonics—for example, a 100-Hz tone combined with 200 Hz, 300 Hz, 400 Hz, and so on. (2) In the case of an air-space resonator, such as a soft-drink bottle, there is a combination of bands of resonant energy: in the example just mentioned the frequencies were 1270–1330 Hz, plus 2150–2250 Hz.

But the sound waves discussed and illustrated in sections 6-3 and 6-4 (except for the aperiodic wave) consisted of *one* frequency alone. What happens in a sound wave when several periodic waves are produced simultaneously? How do they combine?

Several simple sound waves can be added together to form a new **complex** sound wave, which is the sum of the component parts, as shown in Figure 6.10. In this figure one can see the sum of a 100-Hz sound wave plus a 200-Hz and a 300-Hz wave. The resulting complex wave (wave D) is shown at the bottom of the figure. Remember that the rise and fall of the graph line represents the rise and fall of air pressure at a point in space. If two waves, both in the rise phase of their cycle, arrive at the same point at the same time, the resulting rise in pressure will be doubly fast and doubly great. But if the two waves arrive out of phase—that is, one in the rise phase of its cycle and the other in the fall phase of its cycle—they will cancel one another out, since, if the pressure is being influenced to rise and fall simultaneously, it will stay balanced in the middle. It can be seen in Figure 6.10 that when several waves are being added together, the amplitude of the resultant wave at any one point is sometimes *increased* by the additive effect of the component waves and sometimes *decreased* by the subtractive effect of the component waves.

Waves A, B, and C in Figure 6.10, like the waves in Figures 6.2, 6.3, and 6.4A, are termed **simple** or **sinusoidal** periodic waves or simply **sinusoids.**[3] When these are added together, the resultant wave (like wave D in Figure 6.10 or any of the waves in Figure 6.11) is termed **complex.** *The complex wave will be periodic if all of its component waves are.*

Complex periodic waves may have relatively simple or extremely complex shapes (a few are illustrated in Figure 6.11). But no matter how intricate the shape of a complex wave, it is easy to tell if it is periodic or not. If it has a pattern that is repeated, it is periodic; if there is no repetitive pattern, the wave is aperiodic.

*Any* complex periodic wave can be divided up into component sinusoidal waves, according to Fourier's theorem, named for the French mathematician who first proposed it. This means that any complex periodic wave, such as any of those shown in Figure 6.11 (and any of an infinite number of others) can be seen as the sum of simple sinusoidal waves of varying frequencies and amplitudes. (Their precise physical properties can be discovered through the application of Fourier's theorem, which involves mathematics that remain difficult and time-consuming even in this day of computers.) The fact that wave D in Figure 6.10 is the combination of sinusoids is easy to accept; it is perhaps harder to see how such waveforms as the square wave in Figure 6.11A can possibly be the sum of sinusoids. It is far beyond the scope of this book to demonstrate the mathematical derivation; suffice it to say that *any* periodic wave is the sum of a number of sinusoids.

If the sinusoidal components of a periodic wave are different in frequency by more than a few hertz, then our ear hears the complex wave as having a different quality from a simple wave of the same frequency. (People with a good ear for music can often identify the components.)

---

[3] The term **sinusoidal** is derived from the trigonometric function of the same name, whose shape, when graphed, is like the shape of a graphic representation of a simple wave. The name is often shortened to **sine,** both in mathematics and in discussing the shape of sound waves.

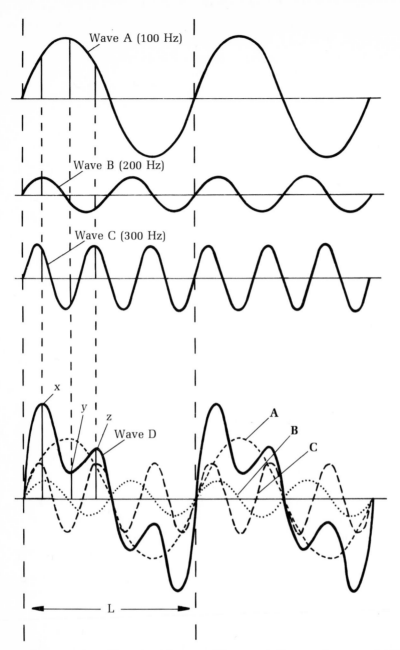

**Figure 6.10.** The operation of Fourier's theorem. Three periodic sound waves of different frequencies and amplitudes (A, B, and C) are shown to add together to give one complex periodic wave (D). Note the different frequencies and amplitudes of the three component waves. Wave D is the sum of these components; its components are indicated with broken lines. The frequency of D is 100 Hz. It can be seen that wave D is simply the result of adding the components: at point x, for example, wave A is still rising, and waves B and C are near their high points; at point y, wave A is near its high point, but waves B and C are descending; at point z, wave A is starting its descent, wave B is near its low point, and wave C is at its high point. Any other point along wave D can similarly be found to be the sum of the components. The rise and fall of the graph line represents

As Figure 6.11 shows, a complex periodic wave has a cycle that can be identified. As with the simple periodic waves we saw earlier, each cycle is exactly like those that precede and follow. The **frequency** of a complex wave is the same measure as for simple waves: the number of times the cycle repeats itself each second. Of course, the components of the complex wave each have their own frequencies, higher than the frequency of the overall complex wave.

A complex periodic wave, like simple periodic waves, will have a somewhat melodic quality, as contrasted with an aperiodic wave, which has a harsh or "noisy" quality. **Melodic,** however, does not imply that the sound is necessarily pleasing musically, only that it is not harsh and noisy. For example, if you pronounce a sustained vowel such as "ah," you are producing a complex sound wave that is predominantly periodic.

With a minimum of equipment you can produce sounds that have the auditory quality of complex periodic waves as opposed to that of simple periodic waves. A tuning fork, tuned to a particular frequency—say the note A on the musical scale—will produce a simple periodic wave. The same note played on any musical instrument will have the *same frequency* but will be complex rather than simple. It strikes the human ear as being "richer" than the note produced by the tuning fork. As mentioned earlier, musical instruments tend to emphasize certain harmonics and de-emphasize others. Similarly, the same note played on different instruments will have the same frequency but will be a complex wave of a different shape, again depending on which harmonics are emphasized. (It is a curious fact that we find certain combinations of harmonics "rich" and others discordant.) Many phonetics and acoustics laboratories are equipped with oscillators that can produce sine waves, square waves, and sawtooth waves of the same frequency.

The additive nature of sound waves, and the fact that a complex wave can be seen as the sum of a number of simple waves, is basic to speech. The resonant speech sounds, such as vowels, result from the combination of several frequencies or tones into a complex waveform.

## 6-7  Acoustic Principles Applied to the Vocal Tract

These principles will now be applied to the human vocal mechanism, and analogies drawn between it and the soft-drink bottle, to clarify the means by which speech sounds are produced. We will at first discuss only resonant speech sounds, that is, the vowels and a few consonants such as "l."

The vocal folds provide a source of "buzzing" sound, quite low in amplitude. A median frequency for this glottal vibration would be around 130 Hz for an adult male and 220 Hz for an adult female. The glottal vibration and its harmonics provide the sound energy to excite resonance within the supraglottal cavities. These cavities—the pharyngeal, oral, and nasal—provide the

---

rise and fall in pressure, so it is apparent that when one component wave is influencing the pressure to rise and another to fall, the result will be an intermediate point. And when all component waves are influencing the pressure to rise, the overall rise will be greater than that of any one component wave. Distance L corresponds to 1 cycle of waves A and D, 2 cycles of wave B, and 3 cycles of wave C.

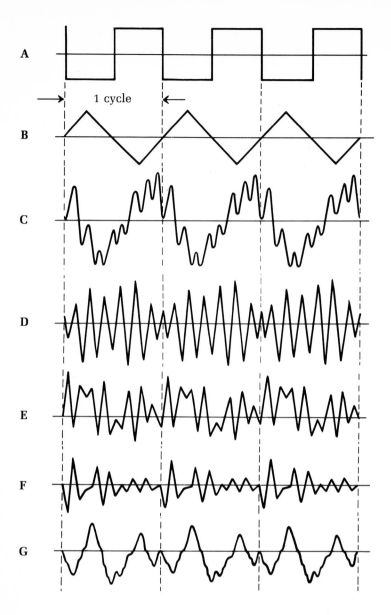

**Figure 6.11.** Some complex periodic waves. Illustrated are seven of the infinite variety of complex periodic waves: A. A "square" wave. B. A "triangular" wave. C. The sum of a 300-Hz, a 2055-Hz, and a 2350-Hz wave. D. The sum of a 400-Hz, a 500-Hz, and a 600-Hz wave. E. The sum of a 100-Hz, a 500-Hz, and a 600-Hz wave. F. The author pronouncing the vowel "ah" (/ɑ/) (fundamental frequency is about 125 Hz). G. The author pronouncing the vowel "oo" (/u/) (fundamental frequency is about 125 Hz). For ease of comparison, the seven waves have been drawn to different scales to make the length of one cycle the same for all. The fundamental frequency of the wave from which C was drawn is 300 Hz, of E 100 Hz, and of F and G about 125 Hz. These different frequencies will of course correspond to different wavelengths and periods, so in scale drawings the lengths of the cycles would differ (for example, E would be 4 times as long as D). But we have made them appear the same length in this drawing so you can compare the different wave shapes.

resonating chamber for speech production. As with the soft-drink bottle, the vocal cavities will have their own characteristic resonant frequencies.

It was stated earlier that resonant characteristics of an air-space resonator could be modified by changing the shape, size, and material of the resonator. At least two of these principles are used in speech production.

1. RESONATOR SHAPE. In order to produce different vowel sounds, the shape of the vocal tract is modified. This changes its resonant characteristics. In turn, this means that the cavity will resonate at different frequency patterns and identifies them as different vowels.

The shape of the oral cavity can be changed by changing the position of the tongue and lips. For example, say "ee," then "oo." [4] The tongue is positioned differently for each sound, and the lips are rounded for "oo" but not for "ee." The size of the space inside the mouth is approximately the same, but the shape has changed. The resonant characteristics are different, so the frequencies produced are different. The ear identifies the combination of frequencies heard as particular vowels.

2. RESONATOR SIZE. The resonating characteristics of the vocal tract can be changed by altering the size of the cavities. For example, pronounce the vowel "ee" and the vowel "a" (as in "cat"). For the second vowel, the jaw was lowered, making the space inside the mouth considerably larger. The change in size modified the resonant frequencies, and different vowels were produced.

Even with the jaw position constant, the effective space inside the mouth can be changed by the tongue position. If the tongue is bunched up it will occupy more space than if it is lying flat on the floor of the mouth.

If we lower the velum, we can change both the size and shape of the resonant cavity by opening the nasal passages. Instead of increasing resonance, as might be expected, the nasal cavity tends to damp or reduce some of the oral resonance. This accounts for the distinctive sound of nasal vowels (such as certain vowels in the French and Portuguese languages).

Finally, the effective size of the resonating cavity may be modified by abnormal growths such as adenoids or enlarged tonsils. However, these conditions produce audible changes in voice quality mostly by interfering with the raising and lowering of the velum. A cold changes voice quality by denasalizing all speech sounds since the nasal passages are blocked.

3. RESONATOR MATERIAL. Of course, the material of which our vocal tracts are made cannot be changed, but it has often been suggested that changing the degree of tenseness of speech muscles would be similar in effect to changing from a soft-walled resonator to a hard-walled resonator. This change is supposed to be responsible for the difference in sound between a "tense" vowel such as "ee" and a "lax" vowel such as the "i" of "bit." The vowel of "beet" does somehow feel "tenser" than the vowel of "bit," but recent studies have shown that the difference in sound is not so much a result of the differing

---

[4] The vowels are given their usual English spelling here. The phonetic symbols for vowels are introduced in Chapter 7, those for consonants in Chapter 8. The vowel "ee" (as in "beet") is symbolized /i/; "oo" (as in "boot") is /u/; "i" (as in "hit") is /ɪ/; "a" (as in "cat") is /æ/.

tension of the vocal tract walls as of a change in the size and shape of the pharyngeal cavity resulting from the position of the tongue root.

In summary, it appears that the differing sounds of various vowels—reflecting differing resonant characteristics of the vocal tract—result from changes in the **size** and **shape** of the resonating chambers of the upper vocal tract.

## 6-7.1 Resonance in Vowels: The Formants

The vocal tract resonates at characteristic frequencies, like the soft-drink bottle. But there is an obvious difference. We recognize the resonant sound of the bottle as a tone, having musical properties, but vocal resonance is recognized as speech sound, having potential for carrying meaning. The main acoustic difference between the two is in the number of resonant bands and their pattern. The bottle has one or perhaps two resonant bands, whereas the vocal tract, having an irregular and complex shape, has five or six resonant bands of acoustic energy, called **formants.**

The first three formants distinguish one vowel sound from another. The higher formants contribute more to personal voice quality than to the identification of the particular vowel, so our discussion will concentrate on the first three formants.

Let us take the example of the vowel "ee" as in "beet." It is characterized by resonance centering at 300 Hz, 2700 Hz, and 3300 Hz, called the first, second, and third formant, or $F_1$, $F_2$, and $F_3$, respectively. Each formant has a bandwidth of 75 to 100 Hz.

Each different vowel sound has a different pattern of formants. The vowel of the word "put" has these formant frequencies: $F_1$, 470 Hz; $F_2$, 1160 Hz; $F_3$, 2680 Hz.

The fundamental frequency ($F_0$)[5] of speech and its harmonics provide the energy to excite the formant resonance. The listener hears the fundamental as well as the three formants. The pattern of formants plus the fundamental, heard simultaneously, is interpreted as a particular vowel. All the formant frequencies plus the fundamental frequency add together in the manner discussed in section 6.6, producing a complex periodic sound wave. In decoding speech, the brain separates them again and recognizes the combination of frequencies as a certain vowel spoken at a certain frequency.

The frequencies of the formants are determined by the two variables discussed earlier: the size and the shape of the vocal tract. This means that the fundamental can be changed *without* changing the vowel sound. You can say "ah" on a high note, a middle note, or a low note, and it still sounds like "ah."

The fact that the perceptual mechanism uses the *pattern* of formants to interpret vowel sounds is shown in two ways: the speech of different individuals and artificial speech.

The formant frequencies given above are averages for women speak-

---

[5] The term **fundamental frequency** (often shortened to **fundamental**) has two uses. For any periodic sound, it is used to distinguish the basic frequency from its harmonics. In speech, it is used to distinguish the audible frequency of the glottal vibration from *both* its harmonics *and* the formants. If we change the pitch of our voice, as when singing, we are changing the fundamental frequency of speech. The harmonics of this fundamental change as the fundamental changes, but the frequency of the formants does not change significantly with a change in fundamental.

ers. Men's formants are generally a little lower, children's a little higher, because of the size of the organs of speech; but while the exact frequencies are a little different, the pattern remains the same. A man, a woman, and a child produce different sounds when they say "ee," but we perceive them as the same vowel.

Artificial speech gives an interesting demonstration of how speech sounds are perceived. If the pattern of fundamental plus formants is duplicated by an artificial tone-generating device, the listener will perceive the appropriate vowel sound.[6]

6-7.2  The Production of Nonresonant Speech Sounds

The foregoing remarks apply to resonant speech sounds, namely the vowels and such consonants as "l" and "r." Our vocal apparatus is capable also of producing sounds that are nonresonant. Two of these methods of producing speech sounds are used in English. (1) Air can be forced through a constricted opening so that its passage generates turbulence and an aperiodic hissing noise. "S" and "sh" are such sounds. (2) Air pressure can be built up and suddenly released, giving an explosive popping noise. "P" and "k" are such sounds. The range of different sounds can be further increased by the use of the vocal folds. The resonant sounds need vocal-fold vibration, but the sounds produced through turbulence or explosion do not, and so this vibration may be used to create variety. "S" is a turbulent sound produced without vocal-fold vibration; "z" uses vocal-fold vibration. "P" is an explosive sound without vocal-fold vibration; "b" uses vocal-fold vibration.

At the end of Chapter 7 (section 7.8), a more detailed description of the acoustics of vowels is given, along with spectrograms of various English vowels. At the end of Chapter 8 (section 8.8), a more detailed description of the acoustics of consonants is given, and spectrograms of various English consonants are shown.

**Classroom Demonstrations on Speech Acoustics**

The following simple demonstrations can be made in the classroom to clarify some of the concepts presented in this chapter. Demonstrations are dependent upon available equipment, of course; they may be given by the teacher or by students as a class project. In any case, these demonstrations have proved useful in helping students to understand the sometimes difficult concepts. Naturally, the inventive instructor or student who has the necessary resources at his/her disposal may design other demonstrations.

Demonstration 1

SUBJECT. Frequency, amplitude, and period.

EQUIPMENT. Oscilloscope (preferably a storage type), oscillator with amplifier and/or attenuator, loudspeaker.

[6] In fact, artificial speech is used in phonetic research. Since the parameters of artificial speech can be controlled accurately, one can conduct research on the question of what aspects of the speech signal are salient for perception, and which are redundant (unnecessary). This is called **analysis by synthesis.** Communications engineers are conducting research into the possibility of sending instructions for synthesizing speech rather than speech itself along telephone wires. This would involve decoding and encoding devices at each end of the telephone lines.

PROCEDURE. Connect the oscillator output to the loudspeaker (through amplifier and/or attenuator, depending on the oscillator) and to the oscilloscope input. Demonstrate the change in frequency (shown visually on the oscilloscope screen) as the pitch of the sound from the loudspeaker changes. Similarly, note how amplitude changes reflect loudness changes. Demonstrate measurement of the period, using information of the oscilloscope scan rate.

Demonstration 2

SUBJECT. Resonance of air chambers.

EQUIPMENT. Party noisemaker, tubes, pipes.

PROCEDURE. Blow on the noisemaker in the open air and in the end of various tubes, noting differences in sound output.

Demonstration 3

SUBJECT. Amplification and attenuation as a function of resonance.

EQUIPMENT. Oscillator (and separate amplifier if needed), small loudspeaker, tube or pipe, microphone, and sound-level meter.

PROCEDURE. Connect the oscillator output to the loudspeaker, using an amplifier if needed (depending upon the oscillator). Tape the loudspeaker to one end of the tube, and the microphone to the other. Connect the microphone to the sound-level meter. Slowly vary the frequency of the oscillator through the audible range and note the variation in loudness at the microphone end of the tube. **Note:** This demonstration is included in the Bell Telephone Laboratories film *The Speech Chain*, mentioned in the Annotated Bibliography.

Demonstration 4

SUBJECT. Vowels, formants.

EQUIPMENT. Commercial sound spectrograph (such as Sona-Graph, manufactured by Kay Elemetrics Corporation).

PROCEDURE. Analyze several vowels to demonstrate presence of formants.

Demonstration 5

SUBJECT. Electrical analog of speech signal, speech envelope.

EQUIPMENT. Storage oscilloscope, microphone, optional: tuning forks.

PROCEDURE. Optionally, demonstrate analog of pure tone (generated by tuning fork) shown as rise and fall of oscilloscope trace. Demonstrate the more complex electrical analog of speech. Prolong vowels to demonstrate periodicity. Discuss Fourier analysis and introduce concept of speech envelope.

**Annotated Bibliography**

The physics of sound is discussed in considerable detail in most college physics textbooks.

The following books discuss sound in relation to speech: Gray and Wise's *The Bases of Speech* [1959], Denes and Pinson's *The Speech Chain* [1963], Joos's *Acoustic Phonetics* [1948], and Ladefoged's *Elements of Acoustic Phonetics* [1962]. The last three chapters in Gerber's *Introductory Hearing Science* (those by Wakita, Gerber, and Haggard) discuss particular aspects of the acoustics of speech; other chapters in the same volume discuss the physics of sound [1974].

Bell Telephone Laboratories makes available a 5-minute recording entitled *Computer Speech*, which gives samples of artificial speech and explains the uses of it.

# Chapter 7

# Articulatory Phonetics: The Vowels

### 7-1 Speech Sounds

Before examining individual speech sounds, we should stress that for speech to serve its communicative purpose, it must be made up of **contrasting** sounds, and there must be a considerable number of contrasts.

Cartoonists sometimes portray cavemen as having a vocabulary based on one syllable, "ugh." While scholars attribute more linguistic ability to these early men (see Lieberman [1975]), let us consider just how such a system might work. If the only vocal capability of an individual were to say "ugh," what possible words could his language have? Well, "ugh," of course, and "ugh-ugh," and "ugh-ugh-ugh," and so on. It is easy to see that only four or five different "words" could be used before the task of speaking and listening became too difficult. Perhaps this number could be doubled by careful use of the tone of voice: "ugh?" could contrast with "ugh!," and just plain "ugh," but a dead end is reached very quickly, limiting the number of messages that can be sent and received. So much for a system based on one phonetic unit.

This "language" would be improved by the addition of one phonetic contrast. Increasing the number of syllables by one, through the addition of "uck," quadruples the number of contrasting "words" that can be made, and the addition of a third contrasting syllable would greatly increase the number of possible words. In fact, the addition of sound contrasts increases exponentially the number of possible words of a given length.

In all natural languages, the number of phonetic contrasts is quite large. English, for example, has about 39 contrasting speech sounds (the number depends upon the dialect). These sounds can be combined in many ways (though not in just *any* way, as will be shown in Chapter 12). The result is a positively enormous number of possible different words, without having to resort to memory-taxing polysyllable words, as would be necessary in a hypothetical caveman language in order to have even twenty different words. The number of different one- and two-syllable words in English is huge, as an unabridged dictionary demonstrates, and many possible words are not used. If we suddenly needed three times the present vocabulary, this could be accomplished without the need for new words longer than two syllables. Strink and plick and so on would be perfectly acceptable new words, having the advantage of being short, pronounceable, easy to remember, and most importantly, easy to distinguish from other English words.

So it is the phonetic **contrasts** of a language that serve as the medium for carrying meaning. Individual speech sounds cannot be said to have any meaning.

For example, the vowel of the word meet is meaningless by itself, independent of the English (or other) language, but, in the context of an English word, since it is distinctively different from other English vowels, this vowel indicates that the word spoken was meet and not mate or might or moat or moot or mitt, or whatever. The speaker, of course, is concerned with the meaning of the word meet and is not conscious of phonetic considerations. He is able to communicate his meaning through the medium of speech only because there are systematic contrasts among the speech sounds of his language.

## 7-2 Vowels and Consonants

If you were asked to explain the difference between vowels and consonants, you might respond by dividing the letters of the alphabet into these two classifications: "vowels" and "consonants." Phoneticians, however, classify speech **sounds,** not letters, into these two groups. Letters may *represent* either type of speech sound, although our English spelling system has a poor correspondence between sounds and letters. In the International Phonetic Alphabet (IPA), there is a better correspondence between letters and sounds, but the terms **vowel** and **consonant** still always refer to **sounds,** never to letters or symbols. The term **phone** or **segment** means a single speech sound.[1] Each distinctly different phone is represented by a different IPA symbol.

Phones are classified as vowels or consonants chiefly on the basis of how they are articulated. For the articulation of vowels, the oral cavity is open at least as far as it is for the vowels of "beat" and "boot"—that is, the airflow is unimpeded—and the vocal folds are generally vibrating. For consonants, the airstream is stopped, impeded, or diverted through the nasal passage, and the vocal folds may or may not be vibrating.

In general, your intuition about what is a vowel and what is a consonant will be correct, with the possible exception of some r-sounds and perhaps some other phones.

This chapter will consider the vowels; the consonants will be considered in Chapter 8.

## 7-3 Vowels

In Chapter 6, it was noted that vowels are defined acoustically by particular patterns of bands of sound energy at particular frequencies (section 6-7.1). We

---

[1] The term **phoneme** is sometimes loosely used to mean a speech sound, but this term properly has a more specific meaning, as will be shown in Chapter 11.

noted that the acoustic patterns typical of vowels are the result of excitation of the vocal tract resonator by the noise of the vibrating vocal folds. The particular acoustic pattern of each individual vowel is dependent upon the resonant characteristics of the vocal tract; these in turn depend upon the size and shape of the vocal tract, which can be changed at will by the speaker. This means that vowels can be classified not only by how they sound (the acoustic quality) but also by the position of the speech organs in producing them (their articulatory features).

In the articulation of vowels, the effective shape and size of our vocal tract are changed through the following movements of the speech organs: (1) by raising or lowering the jaw, which changes the amount of space inside the mouth; (2) by arching the tongue to varying degrees, and in different places (front or back); (3) by rounding or spreading the lips, which changes the resonant characteristics of the vocal tract; and (4) by moving the tongue root, which changes the size of the pharynx. Additionally, vowels in some languages are produced with a lowered velum, bringing the nasal cavities into play.

## 7-3.1 Tongue Position and Jaw Height

The vowel /i/[2] as in "beet" is produced with the jaw raised. The vowel /æ/ as in "bat" is produced with the jaw lowered. Pronounce the two vowels in turn, noting the jaw position and noting also that the tongue stays arched in the forward part of the mouth. Now try the vowels /u/ as in "boot" and /ɑ/ as in "father." Note that /u/ is pronounced with the jaw raised and /ɑ/ with the jaw lowered. Also note that the arch of the tongue is toward the back of the oral cavity. (You may have noted the lip-rounding for the vowel /u/; we will discuss this later.) Figure 7.1 shows stylized diagrams of these articulations.

A quadrangle (four-sided figure) has been overlaid on the diagrams in Figure 7.1. This quadrangle is used to give convenient reference points for specifying the tongue position. It is called the **vowel quadrangle,** and later on the vowel quadrangle will be used without the accompanying sketch of the head and tongue.

The four vowels considered so far—/i, æ, u, ɑ/—are produced with the tongue as far as possible from its rest position. If the tongue were raised any more than for /i/ or /u/, a consonant would be produced. The tongue and jaw positions are as low as practicable for the sounds /æ/ and /ɑ/. These vowels, along with others around the periphery of the vowel quadrangle, are called **cardinal** vowels. They are like the cardinal points of the compass, providing reference points for identifying other, noncardinal vowels.

At this point, it is important to take time to convince yourself that the preceding diagrams are accurate. It is suggested that you use a mirror and a safe object (such as a tongue depressor) to examine the configuration of your mouth during the production of these vowels.

We noted that for /i/ and /æ/ the arching of the tongue is forward in the mouth and the jaw is in the extreme high and low positions, respectively. The jaw can also be between these extremes, as it is for the vowel /e/ as in "bait."

---

[2] IPA symbols are generally placed between slash marks, /i/, and sometimes between brackets, [i]. In Chapter 11 the use of these marks is discussed.

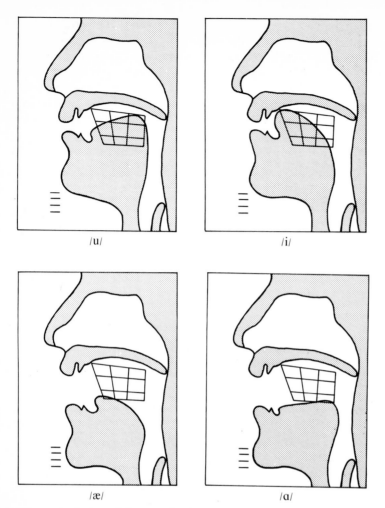

/u/ /i/ /æ/ /ɑ/

**Figure 7.1.** The articulation of four cardinal vowels.

It was noted that for /i/ and /u/ the jaw is in a raised position and the arching of the tongue is toward the extreme front of the mouth for /i/ and toward the extreme back of the mouth for /u/. The arch of the tongue can be between these extremes, however, as it is for the vowel /ə/ in "about."

Therefore, we can see that there are *two dimensions along which the position of articulation of vowels can be identified. In every case, the position of the highest point of the arch of the tongue is considered to be the point of articulation of the vowel.*

The vertical dimension of the vowel quadrangle is known as the vowel **height.** We speak of **high, mid,** and **low** vowels; the **mid** height may be subdivided into **upper-mid** and **lower-mid.** (Some authors use the term **close** instead of **high,** and **open** instead of **low.**)

The horizontal dimension is labeled in terms of how far front the point of articulation is. Vowels produced at the front of the mouth are known as **front** vowels; those produced at the back are known as **back** vowels. We use the term **central** to indicate the position halfway between front and back (do not confuse **central** and **mid**).

In order to identify the point of articulation of a vowel, both dimensions must be given; the height dimension is normally given first. So we identify /i/ as a high front vowel, /u/ as a high back vowel, /æ/ as a low front vowel, and /ɑ/ as a low back vowel. For the low vowels, it is sometimes difficult to locate the arch of the tongue; the jaw position may be used to identify these as low vowels.

There are three more dimensions of vowel articulation: tenseness, lip-rounding, and rhotacization.

## 7-3.2  Tenseness

The first of these additional dimensions is what has traditionally been called **tenseness.** It has been noted that certain pairs of vowels, although they share most of the same articulatory dimensions, differ in "tenseness"—one would be classed as **tense,** the other as **lax.** As the name suggests, the tense vowel was supposed to be pronounced with a general tension of the muscles of speech, and these muscles were more relaxed for the lax vowels. The differing tension of the walls of the resonating cavity was supposedly responsible for the difference in vowel sound produced.

This point of view holds considerable intuitive appeal. If you pronounce /i/ as in "beet"—a tense vowel—and /ɪ/ as in "bit"—a lax vowel—you will probably feel a greater tension in the facial and other muscles of speech when pronouncing the tense vowel. A second pair is the /u/ of "boot" (tense) and the /ʊ/ of "book" (lax). And the vowels /e/ as in "bait" and /ɛ/ as in "bet" are sometimes classed as tense and lax, respectively, although other phoneticians point to height differences in classifying these vowels.

Recent studies have disputed this traditional view. First, physicists tell us that the slight difference in the tenseness of the walls of the resonating cavities would not greatly affect the sound produced; in order to change the sound enough so that it would be recognized as a different vowel, the size and/or shape of the cavities would have to be changed. Studies (e.g., Ladefoged [1968], MacKay [1977], and Stewart [1967]) have shown that the root of the tongue is advanced (moved forward) in tense vowels, widening the pharynx (see Figure 7.2). (If you put your finger on your throat above the Adam's apple and pronounce /i/, /ɪ/, and /u/, /ʊ/, you will note that your finger is forced outward slightly as you pronounce the tense vowel but not as you pronounce the lax vowel.)

The new evidence has led some people to suggest that what used to be called "tense" vowels should be called "advanced tongue root" vowels for the sake of accuracy, but the matter has not been resolved. We are therefore using the more established terminology, which will more likely be found in the literature. It is best not to interpret the term "tense" too literally (though the famous phonetician Daniel Jones [1932] pointed out that while he did not accept tenseness to be what others believed it to be, it is still possible to obtain good results when teaching the sounds in question by instructing the students to tense up or relax their tongues).

Even if tongue-root position constitutes the main difference between

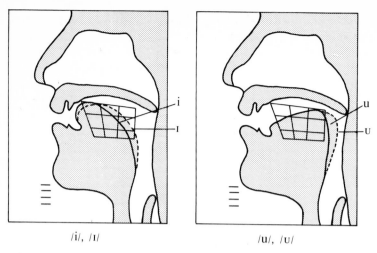

/i/, /ɪ/                     /u/, /ʊ/

**Figure 7.2.** The articulation of tense and lax vowels.

the tense and lax members of a pair, however, we must note other important articulatory differences as well. In the pronunciation of /i/, the mouth is spread wide (see section 7-3.3), while it is relaxed for /ɪ/. And /ɪ/ is less high and less front than /i/. Similarly, we note that /u/ is pronounced with rounded lips, more so than /ʊ/, and that /ʊ/ is less high and less back than /u/. And /e/ is a little higher than /ɛ/, leading some to suggest that height is the only difference between these vowels; however, the evidence shows that /e/ shares some characteristics with other tense vowels, and /ɛ/ with other lax vowels; this can be demonstrated by placing your finger on your throat, as described above, and pronouncing these vowels.

Note that the tense-lax pairs are high or mid vowels—the terms are not used for low front or low or mid back vowels. This makes sense if tenseness is a matter of tongue-root position; with the tongue in position for low vowels, the tongue root may be forced back into a position that cannot be changed without moving the front of the tongue.

### 7-3.3 Lip-Rounding

In pronouncing the vowel /u/, it is necessary to round the lips while in pronouncing the vowel /i/, the lips are spread. In classifying vowel sounds, we sometimes wish to distinguish different degrees of lip-rounding. We can do so by using the adjectives **rounded, neutral** (or **unrounded**), and **spread** in describing the vowel.

Many languages distinguish vowels by lip-rounding alone. This means that these languages may have two vowels that are articulated in the same part of the mouth and whose only difference is that one is rounded while the other is not. In French, for example, there are two high front tense vowels, one rounded, one spread. The French spread vowel, /i/, is similar to the equivalent English sound. The French rounded vowel is transcribed /y/ and has no equivalent in English. So the French words pi, /pi/, and pu, /py/, contrast only by lip-rounding. There are other pairs of rounded and unrounded vowels in French and other languages, making it necessary in those languages always to specify whether a vowel is rounded or not.

In English, vowels are generally not contrasted by rounding alone. There are some vowels that are rounded, and others that are unrounded, but, with one exception, there *are no* pairs of vowels whose articulation is identical except for rounding. Thus, English vowels are often identified without reference to rounding, since this is redundant information.

For example, a high back tense vowel in English is always rounded; there is no high back spread vowel in English (though such a vowel exists in some other languages). Whether or not rounding is mentioned, however, it remains an important aspect of the articulation of this vowel.

The one exception is the pair of vowels /ʌ/ and /ɔ/, as in "cut" and "caught." Their place of articulation is similar, but /ʌ/ is unrounded while /ɔ/ is rounded; so rounding must be specified with these vowels. (In some phonetics texts /ʌ/ is said to be a central vowel, not a back vowel. Such a classification is convenient since it bypasses the problem of having to specify rounding, but it is hardly accurate. Pronounce /ʌ/, /ɔ/ to demonstrate to yourself that it is the lips that change, not the tongue placement.)

## 7-3.4 Rhotacization

To **rhotacize** a vowel means to give it an r-like quality (the name comes from the Greek letter *rho*). Examples of English rhotacized vowels would include the vowels of such words as "bird," "fur," and "heard." Note that while the spelling shows a vowel followed by a consonant r, the sound is just one vowel that is rhotacized, or **r-colored.** There is no consonant "r" in these words, though our ear identifies the sound as being similar to a consonant "r."

The English rhotacized vowel is a central vowel, transcribed /ɚ/.[3]

At least one writer on the subject (Ladefoged [1975]) states that r-coloring of a vowel may come from a number of different articulatory gestures that produce a similar sound and that it is therefore better to classify these vowels by sound than by articulation. The r-like quality of the rhotacized vowels may come from some or all of these articulatory gestures: retraction (pulling back) of the front of the tongue; a bunching up of the back of the tongue; and a retraction of the root of the tongue into the pharynx. The acoustic effect is a drop in the frequency of the third formant.

The vowel of such words as "beard," "far," "board" is made up of a vowel /ɚ/ in combination with another vowel. Again, what is spelled with the letter r is actually a vowel; this will be examined in section 7-5, on diphthongs. The sound spelled with an r in such words as "red" or "try" is a consonant and will be discussed in Chapter 8.

[3] Most transcription systems used for general purposes transcribe a word like "her" as /hər/, suggesting a vowel followed by the consonant /r/. This agrees with our intuition and is generally a satisfactory system. However, it is important to realize that in speech the vowel and the /r/ are combined into one rhotacized (r-like) vowel: /hɚ/. Anyone attempting to teach this sound as a sequence of vowel plus consonant /r/ will not have good results. Note also that some transcription systems distinguish the unstressed [ɚ], as in "father," from the stressed [ɝ], as in "bird." This is redundant if stress is marked in another way, which will be shown in Chapter 9.

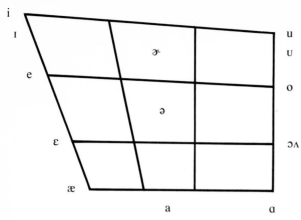

**Figure 7.3.** The vowel quadrangle.

There are many dialects in which there is no rhotacization of vowels. These so-called r-less dialects include many British dialects, and in the United States they include New England, Southern, and Black English. These dialects are not really r-less, since they have the *consonant* "r"; it is just the *rhotacized vowels* they are lacking. In these dialects, the rhotacized vowel is replaced with a nonrhotacized central vowel, or else the preceding vowel is lengthened.

### 7-3.5 Stress and Vowels

Vowels in syllables that are not stressed tend to have a neutral or mid-central articulation; that is, they are neither high nor low and neither front nor back. Examples are the vowels in these words: "terrace," "about," "frustration," "habit," and "frequent." The indistinct vowel sound in these examples is called **schwa** and is transcribed with the symbol /ə/. The effect of stress on vowel sounds is discussed in detail in Chapter 9.

### 7-3.6 The IPA Symbols for English Vowels

The articulatory positions of the various vowels discussed are seen in Figure 7.3.

Sample words that will help in identifying the vowels are given below, but a word of caution is necessary. It is not a good idea to memorize lists of key words as a mnemonic for the IPA symbols. Vowels have slightly different qualities depending on the word in which they occur, and memorizing key words may hinder more than it helps. It is better to try to associate the symbol with the sound and to avoid key words once the vowels have been identified. Also, there is enormous dialect variation in the qualities of vowels, and the example words given may not be correct for your dialect. The words given indicate a "standard American" pronunciation.

| Vowel | Example words |
|-------|---------------|
| i | bee, heat |
| ɪ | bin, hit, sing |
| e | bay, hate |
| ɛ | bet, hen, test |
| æ | ban, hat, hang |
| u | hoot, boot, food |
| ʊ | hook, took, put |
| o | boat, toast, home |
| ɔ | caught, haughty |
| ʌ | buck, mutt, dusk |
| ɑ | cot, f<u>a</u>ther |
| ə | <u>a</u>bout, Cub<u>a</u> |
| ɚ | fath<u>er</u>, butt<u>er</u> |

The vowel /a/ is shown in Figure 7.3. There is no key word for this vowel except as in some Midwestern pronunciations of "f<u>a</u>ther"; this is the vowel of the French word "la."[4] It is normally used in English only to transcribe diphthongs (see section 7-5).

Most of the phonetic symbols are called by their sound or their name as a symbol of the English alphabet. The exceptions are as follows:

| Symbol | Name |
|--------|------|
| ɛ | epsilon |
| æ | ash |
| o | close o |
| ɔ | open o |
| ʌ | caret *or* wedge |
| ə | schwa |
| ɚ | (unstressed) schwar |
| ɝ | (stressed) schwar |

---

[4] The symbol <u>a</u> is sometimes used to replace <u>æ</u> or <u>ɑ</u>, since neither of these symbols is available on a typewriter. The problem is that the use of <u>a</u> for English vowels is inconsistent (some substitute it for <u>æ</u>, others for <u>ɑ</u>) and therefore it is recommended that <u>æ</u> and <u>ɑ</u> be correctly and consistently used. The symbol <u>a</u> should be reserved for English diphthongs, transcription of fine dialect differences, and foreign languages.

## 7-3.7 Using the Descriptive Adjectives for Vowels

Earlier in this chapter, adjectives for describing vowels were given. Note that the terms for tenseness, lip-rounding, and rhotacization are generally used only when needed to prevent ambiguity. Of the two remaining dimensions, the height dimension is given first, and then the front-back dimension. Do not attempt to memorize a description of each vowel; use the examples to confirm your understanding of vowel articulation. You should eventually be able to apply these descriptions to any vowel, including the non-English vowels of foreign languages or misarticulated speech.

| Vowel | Description |
|---|---|
| i | high, front, tense |
| ɪ | high, front, lax |
| e | (upper-) mid, front, tense |
| ɛ | (lower-) mid, front, lax |
| æ | low, front |
| u | high, back, tense (rounded) |
| ʊ | high, back, lax (neutral or slightly rounded) |
| o | upper-mid, back (rounded) |
| ʌ | lower-mid, back, unrounded |
| ɔ | lower-mid, back, rounded |
| ɑ | low, back |
| ə | mid-central, unstressed |
| ɚ | central, rhotacized (unstressed) |
| ɝ | central, rhotacized, stressed |

## 7-4 Vowel Quality and Quantity

Unfortunately, the vocabulary used in everyday language to describe vowel sounds is quite inadequate for the job. Some new terms will be introduced in this section. The words themselves are not new, but their meanings probably will be. It may be necessary to unlearn some meanings for words and to learn new ones instead.

The **quality** of a vowel refers to the particular vowel sound that is heard. The quality of /i/ and /ɪ/ is different because they are different vowels.

The **quantity** of a vowel, more commonly called the **length,** is measured in terms of time. A **short** /ɪ/ sound would be spoken quite quickly; a **long** /ɪ/ would be prolonged. The terms **long** and **short** do *not* refer to vowel quality.

Most of us are in the habit of calling the vowel sound /i/ "long e" and the vowel sound /ɛ/ "short e." The terms "long" and "short," as used in everyday language, refer to vowel quality. The two sounds in question are different vowels; they are *not* long and short versions of the same vowel. The reason these terms are used has to do with the historical development of the English language and our spelling of words. In phonetics, and in the professional description of speech sounds, it is important to remember to reserve the terms **long** and **short** for **temporal length.**

There are two ways to indicate that a vowel is long (in time). The vowel symbol can be written twice (or even many times). This may be useful in indicating prolongations in stuttered speech. The other method is to use a colon (:) after the vowel symbol, which is normally considered to indicate double the length of the sound in question. To indicate that a vowel is a little longer than normal, but not quite twice as long, place just one dot following the vowel. For example, if someone prolonged the vowel of the word "bay," it could be transcribed /bee/ or /be:/. If the prolongation was slight, it would be transcribed /be·/.

Some languages contrast different words by means of vowel length. In Finnish, for example, /tule/ means 'Come' (the imperative), but /tulee/ means 'he comes.' In English, we do not contrast words by vowel length,[5] so we usually do not need to mark the length of vowels at all. Of course, to record speech that has abnormal prolongations—be it deviant speech, dialect variations, or dramatic use of prolongation—length must be indicated. The speech of stutterers, as well as that of the deaf, frequently contains abnormal prolongations, including prolongations of consonants as well as of vowels.

## 7-5  Diphthongs

Diphthongs are vowels made up of two different vowel sounds fused together. For example, the vowel in the word "my" is pronounced by starting with the tongue in a low back position and then moving the tongue up to a high front position. You can demonstrate this to yourself by prolonging the vowel. In Figure 7.4, the starting and finishing positions of the tongue are indicated.

We conventionally indicate diphthongs by their starting and finishing points. So the diphthong in "my" is transcribed as /ai/.

There is usually some dispute as to the precise quality at the beginning and end of most diphthongs, and there is in fact much variation because of dialect differences and the surrounding consonants. For this reason, instead of spending endless time disputing each case, it is best to accept a standard conventional way of transcribing diphthongs. This system may later be modified to suit particular needs in recording dialects or nonnormal speech.

The following are the conventional ways of recording English diphthongs (this follows the convention of Jones [1972, p. 61] but with the addition of the ligature):

[5] It is true that standard North American English does not use vowel length contrastively to distinguish between words. However, some dialects lacking rhotacized vowels compensate for the missing /ɚ/ by lengthening the preceding vowel (section 7-5.1). Thus pairs of words such as pock/park or the names Carter/Kotter may be distinguished phonetically by vowel length: [pɑk]/[pɑːk] and [kɑːtə]/[kɑtə]. Native speakers would most likely point to the r as the difference between these pairs, since society places high importance on literacy. But, as noted in Chapter 3, our intuitions are often wrong or are based on what we think we *ought* to say. In summary, despite the spelling and our intuitions, vowel length is distinctive in some dialects of English.

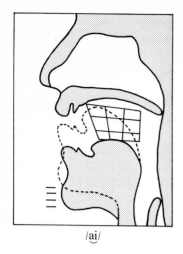

/ai̯/

**Figure 7.4.** The articulation of the diphthong /ai̯/.

| Vowel | Example words |
|-------|---------------|
| /ai̯/ | my, buy, eye, I, might, hide |
| /au̯/ | cow, loud, found, howl |
| /ɔi̯/ | boy, boil, hoist |

A connecting line or **ligature** often joins the two symbols of a diphthong, indicating that the two vowels are together forming one syllable, but common usage often omits this.

While it is not really a diphthong, the first sound of the word "use" sometimes causes confusion and will be clarified here. The letter u of the word "use" and other similar words represents two sounds; the first is like the initial sound of the word "yellow" and is transcribed /j/. So the word "use" would be transcribed /juz/ or /jus/.

One other note on diphthongs: two vowel sounds next to one another, but in different syllables, do not form a diphthong. In the word "doing," for example, the /u/ and /ɪ/ vowels are in different syllables, and do not form a diphthong (this is why the ligature is used for true diphthongs).

### 7-5.1 Diphthongs with Rhotacized Second Element

As pointed out earlier, words such as "beard," "far," and "board" have a vowel sound made up of a schwar (/ɚ/) plus another vowel in most dialects. Phonetically, the vowel is combined with schwar, forming a diphthong, and may be indicated this way:[6]

---

[6] The remark made earlier (p. 95n) applies here. While it is phonetically accurate to say that the word "bar" contains the diphthong /ɑɚ/, for general transcription purposes it is often easier to consider the sound as a sequence of /ɑ/ plus the consonant /r/; that is, /bɑr/. Similarly with the others, which may be transcribed /ir/, /er/, /ur/, /or/, and so on.

| Symbol | Example word |
|--------|--------------|
| ɪɚ[7] | beer |
| eɚ | bear |
| uɚ | boor |
| oɚ | bore |
| ɔɚ | hoarse |
| ɑɚ | bar |

There exists considerable dialect variation in the lower front rhotacized diphthongs. Some dialects make a three-way distinction between "marry," "merry," and "Mary"; others make a two-way distinction; and some pronounce all three alike. If they are needed, one may distinguish /æɚ/, /ɛɚ/, and /eɚ/ (or /ær/, /ɛr/, and /er/—see footnote, p. 100).

As noted above, so-called r-less dialects only lack vocalic (vowel-like) "r"s; they do not lack consonantal "r"s. This lack appears in the rhotacized diphthongs as well. In some dialects, such as New England, a schwa replaces the schwar. In other dialects, such as Southern, the vowel preceding the missing schwar is lengthened. So standard American "for" is transcribed /foɚ/ (or, if you prefer, /for/) but /foə/ in New England and /fo:/ in Southern.

### 7-5.2 The Dipthongal Quality of English Vowels

The vowels /i, e, o, u/ are identified as long vowels in English, since they are usually prolonged slightly as compared to other English vowels. This prolongation goes hand in hand with another peculiarity about these vowels as they are pronounced in most dialects of English. The long vowels in English tend to be slightly diphthongized. This means that their point of articulation changes slightly as they are pronounced. For example, pronounce the word "say" and carefully observe your articulatory gestures. Notice that the jaw is not in a constant position throughout the pronunciation of the vowel; the vowel becomes higher as its articulation progresses. Try the words "see," "sue," and "so" and observe the changing quality as well.

It is useful to compare the way a native speaker of French, Italian, or Spanish pronounces these vowels with the way you pronounce them. This comparison might help you to see the differences. In English, the articulators move considerably during the production of the vowel; in the other languages mentioned, there is very little or no movement during the production of the vowel. The vowels in these languages are often called **pure** vowels. The term pure does not indicate any superiority but simply means that the vowel has a

---

[7] As with other diphthongs, there may be some argument about the exact quality of the vowel sounds. For instance, it may be suggested that /ɪɚ/ (or /ɪr/) is more accurate than /iɚ/ (or /ir/) for "ear." You may also have a similar comment concerning /uɚ/ (or /ur/), or another of the transcriptions given. The rhotacization of the diphthong may affect the tongue-root position, making it difficult to tell whether the first element of the diphthong is tense or lax, and the quality varies from dialect to dialect. As with other diphthongs, it is usually satisfactory to accept one standard transcription for general purposes and to reserve the fine distinctions for special purposes.

single, unchanging quality. A better term for a pure vowel is **monophthong,** in contrast to diphthong.

While the long vowels in English are generally slightly diphthong-ized, the short vowels are more monophthongal or pure. /ɪ/, /æ/, /ɛ/, and the other short vowels do not show a change in quality during their production. However, one frequent peculiarity about the speech of deaf children is their tendency to diphthongize all vowels, short or long. Also, there are dialects, such as that of the American South, in which short vowels are strongly diphthongized: "bit," for example, might be pronounced [bɪ·ət]. Curiously, this same dialect tends to monophthongize certain diphthongs: "my," for example, may be pronounced [ma:].

The importance of understanding the diphthongal nature of English long vowels is that it has practical applications in some therapy situations. The foreign speaker whose native language has pure vowels, or the deaf speaker who has not heard these vowels pronounced, may need guidance in pronounc-ing these vowels with the precise quality of English speech. Even though the differences are subtle, the pronunciation of these vowels without diphthong-ization will cause them to sound foreign or unnatural. Since the pathologist should be able to detect fine differences in speech sounds, it is well for the student to listen for this diphthongal quality just for practice.

The transcription symbols that were introduced in this chapter do not indicate the diphthongal nature of these long vowels but represent them as if they were pure vowels. For the most part, this is satisfactory since we are only concerned with English and since most manuals of transcription use the system indicated in this chapter.

Several systems of transcribing English vowels more precisely are in use, however, and since they may appear in other books, we will mention them briefly. One system was devised by Daniel Jones [1972], the other by the team of Trager and Smith (see Ladefoged [1975, p. 64]); the former was developed in England, the latter in the United States. These two systems represent English long vowels as follows:

| This book | Jones | Trager-Smith |
|-----------|-------|--------------|
| /i/ | /i:/ | /iy/ |
| /e/ | /ei/ | /ey/ |
| /o/ | /ou/ | /ow/ |
| /u/ | /u:/ | /uw/ |

There are other differences among the systems, but for our purposes it is enough to point out the quality of these long vowels, and to prepare for a possible variety of transcriptions of the same sounds. In all cases it is best to pick one system for one's own use, and to stay with it consistently.

7-5.3  Vowel Articulation Summary

The articulation of all the English vowels we have discussed is summarized in Figures 7.5 through 7.8. Each shows the tongue and jaw position, as well as the

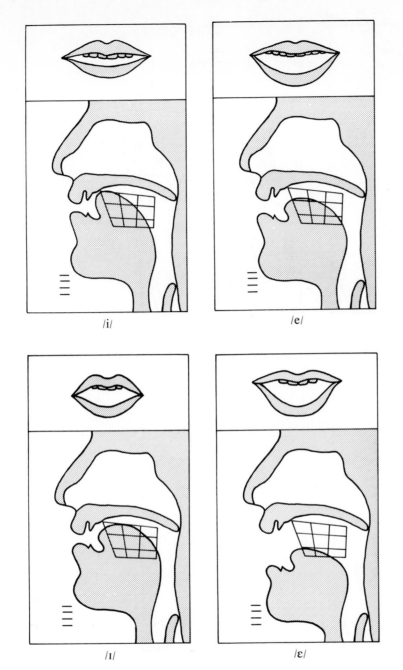

**Figure 7.5.** The articulation of /i/, /e/, /ɪ/, and /ɛ/.

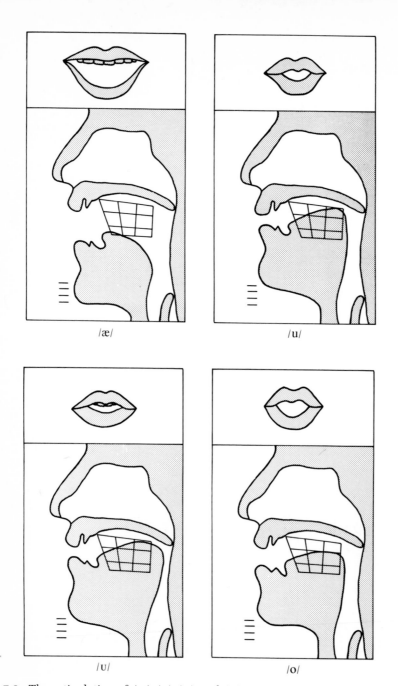

**Figure 7.6.** The articulation of /æ/, /u/, /ʊ/, and /o/.

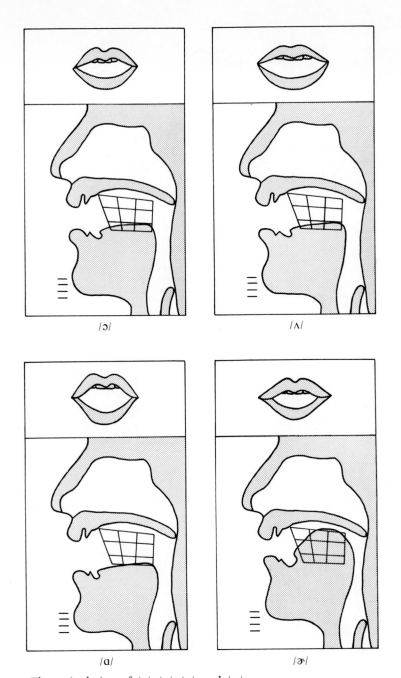

**Figure 7.7.** The articulation of /ɔ/, /ʌ/, /ɑ/, and /ɚ/.

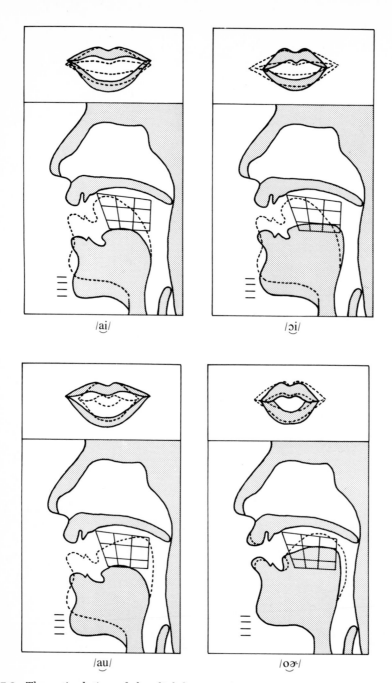

**Figure 7.8.** The articulation of the diphthongs /aɪ/, /ɔɪ/, /aʊ/, and /oɚ/. The solid outlines and shading indicate the starting point; the broken outlines represent the finishing point.

lip posture. Only one example of a rhotacized diphthong is included, to avoid repetition. In the articulatory sketches of the diphthongs, the starting positions of the tongue, lips, and jaw are shown with a solid line, and the finishing positions are shown with a dotted line.

## 7-6 Non-English Vowels

Some vowels characteristic of languages other than English will be considered next. Try pronouncing these vowels, and if possible try identifying them as they are pronounced by someone else.

In English, front vowels are unrounded. Try pronouncing front rounded vowels, such as those characteristic of French or German. Do this by pronouncing the English front vowels /i/, /e/, and /ɛ/ while simultaneously rounding the lips. Practice alternately rounding and unrounding the lips while pronouncing the vowel. Be sure to hold the tongue and jaw position steady, and note the way lip-rounding affects the quality of the vowel. The IPA symbols are /y/, /ø/, and /œ/, respectively, for the rounded cognates of /i/, /e/, and /ɛ/. An articulatory sketch of /y/, for example, would have the tongue position of /i/ and the lip position of /u/.

Similarly, English high back vowels are rounded. In the same way as above, practice producing spread back vowels. Start with the English vowels /u/ and /o/, and spread the lips while pronouncing the vowel. The spread vowels corresponding to /u/ and /o/ are /ɯ/ and /ɣ/ respectively. Most English dialects have both the rounded and unrounded lower-mid back vowels, /ɔ/ and /ʌ/. (In some dialects /ɔ/ is not distinguished from /ɑ/; such words as "cot" and "caught" are pronounced alike, with the /ɑ/ vowel.) But most English dialects lack the low back rounded vowel corresponding in place of articulation to /ɑ/. To pronounce the rounded /ɒ/, pronounce /ɑ/ and then round the lips.

Table 4.1 indicates all these vowels by their place of articulation.

Another excellent practice for the speech pathologist or students of phonetics is the pronunciation of nasalized vowels, such as those found in French or Portuguese. All the other vowels we have discussed are articulated with the velum in the raised (closed) position; nasalized vowels are produced with the velum lowered. We have all learned to lower the velum for pronouncing nasal consonants (and for nasal breathing) and to raise it for other speech sounds (and oral breathing). It is thus difficult at first for us to pronounce vowels with a lowered velum. Some clients of speech therapy may need guidance in controlling their velum, such as the deaf speaker or the individual whose cleft palate has been repaired.

This exercise is helpful in learning the conscious velic control you may have to teach a client. Pronounce a vowel, such as /ɛ/. Stop saying it, but keep your tongue, jaw, and lips frozen in position. If you inhale through your nose, you should feel your velum lowering. Practice trying to hold it in the lowered position while pronouncing the vowel. It may be difficult at first, because you will unconsciously raise the velum as soon as you try to pronounce the vowel. But patient practice should pay off. If you are a smoker, it may help to inhale smoke first. This gives a visual clue as to whether or not the velum is lowered. If it is, smoke should pass out through the nose as you

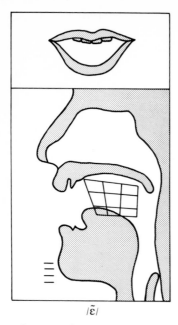

/ɛ̃/

**Figure 7.9.** The articulation of the nasalized vowel /ɛ̃/.

pronounce the vowel. But in any case, the particular acoustic quality of a nasalized vowel should be immediately apparent.

The French nasalized vowels are /œ̃/, /ɔ̃/, /ɛ̃/, and /ɑ̃/; the tilde (˜) indicates nasalization. Figure 7.9 gives an articulatory sketch of /ɛ̃/.

## 7-7 The Glossectomee and Other Theoretical Problems

We have indicated the usual articulatory gestures that are made for the production of English vowel sounds. But the listener attends to the sounds he hears; he does not inspect the gestures made to produce the sound (with the exception, of course, of the deaf "lip-reader" or speech reader). In fact, similar resonant characteristics of the vocal tract can be achieved through different configurations. It is for this reason that glossectomees (those who have had their tongue partially or completely removed) can in some cases produce intelligible speech, and individuals with partial paralysis of the speech organs can make compensatory gestures leading to normal-sounding speech. The end is more important here than the means of achieving it, and if an intelligible vowel sound can be achieved without the tongue positions indicated in this chapter, that vowel may still be used for speaking. The skill of the ventriloquist is in producing normal-sounding speech without the standard "normal" articulatory movements; the ventriloquist's ability demonstrates that it is possible. Obviously, the study of speech by glossectomees is beyond the scope of this book, but it illustrates a point about phonetics that is often ignored in texts on the subject. The articulatory movements that are customarily indicated are only idealized, "normal" gestures. This fact has numerous practical applications in therapy, not the least of which is in the neglected area of aiding the glossectomee in producing intelligible speech.

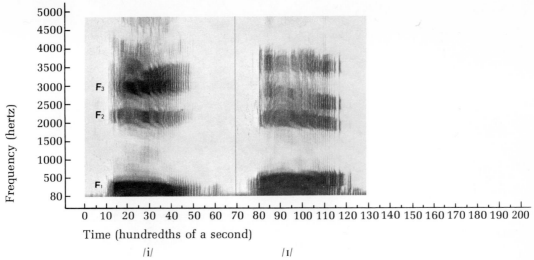

**Figure 7.10.** Spectrograms of the vowels /i/ and /ɪ/.

Furthermore, many people question whether the standard articulatory postures are truly representative of the actual articulatory gestures made in connected speech. The questions about tenseness have already been mentioned. It appears from x-ray data that the vowel quadrangle is closer to an oval, tilted up toward the front. (The standard positions have been given here because they are less confusing, more generally in use, and are close enough to the truth not to be misleading.) It appears that there are additional articulatory gestures not usually mentioned in books on articulatory phonetics. For example, in Perkell's x-ray motion picture study *The Physiology of Speech Production* [1969], the larynx was observed to move up and down a little more than 1 centimeter. This adjustment of the overall length of the vocal tract will undoubtedly affect formant frequencies and is likely an essential part of the pronunciation of English words (it appears to be associated with syllable stress).

The details of these matters are beyond the scope of an introductory text. They are mentioned by way of stressing the complexity of speech articulation, and the limited extent of our understanding of speech articulation. We must be prepared for future advances in these fields. Tongue positions might be easily taught, but movements of the entire larynx, of the sort mentioned above, may be much more difficult to teach because of our lack of awareness of our larynx and the limited feedback we receive from it.

## 7-8 The Acoustics of Vowels

Figures 7.10 through 7.16 are spectrograms of the vowels of American English. They show the acoustic components of the vowel sounds of the speech of an adult male and were made with a commercially available Kay Elemetrics Sona-Graph sound spectrograph.[8] Other details of technical interest are that a wide-

[8] Kay Elemetrics Corporation, 12 Maple Avenue, Pine Brook, New Jersey 07058.

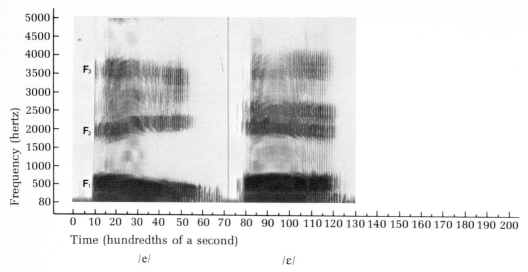

**Figure 7.11.** Spectrograms of the vowels /e/ and /ɛ/.

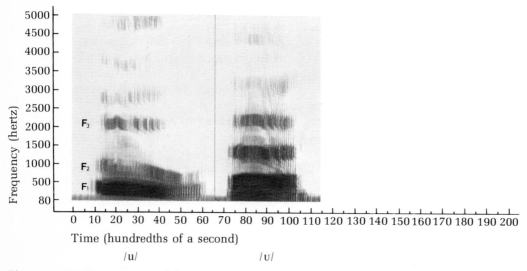

**Figure 7.12.** Spectrograms of the vowels /u/ and /ʊ/.

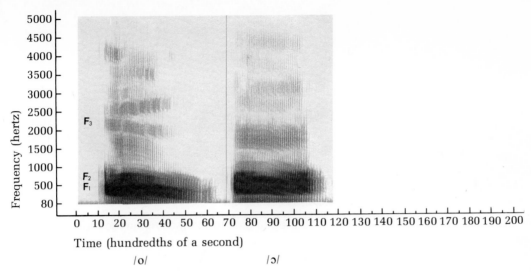

**Figure 7.13.** Spectrograms of the vowels /o/ and /ɔ/.

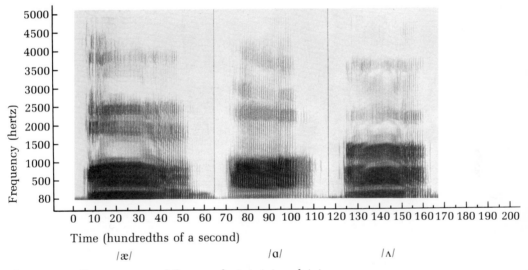

**Figure 7.14.** Spectrograms of the vowels /æ/, /ɑ/, and /ʌ/.

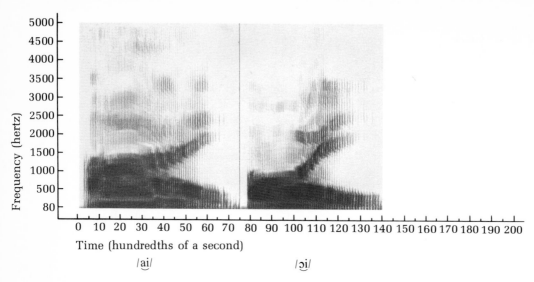

**Figure 7.15.** Spectrograms of the diphthongs /a̯i/ and /ɔ̯i/.

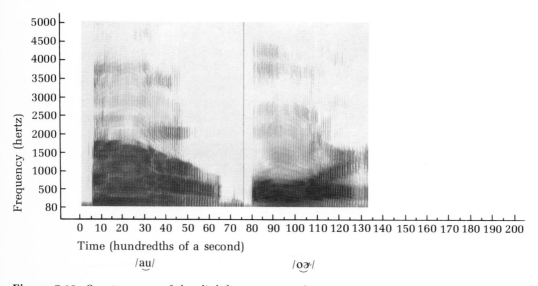

**Figure 7.16.** Spectrograms of the diphthongs /a̯u/ and /oɚ/.

band filter was used in the analysis, and the sounds were recorded with a high-frequency pre-emphasis normally used for speech.

The salient features to look for in the spectrograms are as follows: (1) The **frequency scale** is shown along the vertical axis. (2) The **time scale** is shown along the horizontal axis. (3) The **amplitude** is shown by darkness of shading: the darker the shading, the greater the amplitude. (4) The **formants** show up as darker bands (a few have been labeled to aid in identification). (5) The **vertical striations** visible in the spectrograms reflect individual cycles of the glottal frequency, each vertical line representing the opening of the vocal folds (the higher the pitch of the voice, the closer together these would be). (5) Note that for the diphthongs, the formant frequencies change. (6) Note that the long vowels /i, e, o, u/ are slightly diphthongized, as shown by the change in formant frequencies.

## Questions for Discussion

1. What are some differences in vowel sounds among various dialects you have heard?
2. Remembering your own experience in trying to pronounce nasalized vowels, suggest ways of trying to teach someone else conscious control of movement of the velum.

## Annotated Bibliography

No Annotated Bibliography is included for this chapter, since articulatory descriptions of vowels may be found in any introductory book on phonetics. A number of such books are mentioned in the References.

# Chapter 8

## Articulatory Phonetics: The Consonants

### 8-1 Consonants

As Chapter 7 brought out, vowels are characterized by an oral cavity that is relatively open, at least as open as for the vowel /i/, which gives a resonant or melodic quality to the sounds. This chapter will point out that in the production of consonants the airflow out of the mouth is completely blocked, greatly restricted, or diverted through the nose. This gives consonants a more noisy, less melodic quality than vowels.[1]

The way the airstream from the mouth is modified (i.e., blocked, restricted, diverted, etc.) provides a means of classifying consonants. This dimension is called **manner of articulation.** We will consider five types of English consonants (plosives, fricatives, affricates, nasals, and approximants) and will mention a few of the less-common types, which occur in other languages and occasionally in English.

The exact point in the oral cavity at which the airstream is modified—that is, lips, teeth, alveolar ridge, etc.—gives a second dimension for classifying consonants; this dimension is called **place of articulation.**

A third dimension is **voicing,** which depends upon whether or not the vocal folds are vibrating during the production of the consonant. For example, /z/ is voiced (the vocal folds are vibrating) while /s/ is voiceless (the folds are apart). If you pronounce them out loud, you hear the "buzzing" of the vocal folds accompanying the /z/, and you can feel their vibration if you put your hand on the thyroid cartilage (Adam's apple). Both the buzzing and the vibration are missing from the voiceless /s/.

The **place of articulation** dimension uses the names of the various

---

[1] Note that it is the vowels, not the consonants, that carry the tune when we sing: you can sing an /ɑ/, but you cannot sing an /s/!

parts of the vocal tract mentioned in Chapter 5. To review these terms, they are, starting at the front of the mouth:

An articulation with the **lips** is a **labial** articulation; with **both lips** it is **bilabial;** the combining form is **labio-,** as in labiodental.

An articulation with the **teeth** is a **dental** articulation.

An articulation with the **alveolar ridge** is an **alveolar** articulation; the combining form is **alveo-,** as in alveopalatal.

An articulation with the (hard) **palate** is a **palatal** articulation; the combining form is **palato-,** as in palatovelar.

An articulation with the **velum** is a **velar** articulation; movements of the velum itself are **velic** movements.

An articulation with the **uvula** is a **uvular** articulation.

An articulation with the **glottis** is a **glottal** articulation.

An articulation with the **tongue** is a **lingual** or **glossal** articulation, though it is normal practice not to specify the tongue in consonant articulation.

An articulation with the **tip** of the tongue is an **apical** articulation; with the **blade** of the tongue is a **laminal** articulation.

One more note before examining individual consonants. Chapter 5 presented a number of different airstream mechanisms. In the following discussion, all consonants are assumed to be pulmonic egressive—the air is being pushed out of the lungs.

The individual consonants discussed below are organized into major groups by manner of articulation and into subgroups by place of articulation and voicing (Figures 8.1 through 8.4).

## 8-2 The Plosive

A **plosive** consonant is formed by blocking the oral cavity at some point. The velum is raised, effectively shutting off the nasal passages. Pressure is built up inside the oral cavity and suddenly released with an explosion or "popping." /p/ as in "pan," is such a plosive sound, as is /t/ in "tam." Notice that plosives cannot be pronounced alone. If you try to say /p/ alone, it will invariably be followed by a vowel.

### 8-2.1 Bilabial Plosives

The plosive /p/ is a bilabial sound. The blockage of the oral cavity is made with the two lips. /p/ is a voiceless sound; the vocal folds are not vibrating. In an attempt to verify this by placing a hand on the throat, it is important not to mistake the voicing of the following vowel for the voicing of the consonant.

If the same articulatory gesture is produced as for /p/, but with glottal vibration, /b/ will be pronounced. /p/ and /b/ form a pair of **cognate** sounds; they are produced by the same articulatory gestures, and differ only in voicing. For the convenience of classification here subsequent consonants will be arranged in cognate pairs.

### 8-2.2 Alveolar Plosives

Moving toward the back of the mouth, the next point of articulation for stops is the alveolar ridge behind the teeth. For the stops /t/ and /d/, oral blockage occurs by placing the blade of the tongue against the alveolar ridge. The sides of the tongue are placed along the upper teeth, completing the seal. The release occurs by lowering the blade of the tongue and allowing the pressure to explode over the top.

/t/ and /d/ are called **alveolar plosives.** This terminology needs some comment. In producing consonants, two articulating organs are usually brought into play. When consonants are classified, it is generally assumed that one of the two will be the tongue, and both articulators are specified only when *neither* is the tongue. /p/ is called a **bilabial plosive,** specifying both articulators (two lips). On the other hand, /t/ is an alveolar plosive, specifying only one articulator, since the second is the tongue. Some texts call the /t/ a **lingua-alveolar** plosive; however, there is generally no confusion produced by leaving out the specification for the tongue.

/t/ is the voiceless alveolar plosive; /d/ is voiced. In some languages, these two sounds are produced, not as in English with the blade of the tongue against the alveolar ridge, but with the tip of the tongue against the upper teeth. In such languages, we would specify /t/ and /d/ as **dental** plosives. In French and Spanish, /t/ and /d/ are generally apicodental (i.e., the tip—apex—of the tongue against the teeth), as compared to English where the articulation is laminoalveolar (i.e., the blade of the tongue against the alveolar ridge).

## 8-2.3 Velar Plosives

The next point at which English produces plosives is with the **back** of the tongue against the soft palate or **velum.** The two **velar plosives** are /k/ and /g/; /k/ is voiceless while /g/ is voiced.

## 8-2.4 Glottal Stop

The **glottal stop** is usually classified with the other plosive sounds, though its manner of articulation is somewhat different. The glottis is the space between the vocal folds. If the vocal folds are brought together and released under pressure, an audible speech sound will be produced. It is not usually counted among the speech sounds of English, but it is used in several dialects of our language. Scottish speakers, for example, often substitute the glottal stop for /t/. Most of us use a glottal stop between the two vowel sounds in the expression "uh-uh," meaning 'no.' The transcription symbol for the glottal stop is /ʔ/, like a question mark with a bar instead of a dot. Because of its importance in certain communication disorders, it would be useful to become familiar with this sound.

Since the glottal stop involves the vocal folds, there can be no voiced and voiceless varieties; it is classified as voiceless.

## 8-2.5 Summary of English Plosives

In summary, there are six plosives in English (plus the glottal stop). They are produced at three places, and at each place of articulation there is a pair made up of a voiced and a voiceless cognate.

Plosives, as we said, require the build-up and sudden release of oral pressure, requiring closure of the nasal passages with the velum. The individual with a cleft palate has never learned to control the movements of the velum, since even with the velum raised, air pressure escapes through the cleft into the nasal cavity. After reconstructive surgery or fitting of a prosthesis, such an individual needs guidance in controlling the velum to produce plosive sounds. Very often these individuals substitute a glottal stop for the plosives they cannot pronounce.

Deaf speakers also will have articulatory difficulty with plosive sounds, and often need guidance with building up sufficient pressure for audible plosives. Additionally, deaf speakers often voice *all* plosives, whether or not it is appropriate; this voicing problem is evident with other consonants as well.

In review, the following table lists English plosives by voicing and place of articulation.

|  | Bilabial | Alveolar | Velar | Glottal |
|---|---|---|---|---|
| Voiceless | p | t | k | ʔ |
| Voiced | b | d | g | |

## 8-2.6 Pressure and Release

Plosives may vary in the amount of pressure built up inside the mouth before release (**intraoral air pressure**). In English, and in many other languages, the voiceless plosives are produced with considerably greater pressure than the voiced plosives, at least at the beginning of a stressed syllable. You can test this fact by putting your hand in front of your mouth and saying "pit" and "bit"; you should feel a stronger puff of air accompanying the /p/ than the /b/ sound.[2]

The plosives having higher intraoral pressure are often called *fortis*, and the weaker ones *lenis*, from the Latin words for 'strong' and 'weak.' In some languages, such as Spanish and French, both the voiced and voiceless plosives are lenis. For this reason, English speaking people sometimes have difficulty distinguishing /p/ from /b/, /t/ from /d/, etc., in those languages, and this fact contributes to the accent Spanish and French speaking people have when speaking English (and vice versa). Voiceless plosives that do not occur at the beginning of a syllable are also lenis in English. Using the test of the hand or match in front of the mouth, compare the /p/ of "pin" (fortis) and "spin" (lenis). More will be said about this in Chapter 10.

Also notice that at the end of a phrase or sentence the oral cavity may or may not be opened after producing a plosive. If you say only the word "stop," for example, you may keep the lips closed after saying /p/. This may be called an **unreleased** plosive as contrasted with a **released** plosive (as in "pan").[3] In English, whether or not a phrase-final plosive is released is optional

---

[2] A dramatic demonstration can be made by holding a lighted match in front of the mouth. "Bit" will usually disturb the flame slightly, while "pit" will usually snuff it.

[3] A note on terminology. We have used the term **plosive** and distinguished **released** and **unreleased** forms. While this is common practice, there are other terms in use by other authors: (1) The term **stop** is sometimes used to mean exactly what is here called a plosive. (2) The term **stop** is sometimes used to mean 'unreleased plosive' and **plosive** to mean 'released plosive.' (3) The term **stop** is sometimes used for any sound requiring oral blockage, namely, released and unreleased plosives and the nasals (section 8-5).

with the speaker: he may or may not do it. In some languages, such as French, *all* plosives are released. When you speak very clearly, as when speaking to a group or to a person who has difficulty understanding you, you tend to release all plosives.

## 8-3  The Fricative

Fricative sounds are produced by forcing air through such a narrow passageway that a turbulent hissing noise is produced. This is accomplished in the oral cavity (or, in some languages, in the pharynx); as for plosives, the velum is raised to close off the nasal passage (Figure 8.2). Like the plosives, each place of articulation has a voiced and a voiceless cognate; these will be considered in pairs, beginning at the front of the mouth and working back, as with the plosives.

### 8-3.1  Labial Fricative

In English, as it happens, there are no bilabial fricatives, though there are in some languages, like Spanish. English, however, does have a pair of labiodental fricatives. This means that the small passage through which the air must pass is formed with the teeth and the lip. The upper teeth and lower lip are used in English and in other languages that have labiodentals. The voiceless labiodental fricative is /f/, and its voiced cognate is /v/.

### 8-3.2  Dental Fricatives

In English, there are two fricative sounds produced with the tongue and the teeth. In some dialect regions, the tongue is placed behind the front teeth; here, we refer to a **dental** fricative. In other dialect regions, the tongue is placed between the upper and lower teeth; here, we refer to an **interdental** fricative. In either case, the sound produced is the same. This is the sound we spell th. We do not distinguish in spelling between the voiced and voiceless cognates, but they are pronounced differently. The voiceless variant occurs in the words "thin," "thought," "ether," and "both." It is transcribed with the Greek letter theta, /θ/. The voiced variant occurs in the words "the," "this," "either," and "lathe." It is transcribed with a symbol called **bar-d** or **eth,** which is a script d with a crossbar, /ð/.

The production of both dental and labiodental consonants—as well as some plosives—will be affected by missing teeth. Frequently children are referred to speech pathologists for problems caused by the transition to adult dentition. Usually the problem will correct itself as new teeth grow in. On the other hand, some speech problems in adults can only be corrected through dental work.

### 8-3.3  Alveolar Fricatives

There is a pair of fricatives produced with the blade of the tongue close to the alveolar ridge. These alveolar fricatives are /s/ (voiceless) and /z/ (voiced). This pair has one other characteristic distinguishing them; they are produced with the tongue slightly **grooved.** Notice that in pronouncing /θ/, the blade of the tongue is quite flat, but in pronouncing /s/, the sides of the blade are curled up slightly, forming a groove in the center. Failure to form the groove is responsible for certain types of lisp. If the front teeth are missing, the air will not have to pass by the same route, and a less sibilant fricative sound is produced: an attempt to articulate /s/ produces a /θ/-like sound, which is identified as a lisp.

### 8-3.4 Alveopalatal Fricatives

The alveopalatal fricatives are articulated by bringing the blade of the tongue close to the part of the roof of the mouth where the alveolar ridge and the hard palate join. These are sometimes called palatoalveolar, or not very accurately, palatal fricatives. Unlike the alveolar fricatives, there is no grooving of the tongue; it is more or less flat at the point of restriction. For this reason, they are often called **slit** fricatives.

The voiceless alveopalatal fricative is usually spelled sh in English; it is the sound in the words "shore," "bush," "sugar," and "position." There are two symbols used to transcribe this sound: /š/ and /ʃ/. Either symbol can be used, but it is important to be consistent in using one or the other. The wedge over the s is called **hachek;** it is borrowed from the Czech alphabet.

The voiced alveopalatal fricative is less common in English. It is the sound that occurs in the words "measure," "version," and "leisure." It is transcribed either of two ways: /ž/ and /ʒ/.

In some pathological conditions (e.g., cerebral palsy), /s/ and /š/, as well as /z/ and /ž/, are not distinguished. This situation is also labeled with the rather loose term **lisp.**

### 8-3.5 Glottal Fricative

The sound /h/, as in "house," is usually classified as a fricative. It is different from the other fricatives in that the vocal tract is wide open, so there is little friction. Also /h/ is voiceless, and there is no voiced cognate for it. For these reasons, /h/ is classified as a **glottal** fricative.

This classification is convenient for labeling purposes but should not be interpreted as indicating that the source of friction is the glottis alone. The vocal folds may be brought relatively close together for the production of /h/, producing some frictional noise, but some will also come from the entire vocal tract; this is called **cavity friction.**

In review, the following table lists English fricatives by voicing and place of articulation.

|  | Labio-dental | Dental | Alveolar | Alveo-palatal | Glottal |
|---|---|---|---|---|---|
| Voiceless | f | θ | s | ʃ or š | h |
| Voiced | v | ð | z | ʒ or ž | |

## 8-4 The Affricate

An affricate is made up of the close sequence of two speech sounds acting as a single linguistic unit, namely, a plosive followed by a fricative having a similar place of articulation. Phoneticians sometimes express this by saying that the plosive is followed by a **homorganic** ('the same speech organ') fricative. In English, the sounds that are usually spelled ch and j are affricates.

The voiceless alveolar affricate occurs in the words "chin," "batch," and "hatchet." It can be analyzed as a /t/ followed by /š/. It is usually transcribed /tš/, /tʃ/, or /č/.[4]

The voiced alveolar affricate occurs in the words "jam," "fudge," and "badger." It can be analyzed as a /d/ followed by a /ž/. It is usually transcribed /dž/, /dʒ/, or /ǰ/. If you have difficulty distinguishing /ǰ/ from /ž/, you can hear these sounds contrasted in the words "virgin" and "version," in the words "ledger" and "leisure," and in the words "pledger" ('a person who pledges') and "pleasure."

Note that the English affricates are made up of alveolar plosives and alveopalatal fricatives. The place of articulation need not be identical for affricates, only similar, but in any case, the plosive is likely pronounced further back than when it stands alone, and the fricative further forward. This gives the two almost identical places of articulation, allowing a quick transition from one to another. Thus, the two are pronounced as a single unit.

English has only the two affricates, but others are common in other languages. German has the affricate /pf/, and German and Italian have the affricate /ts/ (as in the borrowed words "Nazi" and "pizza").

It is important to distinguish the affricate, in which two sounds act as a single unit, from a simple sequence of sounds. For example, there is an affricate at the beginning of the word "chocolate," but in the expression "chocolate shop" there is a /t/ followed by /š/ (indicated by underlining).

We can see that the affricate, functioning as a single unit, is different from a sequence of two sounds that just happen to come together in a phrase. For this reason, the affricate is best written with a symbol showing that it functions as one unit; consistent use of the ligature or the single symbols /č/ and /ǰ/ best represents these English phones.

In review, the following table lists English affricates by voicing and place of articulation.

|  | Alveolar (or Alveopalatal) | | | | | |
| --- | --- | --- | --- | --- | --- | --- |
| Voiceless | tš | or | tʃ | or | č | |
| Voiced | dž | or | dʒ | or | ǰ | |

## 8-5 The Nasal

The nasal consonants, as the name implies, are produced through the nose. The oral cavity is completely blocked during their production, and for this reason some books refer to them as nasal stops. The nasal consonants are all produced with velic opening; that is, the velum is lowered at the same time the oral cavity is blocked (see Figure 8.4).

All English nasals are voiced, as they are in most languages (voiceless nasals, such as those of Burmese and Icelandic, sound to us like a snort!).

---

[4] As with the diphthongs, a connecting line or ligature is often used with affricates, to distinguish them from a sequence of consonants. Again, this convention is frequently ignored. For this reason, the symbols /č/ and /ǰ/ may be preferable, since they indicate the affricate as a single unit.

For this reason, the nasals of English do not need to be classified by voicing: just the place of articulation is sufficient. The place of articulation refers to the point in the oral cavity where there is closure.

The bilabial nasal is /m/, as in the English words "mouse," "hammer," and "lame."

The alveolar nasal is articulated at the same place as /t/ and /d/; it is /n/, as in the English words "no," "banner," and "fan."

The velar nasal corresponds in place of articulation to /k/ and /g/. It is usually spelled ng and nk in English, as in the words "sing" and "sink." It is represented in transcription with this symbol: /ŋ/.

A palatal nasal occurs in French, Spanish, and Italian. In the spelling of French and Italian, it is represented by gn; in Spanish it is spelled ñ. The transcription symbol is /ɲ/. While this is not a distinctive sound in English, we articulate it in words such as "canyon" or "onion."

In review, the following table lists English nasals by place of articulation.

|  | Bilabial | Alveolar | Velar |
|---|---|---|---|
| Voiced | m | n | ŋ |

## 8-6 Approximants

As the name suggests, these sounds are produced with the articulators **approximated,** or brought close together, during their articulation (Figures 8.3 and 8.4). The approximation is not enough to cause frictional sounds like the fricatives (for this reason, the sounds are sometimes called **frictionless continuants**). There are two subcategories of approximants: the **glides** and the **liquids.** Each type shares certain qualities with both vowels and consonants, which makes the approximants a particularly difficult group to classify.

### 8-6.1 Glides

Glides share with vowels the fact that the articulators are no closer together than for /i/. They are like consonants in that they cannot stand alone; they must precede (or follow) a vowel in order to form a syllable. The first of the glides is the sound at the beginning of the word "yellow." It is voiced and its place of articulation is palatal. This sound is usually spelled with the letter y in English, but the phonetic symbol for it is /j/. (The letter /y/ as an IPA symbol is reserved for a high front rounded vowel, as in the French word tu.) Notice that this sound often precedes the vowel /u/, as in such words as "use," "beauty," and "mute." These words would be transcribed /juz/, /bjuti/, and /mjut/.

The second glide we will look at is the one at the beginning of the word "want." It is voiced and is produced by rounding the lips; its place of articulation is bilabial with an additional arching of the tongue in the velar region. Its phonetic symbol is /w/.

Some dialects of English pronounce the word "which" differently from the word "witch." The sound at the beginning of the word "witch" is /w/; the sound at the beginning of the word "which" is similar in articulation but voiceless. In most American dialects, this sound does not appear, but when it is necessary to transcribe the sound, there is a choice of several commonly used symbols. The upside-down w, /ʍ/, is often used in printed material, but when hand-written it may be easily confused with an m. For this reason, in hand-written work, I prefer an unofficial symbol that is an h and a w written together as one: /ʜw/. Sometimes this sound is indicated with the simple sequence of an h and a w: /hw/.

These three sounds /j/, /w/, and /ʜw/ are collectively called **glides.** The first two, /j/ and /w/, are sometimes called **semivowels,** and it may be said that they are the consonantal forms of the vowels /i/ and /u/.


## 8-6.2 The Liquids

The term **liquid** is often used to classify the consonants /l/ and /r/. The word is not very meaningful but provides a convenient cover-term for these two speech sounds that show some similarities. Like the other approximants, the liquids share qualities with both vowels and consonants. They are like vowels in being resonant or melodic in nature and in being able to form a syllable by themselves. They are like consonants in having more of the oral cavity blocked than most vowels; indeed, r's in English are sometimes pronounced as fricatives, as are r's and l's in some other languages.

The /l/ is articulated in the alveolar region, with the blade of the tongue in almost the same position as for /t/ and /d/. The manner of articulation of the /l/ is lateral. The term **lateral** refers to 'the sides,' and indeed /l/ is produced by blocking the center of the oral cavity with the tongue, allowing air to pass on both sides. This can be demonstrated thus: pronounce the sound /l/; stop pronouncing it, but keep your tongue and jaw in the same position; now inhale through the mouth. You will be able to feel the cool air passing on either side of the tongue.

The /l/ is a voiced sound, more resonant than most other consonants. In fact, it is almost vowel-like and does not need a vowel with it to produce a syllable. In some people's pronunciation of English words, the /l/ forms a whole syllable by itself. For example, the second syllable of the word "bottle" may have no separate vowel; some speakers pass directly from the /t/ to the /l/ with no intermediate vowel sound. This is called a **syllabic** consonant and is indicated in transcription with a short vertical line under the consonant symbol. Syllabic /l/ would be indicated as /l̩/.

If you listen carefully to the sound of the /l/ in the word "leave" as compared to the word "dull," you will detect a difference in the quality. The /l/ of "leave" is alveolar, as described above, having the approximate tongue position of /t/. It is sometimes called a light or clear /l/. The /l/ of "dull" is similar except that there is an additional arching of the tongue in the velar region, giving it a "darker" quality. It is called a **dark** or **velarized** /l/, transcribed /ɫ/. More will be said on the two kinds of l's in Chapter 10.

The English consonant /r/ is more difficult to classify. The r-sounds are produced in widely different ways in various languages. French, Spanish, and German illustrate some of these different types of /r/. Some dialects of British English have a different /r/ from North American English, and we tend to think that some speakers of British English say "veddy" for very. As with /l/, one of the best ways of analyzing your own speech articulation is to breathe in through the mouth with your articulators in position to pronounce the sound. Unlike the /l/, in pronouncing /r/ the mouth is closed off at the sides of the tongue, and the air passes centrally, over the body of the tongue. The tongue is arched in the velar region and the root is retracted into the pharynx. The /r/ sound is voiced in English and is somewhat resonant in nature (this is not necessarily true for the r-sounds of other languages).

In some cases, a less resonant form of /r/ is produced by English speakers. For example, the r̠ in the word "try" is often pronounced as a fricative. This sound may be voiced or voiceless and is somewhat similar to /š/. Thus, there is a tendency for children to pronounce "try" as [ts̬rai].

The consonant /r/ may, like the /l/, become syllabic. This is indicated [r̩],[5] which is really no different from the schwar [ɚ]. The /r/ is consonantal in a word such as "string" but is syllabic or vocalic in a word such as "stirring."

Indeed, all of the approximants are both vocalic (vowel-like) and consonantal. There is a very fine dividing line, which may be crossed at any time. Even the nasal consonants act sometimes vocalically. The consonantal and corresponding vocalic forms of these phones are shown below:

| Consonantal | Syllabic or vocalic |
|---|---|
| j | i |
| w | u |
| l | l̩ |
| r | r̩ or ɚ |
| n | n̩ |
| m | m̩ |

To take one example, the word "brilliant" is pronounced [brɪljənt] usually, but when stressed (as when congratulating someone) may be pronounced [brɪliənt].

## 8-6.3 Summary

In review, the English approximants are as follows:

|  | Bilabial | Alveolar | Palatal | Velar |
|---|---|---|---|---|
| Glides | | | | |
| Voiced | w | | j | (w) |
| Voiceless | ʌ | | | (ʌ) |
| Liquids (voiced) | | l | r | |

[5] The use of square brackets [  ], as opposed to slash marks /  /, is discussed in Chapter 11. For the moment, suffice it to say that the square brackets are used for more detailed transcription than is normally necessary.

## 8-7 Summary of Consonant Articulation

Figures 8.1 through 8.4 provide stylized sketches of the articulations of English consonants. Note the position of the tongue, lips, and velum, particularly. Voiced and voiceless pairs such as [b]/[p] are not distinguished in the figures; of course, the vocal folds are differently positioned for each. There is no separate sketch for the affricates since their articulation is a rapid sequence of plosive and fricative. The glottals [h] and [ʔ] are not sketched since their articulatory positions depend so heavily on surrounding sounds. Indeed, as Chapter 10 will show, a great deal of modification of the articulatory positions for *all* phones results from the neighboring sounds.

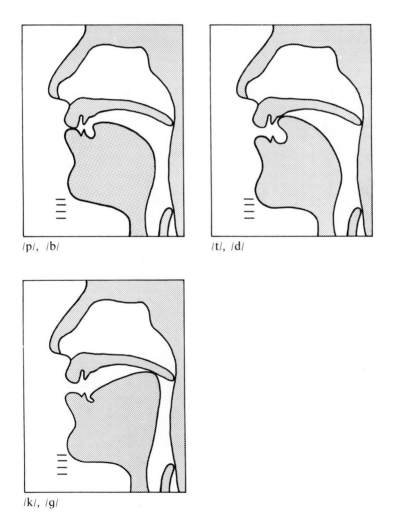

/p/, /b/        /t/, /d/

/k/, /g/

**Figure 8.1.** The articulation of the plosives /p/ and /b/, /t/ and /d/, /k/ and /g/.

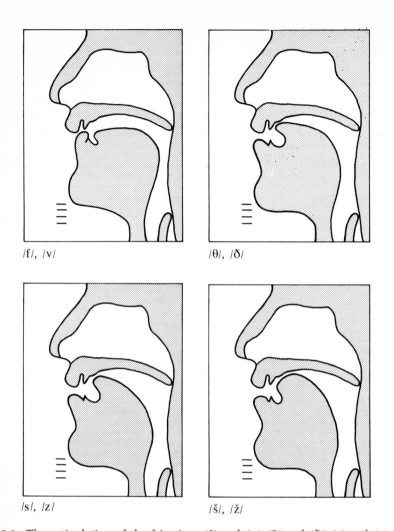

/f/, /v/    /θ/, /ð/

/s/, /z/    /š/, /ž/

**Figure 8.2.** The articulation of the fricatives /f/ and /v/, /θ/ and /ð/, /s/ and /z/, /š/ and /ž/.

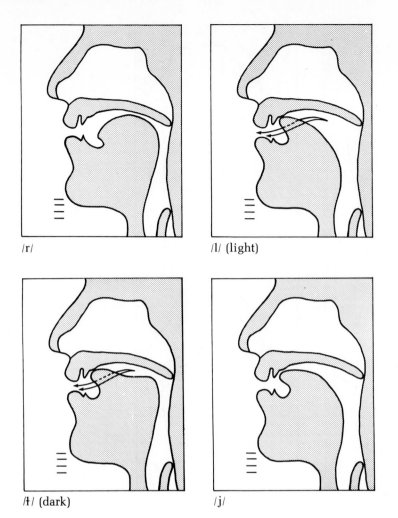

/r/

/l/ (light)

/ɫ/ (dark)

/j/

**Figure 8.3.** The articulation of the approximants /r/, "light l" [l], "dark l" [ɫ], /j/.

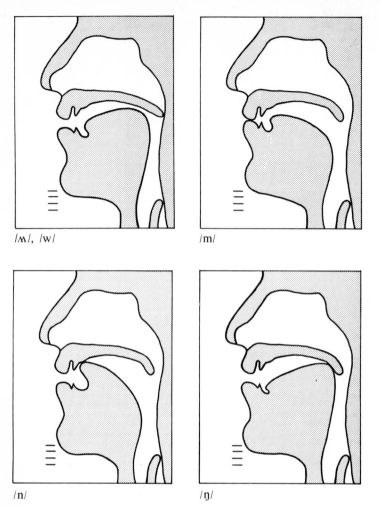

/ʍ/, /w/                           /m/

/n/                              /ŋ/

**Figure 8.4.** The articulation of one approximant and the nasals /ʍ/ (or /hʊ/) and /w/; /m/; /n/; /ŋ/.

## 8-8 Other Consonant Sounds

### 8-8.1 The Flap

When a /t/ is pronounced, for example, the blade of the tongue is placed against the alveolar ridge and then pulled away again. Such a movement produces a plosive. But if the tongue is moved very rapidly and with less tension against the alveolar ridge, it will tend to bounce off again very quickly. A sound produced in this way is called a **flap.** When a word like "butter" is pronounced quickly, the /t/ is not pronounced in the same way as in a word like "table." In the quick pronunciation of "butter," the /t/ is replaced by a flap sound. This is represented with the symbol [ɾ]: [bʌɾɚ]. Some British dialects use a flap r, [ř], between vowels, which is why their pronunciation of <u>very</u> sounds like "veddy" to North Americans. The single <u>r</u> in Spanish spelling represents a flap; e.g., <u>pero</u> is pronounced [pɛřo].

### 8-8.2 The Trill

A trill is produced by the vibration of an articulator under the influence of air passing rapidly over it, similar to the way a kazoo produces a sound. The articulator does not move back and forth by muscle movement but is acting like a flag flapping in the wind. The lips, the tongue, and the uvula may be used to produce trills. We sometimes make a bilabial trill inadvertently when we are cold and shivering. A trilled [r̃] is used in Spanish and contrasted with the flap [ř], which Spanish also uses. For example, the Spanish word <u>perro</u> is pronounced [pɛr̃o], that is, with a tongue-tip trill. A similar trill is used by children in imitating the sound of an airplane or a machine-gun. The uvula is trilled in some languages to produce an <u>r</u>-like sound.

Figure 8.5 shows the articulation of the flap and trill.

### 8-8.3 The Lateral Fricative

The one lateral we looked at, /l/, is resonant rather than fricative in nature. However, a voiceless fricative /l/ (transcribed /ɬ/) is used in many languages. You can pronounce this sound in the following way: Pronounce an /l/; stop saying /l/, but hold your tongue in the same position; now blow air out of the mouth, lightly resisting the tendency of your cheeks to puff out slightly. Some types of bilateral lisp are produced in this manner.

### 8-8.4 The Retroflex

Retroflex consonants are produced with the tongue bent back on itself (*retro* means 'backward'; *flex* means 'bend'). The tip of the tongue is pointing vertically upward, or slightly back, in the articulation of retroflex consonants. While it seems apparent that this would be a manner of articulation, it is best to classify it as a place of articulation since it is possible to produce retroflex stops, fricatives, or even liquids.

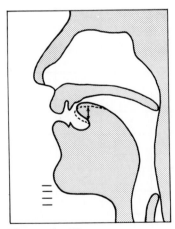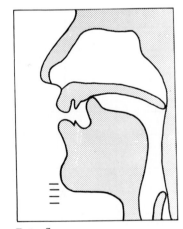

Flap and trill        Retroflex

**Figure 8.5.** The articulation of the flap, apical (tongue-tip) trill, and retroflex.

The English /r/ is sometimes classed as a retroflex for convenience; however, this is inaccurate, at least for most dialects of English, since in a true retroflex the tongue tip is actually pointing upward or backward. The English /r/, as we noted, is articulated with the whole tongue retracted: the tongue tip is pulled well back but is not retroflexed. Of course, some dialects and some individuals may show other articulations.

In parts of the southwestern and south central United States the /s/ is produced with retroflexion, giving it a particularly high-pitched sibilant quality. (Former President Lyndon Johnson frequently exhibited this dialect characteristic.) In Chapter 2, it was suggested that the speech pathologist should be familiar with dialect variation so as not to diagnose a dialect feature as a pathological condition. I know an individual who as a youngster was sent by his teacher to a "speech correctionist" because he spoke with retroflex /s/'s, even though this was simply a characteristic of his regional dialect and the school was located near where this dialect feature prevails. Fortunately, the speech pathologist knew her job and sent a note back to the teacher saying there was nothing wrong with the youngster.

Certain of the languages of India have a whole series of retroflex consonants, a fact that contributes to the distinctive accent many East Indians display in speaking English as a second language.

The symbols for retroflex consonants can be found in Table 4.1. Figure 8.5 shows the articulation of a retroflex plosive.

Table 8.1 summarizes, by place and manner of articulation, the consonants that have been discussed.

**Table 8.1.** Summary of Consonants

|  | Bilabial | Labio-dental | Dental, Inter-dental | Alveolar | Alveo-palatal | Palatal | Velar | Glottal |
|---|---|---|---|---|---|---|---|---|
| Plosives | p    b |  |  | t    d |  |  | k    g | ʔ |
| Fricatives | ɸ    β | f    v | θ    ð | s    z | š    ž |  |  | h |
| Affricates | p͜f |  |  | t͜s    d͜z | č    ǰ |  |  |  |
| Nasals |    m | m̩ |  | n |  | ɲ | ŋ |  |
| Approximants<br>Glides | ʍ    w |  |  |  |  | j | (ʍ) (w) |  |
| Liquids |  |  |  | l |  | r |  |  |
| Flaps |  |  |  | ř<br>ɾ |  |  |  |  |
| Trills |  |  |  | r̃ |  |  |  |  |
| Lateral fricative |  |  |  | ɬ |  |  |  |  |

This table includes those consonants discussed in Chapter 8, as well as a few others. Differences between this table and the official International Phonetic Alphabet presented in Chapter 4 reflect a number of changes common to North American phoneticians for ease of typesetting. See section 4-8.1. Voiceless phones are at the left in each space, voiced ones at the right.

## 8-9 The Acoustics and Perception of Consonants

To appreciate fully the following discussion of the physical properties of the sound of consonants, reference should be made to the spectrograms of the consonants under analysis (Figures 8.9 to 8.16). These spectrograms are the same in principle as those in Chapter 7; time is shown on the horizontal axis, frequency on the vertical axis, and amplitude by darkness of shading. In these spectrograms the consonant is always accompanied by a vowel since the plosives cannot be pronounced alone.

### 8-9.1 The Plosives

Of all speech sounds, the plosives have the most peculiar acoustic pattern, for after all, during most of the time that the plosive is being articulated, the mouth is closed and little or no sound is coming out. During this phase of the articulation, the spectrogram is primarily blank, showing the relative silence. (This may be clearest in Figure 8.16. The /t/ of "took" comes between vowels, and one can see the period of relative silence quite clearly.)

You recall that voiceless plosives are articulated with greater intra-oral air pressure and are released with a stronger puff of air, as compared to the voiced stops. This puff of air is called **aspiration** and is visible on the spectrograms of the voiceless plosives (Figure 8.9). It shows up as a shading covering a wide frequency range, immediately preceding the vowel. (The vowel begins with the visible vertical striations representing voicing.)

During the production of voiced plosives, the vocal folds are vibrating. Since the mouth is closed, this fundamental frequency is not very loud—on the spectrograms of some voiced plosives (Figure 8.10), you can barely make out the low-frequency, low-amplitude **voice murmur** just preceding the vowel. However, since the vocal folds are vibrating during the closure, their pulsing is audible *immediately* upon the release of the plosive. On the other hand, there is no vocal-fold vibration during the closure phase of the voiceless plosives, so after the release of the consonant, voicing must be initiated. There is usually a delay between the release of the plosive and the start of the voicing of the following vowel. This delay can be seen in Figure 8.9. The point of release of the plosives can be seen by the aspiration. Notice that voicing does not begin for a few hundredths of a second. This delay, known as **voice onset time** (VOT), is the most important cue to the perception of voicing in stops; it helps us distinguish /p/ from /b/, /t/ from /d/, and /k/ from /g/.

Thus, the voiceless plosives are acoustically distinguished from voiced plosives by the delay in the onset of voicing and by the noise of aspiration. What distinguishes plosives of one place of articulation from those of another, that is, /p/ from /t/, /t/ from /k/, or /b/ from /g/?

Figures 8.9 and 8.10 show that formants 1 and 2 (the two dark bands of resonance) of the vowel following the plosive change in frequency in the first 40 to 50 milliseconds (thousandths of a second) after the release of the plosive and that the pattern of this change is different for each plosive. Thus, the main acoustic difference distinguishing plosives having different places of articulation is a small change—lasting a few milliseconds—in the frequency of the formants of the following vowel. These changes are called **formant transitions,** and they represent the primary feature that the ear receives and the brain decodes to perceive individual plosives.

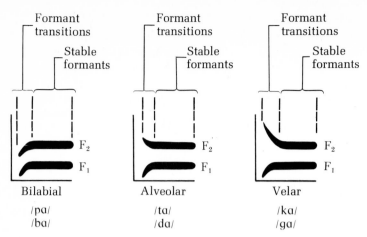

**Figure 8.6.** Stylized spectrograms showing formant transitions for each place of articulation and the vowel /ɑ/. The formants are determined by the vowel (note that these remain constant for all syllables containing the vowel /ɑ/), but the shape and direction of the transition is determined by the place of articulation of the plosive. Thus the transitions for /pɑ/ and /bɑ/ are similar, as are those for /tɑ/ and /dɑ/, as well as those for /kɑ/ and /gɑ/. The members of the pairs are distinguished by another factor, discussed previously. The formant transitions are perceived by the human ear as the plosive consonant; the stable period is perceived as the vowel.

Let us look at these formant transitions in stylized sketches to isolate this particular feature. In Figure 8.6, the basic transitional patterns are shown for plosives followed by the vowel /ɑ/. What happens when a different vowel follows the plosive? As can be seen in Figure 8.7, the transitions are different for each combination of plosive and vowel. However, this does not mean that the syllables /di/, /dɛ/, and /dɑ/, for example, have nothing in common. To see this, let us superimpose the stylized formants for these syllables, as given in Figure 8.8. Notice that the $F_2$ transitions for all the syllables beginning with /d/ point to the same spot; the $F_1$ transitions all point to another, different spot. The other syllables beginning with /d/ would have transitions pointing to the same spot as well. Each of these spots (X in Figure 8.8) is called a **locus** (plural **loci**); notice that their actual location on the spectrogram is in the silent portion of the plosive articulation. As can be seen by extrapolating the formants in Figure 8.7, the labials and velars each have distinctive loci, and the locus for $F_2$ is different for each place of articulation. (That is, extend the formant transitions backward in the direction they point such that they meet, as was done in Figure 8.8. The meeting point for all the extrapolated $F_2$ transitions of syllables beginning with the same plosive indicates the frequency of the locus for that place of articulation. Note that there are two different $F_2$ loci for velars; the division comes between /gɑ/ and /gɔ/ in Figure 8.7.)

The formant transitions appear at the end of the vowel when the stop *follows* the vowel, and if the plosive is situated between two vowels, there are two sets of transitions: those leading into and those leading out of the plosive. For this reason, plosives are likely to be more intelligible when situated intervocalically than at the beginning of a word, preceding a vowel. Stops situated at the end of a word are least intelligible.

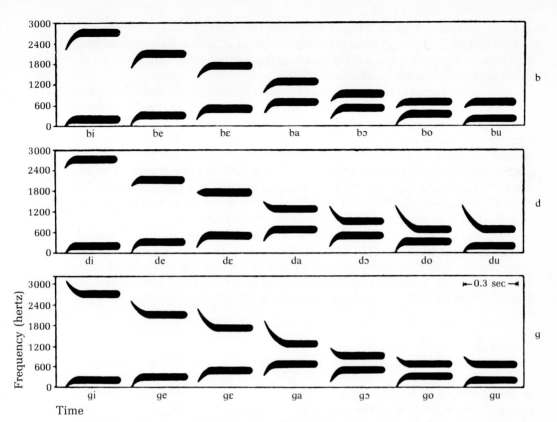

**Figure 8.7.** Spectrograms of synthetically produced syllables, showing second-formant transitions that produce the voiced stops before various vowels. (From Acoustic Loci and Transitional Cues for Consonants by Pierre C. Delattre, Alvin M. Liberman, and Franklin S. Cooper. *Journal of the Acoustical Society of America*, Vol. 27, July 1955. Used by permission of the authors and the American Institute of Physics.)

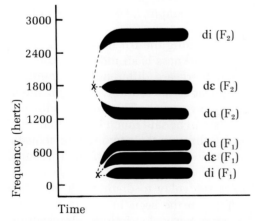

**Figure 8.8.** The loci of the formant transitions of the alveolar plosives /d/ or /t/. While the shape of the formant transition changes according to the formant frequency of the following vowel, the locus remains constant. That is, the formant transitions of the alveolar plosives always "point" to the same frequency (X in the illustration), no matter what vowel follows. It is thus the frequency of the locus that our ear perceives in identifying the place of articulation of the plosive consonant.

Finally, note in Figure 8.16 that the final /t/ of the sentence is weakly released. The aspiration is faintly visible as a "spike." If there had been no release of the final stop, as often occurs at the ends of sentences, there would be no aspiration visible in the spectrogram.

The acoustic shape of plosive consonants suggests that our perceptual mechanism is quite remarkable. Consider, for example, the fact that if formant frequencies change slowly, we perceive a diphthong, while rapid formant transitions are perceived as a sequence of vowel plus consonant. As another example, a plosive consonant such as /d/ does not have a single unchanging acoustic quality; rather, the syllables /di/ and /dɑ/ appear to be less similar acoustically than are /bi/ and /di/. Apparently, our perceptual mechanism abstracts out the loci and identifies them, even though they are just hypothetical dots on a graph in a period of relative silence!

In summary, there are several acoustic cues leading to our perception of different plosives: (1) voiced and voiceless plosives having the *same* place of articulation are distinguished by aspiration and the delay in the onset of voicing in the voiceless variety; and (2) different places of articulation are distinguished by different patterns of formant transitions.

## 8-9.2 The Fricatives

Fricatives are produced with audible air turbulence. This turbulence creates "noise," that is, sound that is aperiodic in nature. Aperiodic sound shows up on the spectrogram as an uneven shading across a wide frequency range. For example, the aspiration of the voiceless plosives is aperiodic.

Figure 8.11 shows that each of the voiceless fricatives has a distinct pattern of aperiodic noise: /f/ has a frequency range of 2000 to 8000 Hz (actually higher, but the upper limit for the spectrograph is 8000 Hz); /θ/ has a similar frequency range, though its lower limit is closer to 100 Hz and it is much weaker overall; /s/ has a frequency of 3500 to 8000 Hz; and /š/ has a range from about 1500 to 6000 Hz. Each fricative is identified by a distinctive frequency range, and this agrees with our intuitions. For example, /s/ sounds higher to us than /š/.

You will note another difference among the fricatives. Some show up darker than others on the spectrograms. Darkness is an indicator of amplitude (loudness), and so you can see that there are differences in loudness among the various fricatives. /s/ and /š/ appear as the loudest; /f/ is considerably less loud; and /θ/ shows up as being very weak. This agrees with our intuition, for it is easy to demonstrate that /s/ can be said much louder than /θ/.

Thus, the fricatives are perceived through their two salient acoustic features: (1) the frequency range of their aperiodic sound, and (2) their relative loudness.

A third feature, voicing, comes into play to distinguish voiceless fricatives from their voiced cognates. This can be seen in Figure 8.12, the spectrogram of the voiced fricatives. Note that vertical striations, representing voicing, are visible as the fricative is articulated. This tends to obscure the aperiodic sound to some degree on the spectrogram, but for the most part, it should be possible to see the simultaneous voicing and aperiodic sound. This is most clearly visible on the spectrograms of /zɑ/ and /žɑ/.

In all cases, the aperiodic noise of the voiced fricatives has less loudness than that of the voiceless fricative, and this is clearly visible in the spectrograms if /sɑ/ and /zɑ/ are compared. The reason for this is related to the articulation of these sounds. In voiced sounds, the amount of air that may pass out of the lungs is restricted by the vocal folds, which open and close rhythmically. This decreased amount of air and decreased pressure reduce the amount of turbulence and hence the loudness of the voiced fricative sounds.

## 8-9.3 The Approximants

Figure 8.13 gives spectrograms of four approximants followed by the vowel /ɑ/. These syllables resemble diphthongs as much as they do consonant-vowel sequences. The approximants show distinct formant patterns, just like the vowels. This is most obvious in the case of /j/. It is less apparent on the spectrograms of /r/, /w/, and /l/ because of the degree of oral closure, which renders the upper formants ($F_3$, $F_4$, etc.) very weak.

## 8-9.4 The Nasals

As can be seen in Figure 8.14, the nasals have formant patterns, similar to those of the vowels, that serve to identify the particular speech sound. The nasals show a slightly reduced loudness as compared to the accompanying vowel, the result of oral closure.

## 8-9.5 The Glottal Stop and Fricative

In Figure 8.15, the glottal stop appears to be similar to the plosives in having a period of silence and a slight delay in the onset of voicing; however, it lacks the formant transitions characteristic of other plosives. The formant transitions in the other plosives are a result of the changing resonant qualities of the oral cavity as the articulators move from the position for the plosive to the position for the following vowel. With the glottal stop, there is no such movement and therefore no formant transitions.

The so-called glottal fricative /h/ (Figure 8.15) shows an acoustic pattern similar to the other fricatives. One essential difference, however, is that the aperiodic noise tends to center around the frequencies of the formants of the following vowel. This is because /h/ is pronounced with the oral configuration of the following vowel, which means that the oral cavity has the same resonant characteristics as it does for the vowel that follows, and while there is no glottal pulsing (voicing), noise at or near the formant frequencies is emphasized.

## 8-9.6 The Sentence

Let us look at the spectrogram of a sentence (Figure 8.16) in order to see what can be learned about the acoustic shape of units longer than one syllable. Some of the features mentioned here will be the subject of more detailed discussions later in the book.

Perhaps the most immediately apparent feature of the sentence is the way that the words are run together. Because of the emphasis placed on

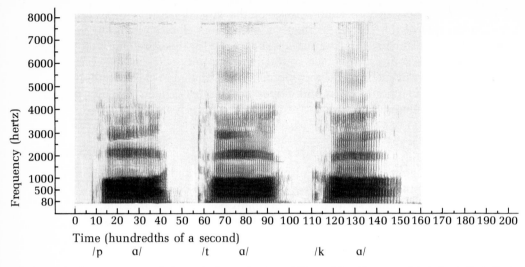

**Figure 8.9.** Spectrograms of the voiceless plosives followed by the vowel /ɑ/: /pɑ/, /tɑ/, /kɑ/.

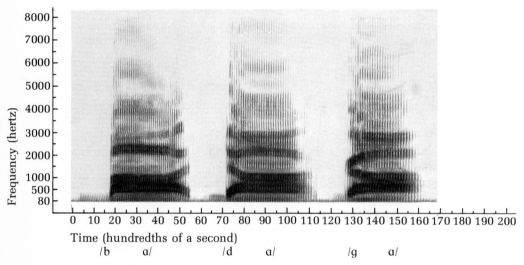

**Figure 8.10.** Spectrograms of the voiced plosives followed by the vowel /ɑ/: /bɑ/, /dɑ/, /gɑ/. Notice the transitions at the end of the syllable /bɑ/, made as the speaker prepares to pronounce the following /d/.

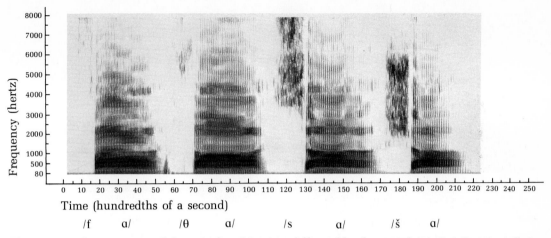

Time (hundredths of a second)

/f    ɑ/        /θ    ɑ/         /s    ɑ/       /š    ɑ/

**Figure 8.11.** Spectrograms of the voiceless fricatives followed by the vowel /ɑ/: /fɑ/, /θɑ/, /sɑ/, /šɑ/. The noise of the /f/ and /θ/ is of low amplitude and shows up only faintly.

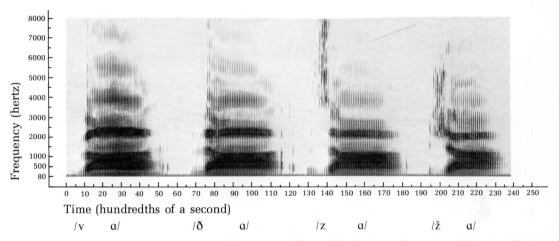

Time (hundredths of a second)

/v    ɑ/        /ð    ɑ/         /z    ɑ/       /ž    ɑ/

**Figure 8.12.** Spectrograms of the voiced fricatives followed by the vowel /ɑ/: /vɑ/, /ðɑ/, /zɑ/, /žɑ/. The noise of the /v/ and /ð/ is of very low amplitude, not showing up at all. The noise of the /z/ and /ž/ is less strong than that of /s/ and /š/, above.

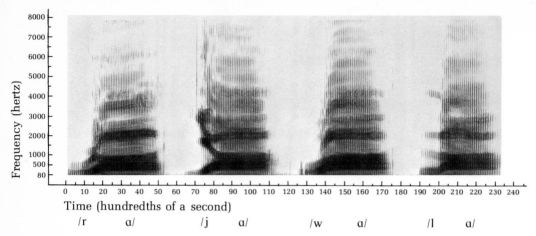

**Figure 8.13.** Spectrograms of the approximants followed by the vowel /ɑ/: /rɑ/, /jɑ/, /wɑ/, /lɑ/.

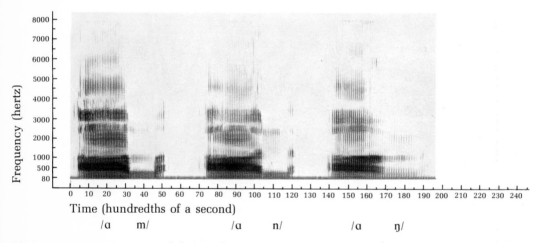

**Figure 8.14.** Spectrograms of the nasals preceded by the vowel /ɑ/: /ɑm/, /ɑn/, /ɑŋ/.

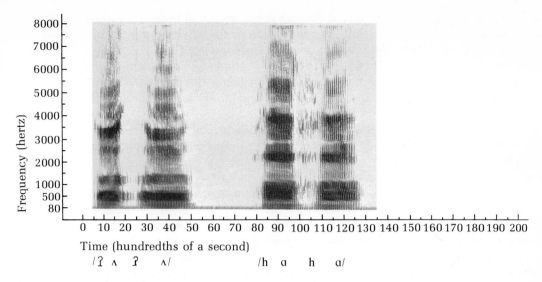

**Figure 8.15.** Spectrograms of the glottal consonants accompanied by vowels: /ʔʌʔʌ/, /hɑhɑ/. /ʔ/ is a stop, /h/ a fricative.

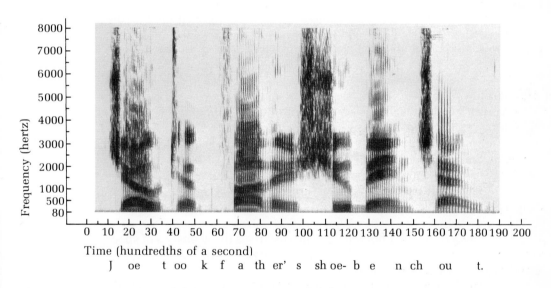

**Figure 8.16.** Spectrogram of the sentence "Joe took father's shoe-bench out."

writing, we tend to think of words as distinct items separated from other words by a space, not only on paper, but in time as well. In speech, however, there is usually no space of time left between words. The sentence "Joe took father's shoe-bench out" is pronounced as if it were a single seven-syllable word. Remember that plosives are characterized by silence during their closure phase, and so the apparent space between "Joe" and "took" is only the articulation of /t/, not a pause.

Second, notice the way similar sounds are modified in context. In the sequence "father's shoe-," there is a /z/ followed by a /š/, but notice that only the /š/ shows up; the /z/ is not pronounced. Such phenomena are considered in Chapter 10.

Third, examine the vertical striations representing individual pulses of the vocal folds. Notice how the distance between them varies. A change in this distance represents a change in the fundamental frequency; the further they are apart, the lower the fundamental frequency. Notice how the frequency drops through the phrase "Joe took father's," rises sharply on "shoe," and drops to its lowest point on "out." Such patterns of frequency are known as **intonation,** which is discussed in Chapter 13.

## Questions for Discussion

1. From your experience, what variant forms of consonants are used in different dialects of English?
2. Is there more regional (dialectal) variation in vowels or in consonants? Why?

## Annotated Bibliography

Consonant articulation is discussed in all introductory phonetics texts. See also the References in this volume.

For details on the consonants of exotic languages, one of the best sources is Smalley's *Manual of Articulatory Phonetics* [1963] with its accompanying workbook and tapes.

The position that affricates are one linguistic unit rather than a sequence of two is given some empirical support in an article by Fromkin [1971].

Joos's *Acoustic Phonetics* [1948] discusses the acoustics of speech in some detail, though it is now rather dated. Articles in the Lehiste anthology [1967] also discuss speech acoustics.

The acoustics of speech are discussed in a very technical text by Flanagan [1972], but the beginner will find this very heavy reading.

See also other sources in the References.

# Chapter 9

## Word Stress

**9-1 Stress**

    Stress in words and sentences plays an important role in the overall phonetic quality of speech. It is to a great extent responsible for carrying meaning, and abnormal stress placement will render otherwise good speech completely unintelligible. So the individual correcting speech in a professional capacity must come to an understanding of the role of stress in speech.

    Stress is perhaps a less tangible aspect of phonetics than, say, the individual phones; it is harder to determine just what is wrong when someone pronounces a word with inappropriate stress. This fact is reflected in the rather vague terms we use in our everyday speech for this and other aspects of general phonetic quality. For example, we may say that a foreign speaker of English has an "accent." This may mean that his vowels, consonants, stress, intonation, assimilation, or other aspects of his speech are peculiar in some way. Clearly, such a term is not precise enough for our needs.

    While stress might be called accent or accentuation, we will stay with the term **stress** and give it a rather precise meaning (this cannot be accomplished in a short definition but will emerge from the entire chapter). This specific meaning should not be interchanged with the vague, everyday uses of words like stress and accent. And, while stress may be less tangible, more variable, and more open to differences in opinion than some other aspects of phonetics, it is no less important. Indeed, it may be more important, since it is one aspect of speech that is highly susceptible to distortion by the deaf speaker, foreign speaker, or individual with certain voice disorders.

9-1.1 Locating the Stressed Syllable

    What is stress? In its simplest terms, it is an increase in the loudness of a word or syllable. If you say a word such as "payment" out loud, you will perceive that the first syllable carries a greater stress than the second, that is, it is pronounced louder: PAYment. Many people find this difficult to perceive at first. But the student of phonetics should have had some practice analyzing his own speech. If you need a trick to help you to perceive stress, this technique may be helpful: you can discover which syllable is stressed by intentionally placing the stress on the *wrong* syllable. By this method of elimination you will discover the correct stress pattern, since the wrong one will sound strange to you. For example, say payMENT, intentionally stressing the second syllable. If you have done this correctly, the word will sound very similar to the first two syllables of the word "pimento" and will rhyme with "invent." It will be obvious to your ear that the second syllable of "payment" is not the correct one to stress, so the stress must fall on the first syllable.

Let us look at a three-syllable word from the point of view of trying to find which syllable is stressed: "discover." If you have a good ear for stress, you need only to say the word (out loud or, better yet, to yourself) to find the stressed syllable. If you are not used to locating the stress, you will need to use the test of stressing the wrong syllable. Say the word "discover" three times, each time stressing a different syllable: DIScover, disCOVer, discovER. The second one should sound most natural to you. After you have used this technique for a while, you should be able to abandon it and be able to find stress in a word just by saying the word to yourself.

## 9-1.2 The Phonetic Effects of Stress

A stressed syllable sounds louder to us; we consciously perceive stress as loudness. In fact, loudness is not the only characteristic of stress, and it may not be the most important factor in our unconscious perception of stress. Let us compare the "same" syllable in a stressed and an unstressed environment. Take the syllable <u>ment</u> in the words "payment" and "mental"; it is unstressed in the first word, stressed in the second.

Certainly there is a difference in loudness between the two. But there is also a difference in length. (Remember that length is a matter of duration or time, not of quality.) The vowel and the whole syllable are longer in the stressed syllable. The vowel quality also changes: it is a distinct /ɛ/ in the stressed syllable; it is not so distinct in the unstressed syllable, where it is **reduced** to a schwa. (As will be shown, there may also be differences in the amount of diphthongization with certain vowels.)

In summary, the effect of stress is to: (1) increase the duration of the syllable, (2) increase the loudness (amplitude) of the syllable, and (3) increase the distinctness of the vowel quality. All these factors, or any combination of them, may play the role of signaling stress in any particular syllable. The changes in loudness and vowel quality are probably the easiest for us to hear, but, being used to normal English pronunciation, we often find even these features hard to hear.

By contrast, an unstressed syllable will tend to have: (1) a shorter duration, (2) less loudness (amplitude), and (3) a less distinct vowel (tending toward, but not always, schwa).

While stress may affect the entire syllable and all the phones in it, it affects the vowel most strongly. The consonants tend to be less modified by different degrees of stress.

Stressed and unstressed, as outlined here, are two extremes of a continuum. We cannot say that a particular syllable is always either fully stressed or completely unstressed. There are an infinite number of points in between.

## 9-1.3  Levels of Stress

For most practical purposes, the continuum from strongest to weakest stress is divided into three identifiable **levels of stress.** (Phonologists and other linguists distinguish a fourth level, which comes into play in phrases and sentences; we will disregard this in the present discussion.) The three levels are **primary** (the strongest), **secondary** (medium), and **weak** or **tertiary.**[1]

A word like "pimento," however, has three levels of stress in English. The most strongly stressed syllable is the second one, /mɛn/. The last syllable, /to/, has less stress than the second syllable but more than the first. The first syllable has weak stress. These different levels of stress are generally marked, ´, `, and ˆ, respectively, for primary, secondary, and weak. These symbols are convenient, because they are available on a typewriter with an international keyboard. The word "pimento" could be transcribed /pə̂mɛ́ntô/.

Other systems are sometimes used to mark stress. For example, the syllable with primary stress may be written in capital letters as was done above. The disadvantage is that only two levels of stress can be marked. The official IPA system uses a raised vertical line to mark primary stress, a vertical line at the level of the base of the letters to mark secondary stress, and nothing to mark weak stress: /pə'mɛn,to/. This system forces the transcriber to divide every word into syllables, which is not always convenient.

## 9-2  The Effect of Stress upon Vowels

As noted earlier, vowels in syllables having secondary or weak stress tend to be **reduced** to schwa. What is a reduced vowel? It tends to be shorter in duration and to have a less distinctive quality. This results from the fact that in unstressed syllables the tongue movements tend to be more relaxed and not to arrive at articulatory positions distant from the mid-central position. However, it is not accurate to think of vowels as either reduced to schwa or not reduced. There is a continuum, and any point between the extremes may be represented in an actual articulation. Syllables having secondary stress are reduced as compared to those having primary stress, and syllables having weak stress may be completely reduced.

Are there any differences between vowels in syllables having primary stress and those in syllables having secondary stress? The differences are small, but these differences are important in contributing to a natural-sounding pronunciation of English. For that reason, it is important to pay attention to

---

[1] Unfortunately, this is another area in which there has been little standardization of terminology. Ladefoged [1975] uses the terms **stressed, unstressed,** and **reduced,** respectively, for what is here called **primary, secondary,** and **weak** stress. Further, if four levels of stress are distinguished, the terms **tertiary** and **weak,** which are synonymous here, must be differentiated in order to have four different names to identify the four levels. The terms used in this chapter are in widespread use, and they will be used consistently to prevent possible confusion, but sometimes inconsistencies in terminology will be encountered in one's reading.

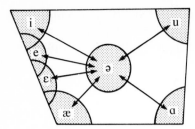

**Figure 9.1.** Vowel reduction. For the sake of clarity, not all vowels are indicated. When stressed, the vowels are articulated nearer to their cardinal positions, close to the outer edges of the vowel quadrangle. When weakly stressed, or unstressed, they tend to be reduced toward schwa (/ə/), or pronounced nearer to the mid-central position of the vowel quadrangle.

them. What are these differences? A good way to start, as usual, is to listen analytically to some speech sounds. The syllable /to/ in the word "pimento," as has been shown, is an example of secondary stress; in the expression "tow truck," it has primary stress. When these two are pronounced out loud in a normal voice, some small difference will be noticed between the syllable /to/ in the words "pimento" and "tow truck." There is less of a diphthongal character to the vowel in the syllable having secondary stress, and it is shorter in duration. Further, its position of articulation may be a little more central.

What is occurring is that for each vowel there is a point anywhere between schwa and the full value of that vowel that can be pronounced. We must therefore make a judgment about which end of the continuum a pronunciation is closer to. In the vowel quadrangle shown in Figure 9.1, the arrows represent the continua along which each vowel might be pronounced. The enclosed areas on Figure 9.1 represent the range of pronunciations that would be clearly and consistently identified as particular vowels. Note that while not all vowels are included on this diagram, the same principle applies to /o/, /ɔ/, and the other vowels.

Suppose we consider one vowel, say /e/, in greater detail. Figure 9.2 shows that, depending upon stress, there are numerous realizations of an English vowel (as before, the principle applies equally to vowels not shown in the diagram). Although it is not diagrammed, a very important phonetic change brought about by stress is the fact that /e/ under primary stress is diphthongized

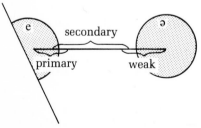

**Figure 9.2.** Levels of stress for /e/. An enlargement of a portion of the vowel quadrangle in Figure 9.1, showing the approximate position of articulation of the vowel /e/ under primary, secondary, and weak stress.

(see section 7-5.2), but under secondary stress it is not or is less so. All four of the English long vowels (/i, e, o, u/) behave similarly. For example, compare the pronunciation of /i/ in the words "foresee" and "hippy." Further examples will be found in section 9-2.1 below.

The high front vowels present a special problem, though, in many dialects of North American English. They tend to remain high when they are reduced, giving a high central vowel in these dialects. On the vowel quadrangle, this vowel is located midway between /i/ and /u/, above /ə/; its IPA symbol is /ɨ/. This vowel is present in many speakers' pronunciation of the word "roses" (as opposed to "Rosa's," which has /ə/). Usually, the symbol /ɨ/ is not used in the broad transcription of English, though of course it is used for detailed transcription as in the case of fine dialect differences or communication disorders. The result of the slightly peculiar behavior of /i/ and /ɪ/ under reduced stress is that a number of different—and therefore confusing—conventions are used in the transcription of these vowels when they do not have primary stress. These will be examined in section 9-2.2.

It seems apparent in general that the idealized full articulatory movements for vowels are made only under primary stress, and reduced stress leads to articulatory gestures that do not fully reach their target. As noted in our discussion of vowel articulation in Chapter 7, tongue position is not the only factor in vowel articulation. Lip posture and tongue-root position play a role as well. It is apparent that each of these features, too, will vary along a continuum, and that stress will influence whether or not the idealized articulatory position is reached. For example, an /i/ under secondary stress will have a more neutral (i.e., less spread) lip posture than an /i/ under primary stress. This leads some phoneticians to identify /i/ under secondary stress as an /ɪ/ and contributes to the differences in transcription systems that we will examine in section 9-2.2. In addition, the tongue-root position, which varies according to the "tenseness" of a vowel, may be subject to some variation according to level of stress and thus may contribute to some of the acoustic differences between a vowel under primary stress and the same vowel under secondary stress; this is at present unconfirmed.

## 9-2.1 The Reduced Form of Vowels

Let us now look at some examples of English vowels under the influence of different degrees of stress. At this time, it would be well to recall a point that is relevant throughout this or any other phonetics book: namely, that the examples may not be appropriate in all dialects. In Table 9.1, the vowels may not in all cases be appropriate to your pronunciation.

It may at first seem arbitrary that a certain reduced vowel is stated to be a reduced form of a particular cardinal vowel. For example, why is the e of "homogenize" a reduced /i/ and not, say, a reduced /e/? By looking at a related word in which the particular vowel is stressed, one can find the "true" [2] value

---

[2] This "true" value is what phonologists call the **underlying** vowel. As the word "homogenize" is pronounced (its **surface** form), one can only tell that there is a schwa. An examination of related words shows that this sound is an /i/ that has been reduced to schwa through the operation of phonological rules (as discussed in Chapter 2). Thus, the underlying vowel is /i/; the surface vowel is [ə].

**Table 9.1.** Reduced Forms of Vowels

| Vowel | Primary Stress | Secondary Stress | Weak Stress |
|---|---|---|---|
| i | scheme | schematic | |
| | homogeneous | hippy | homogenize |
| ɪ | simple | simplistic | simplistic |
| | morbidity | morbid | insipid |
| ɛ | tempestuous | tempestuous | tempest |
| e | maintain | | maintenance |
| | Canadian | | Canada |
| | grade | gradation | |
| æ | Canada | | Canadian |
| | nationality | | nationalism |
| | extrapolate | extrasensory | extra |
| | | acknowledge | |
| u | moving | removability | |
| ʊ | hoodwink | motherhood | |
| o | photo | photosynthesis | photograph |
| | Oklahoma | Oklahoma | |
| ɔ | auction | auctioneer | |
| ʌ | confront | confrontation | |
| ɑ | monotone | monocular | (carbon) monoxide |
| ai | license | licentious | |
| | digest (noun) | digestion | digest (verb) |
| au | sauerkraut | sauerkraut | |
| ɔi | employ | employability | |
| ju | refute | refutation | jugular |

*Rhotacized vowels:*

| Vowel | Primary Stress | Secondary Stress | Weak Stress |
|---|---|---|---|
| ɚ | circle | semicircle | circumnavigate |
| | imperfect | imperfection | perfection |
| iɚ | commandeer | | commander |
| | ethereal | | ether |
| eɚ | primarily | primary* | primary* |
| uɚ | injurious | | injury |
| oɚ | laborious | laboring | labor |
| | professorial | | professor |
| | record (verb) | | record (noun) |
| ɑɚ | partner | | orchard |

\* Depends upon dialect.
Note: There are considerable dialect differences in the degree of stress placed on each syllable. Also, the stress may be modified when the word is used in a sentence as compared to being pronounced in isolation.

of the vowel. In this case, the word "homogeneous" provides the clue to the value of this vowel. If there is no related word in which the particular vowel is stressed (as, for example, "orchard") knowledge of the history of the word (often reflected in the spelling) is used in making this judgment.

Table 9.1 indicates various English vowels and diphthongs under the three levels of stress. Several aspects of the influence of stress on vowels should be noted in the examples.

(1) Note that the long vowels (/i, e, u, o/) are fully diphthongized under primary stress but are shorter and "purer" under secondary stress. And, like the short vowels, they are reduced to schwa under weak stress. (2) Note

that there are few examples of the diphthongs /ai/, /au/ and /ɔi/ under weak stress. Because of the historical development of these sounds, most are in syllables taking primary or secondary stress. There are a few examples of fully reduced diphthongs, however. The noun "digest" (*Reader's Digest*) has primary stress on the first syllable, /dáiǰèst/, but this syllable is reduced in the verb form ('to digest food'): /dəǰést/. Again because of historical development, diphthongs often alternate with different vowels: for example, "pronounce" is related to "pronunciation," "denounce" with "denunciation," etc. (3) Notice that the reduced form of /ju/ is usually /jə/; that is, the /j/ glide is retained under weak stress. (4) A vowel followed by an r-sound is generally reduced to one single vowel, /ə/ or /ɚ/, depending on the dialect. For example, note the relationship between "laborious" and "labor." [3]

## 9-2.2 The Transcription of Stress

It is normal practice in transcription to differentiate two levels of stress in our representation of *vowels*; that is, when a vowel has weak stress, it is transcribed with a schwa, but when it has either primary or secondary stress, it is transcribed with its full quality (/e/, /i/, etc.). Thus, while the three levels of stress can be indicated with stress marks, there is no generally accepted way of transcribing the effect of secondary stress on vowel quality.

This lack is usually not a problem. For one thing, the stress marks are available when needed, and second, it is often satisfactory to ignore the differences in vowel quality under primary and secondary stress *for the purposes of transcription*, although one *cannot* ignore the phonetic differences for the purposes of speech correction. The real phonetic differences between vowels under primary and secondary stress contribute to natural-sounding speech. Clients or students will need to become aware of the subtle differences in vowel quality resulting from stress in order to improve their pronunciation.

Some authors try to represent in transcription the effect of secondary stress on vowels but use inconsistent notation, which may confuse students more than it helps. Some methods for representing secondary stress vowels, and the actual phonetic differences that these systems are trying to represent, will be discussed next. These are not recommendations to follow in transcription (that will come later) but, rather, an explanation of some systems that may be encountered in your reading.

THE VOWEL /i/. Some books recommend using the symbol /ɪ/ for the secondary-stressed version of the vowel /i/. So, it is recommended that a word like "happy" be transcribed /hæpɪ/. Many students of phonetics find this very confusing and inconsistent. In fact, it is an attempt to show that the last syllable of "happy" does not have as full a vowel as, for example, that of "foresee"; we noted in section 9.2 that under secondary stress the articulation of /i/ may approach that of /ɪ/. How should this vowel be transcribed? Of course, you should be consistent with your teacher or lab manual, but it is recommended that you use the symbol /i/ rather than /ɪ/, since the latter causes so much confusion.

---

[3] Alternations such as labor/laborious provide one argument for calling a sequence such as the -or- of "laborious" a diphthong rather than a vowel plus consonant.

LONG VOWELS. Chapter 7, on vowels, showed that all long vowels in English are to some extent diphthongs. We discussed the fact that some authors prefer to show that these are diphthongs in the transcription while other authors feel that if one is dealing only with English, the simpler system is better. The vowel in the word "boat," for example, can be written /o/, /oṵ/, or /ow/ (cf. section 7-5.2).

Long vowels tend to be more diphthongized in syllables of primary stress. In syllables with secondary stress, they tend to retain their distinct character—the long vowel does not become a schwa—but they are less diphthongized. So, for those transcription systems that indicate the diphthongal character of long vowels, sometimes the diphthongal quality is not marked in secondary-stress syllables. For example, "tow truck" /toṵtrʌk/ but "pimento" /pəmɛnto/. The syllable with the /o/ has primary stress in "tow truck" but secondary stress in "pimento."

The important point here is that, phonetically, there is less of a diphthongal character to long English vowels in syllables having secondary stress than primary stress; this is true no matter what system is used to transcribe the vowels.

DIPHTHONGS. The true diphthongs, like /ai/ and /au/, retain their diphthongal character when in positions of secondary stress. They will be a little shorter in duration, and the starting and finishing points of the diphthong may both be a little closer to the neutral rest position of the tongue, than if the diphthong were under primary stress, but the best transcription is to use the same symbol as for the fully stressed versions. For example, in the expression "White House" (meaning the president's residence), "House" has secondary stress. If you have a good ear, you may be able to detect the fact that the diphthong in "House" is a little reduced from its realization in a stressed articulation of "house." But the best transcription is to use the same vowel for both and, where necessary, to mark stress separately.

The above examples should make it clear that the first two levels of stress are not well distinguished by transcribing different vowels according to the degree of stress. A much better system, where it is important to mark stress, is to use the accent marks given earlier in this chapter in conjunction with the full vowel quality for both primary and secondary stress, and schwa for the vowels under weak stress.

## 9-3  How Languages Use Stress

Languages can make use of stress at three levels: in the word, in the short phrase, and in the sentence.

Word stress refers to the way the different syllables of words are stressed in a particular language. For example, the word "exploit" is stressed differently depending on whether it is a verb or a noun ("to exploit resources" and "the hero's exploits," respectively). A word must have more than one syllable before we can talk about word stress.

In the short phrase, special patterns of stress (sometimes in combination with intonation) are used to make distinctions in meaning. For example, "the white hóuse" (the house that is white) has a different stress from "the White Hoùse" (the official residence of the president of the United States).

In a sentence, we often make use of stress to emphasize certain words and thereby change the meaning. For example "I didn't break it" means "Someone else did"; "I didn't break it" may mean something like "I just dismantled it; I can easily put it back together." Note that, in writing, we often show stress by underlining (handwriting or typewriting) or italic script (printed matter).

Word stress is the topic of this chapter. Phrase stress and sentence stress will be among the topics of Chapter 13.

## 9-3.1 How Languages Use Word Stress

Different languages use word stress differently. We can arbitrarily divide the world's languages into four types, but we will take a detailed look only at those like modern English. The student who is familiar with the languages given as examples may find cases that do not behave exactly as stated. In general the principles operate as stated; an effort has been made to select familiar languages rather than exotic ones that might serve as more perfect examples.

In a language such as French, every syllable has equal stress. There is a schwa in French, but it is not a reduced form of some other vowel, it is a separate and distinct phoneme.[4] In such a language, stress cannot be used to contrast two words that are otherwise similar.

In some languages, such as Old English as it was spoken by King Arthur, the syllable that takes primary stress is determined by simple rules. In this type of language, stress is completely predictable; it does not have to be learned for each word the way it does for Modern English. However, two words could not differ by stress placement alone. For the most part, Modern German has predictable stress, and stress placement is not used to carry meaning distinctions.[5]

In a language such as Spanish, the syllable taking primary stress is usually determined by rule. There are some exceptions, allowing contrasts on the basis of stress alone. In Spanish spelling, stress is unmarked when it is predictable by the rule, and it is marked with an accent if it falls on a syllable other than the one predicted by the rule.[6] For example, these words contrast in Spanish: termino ('I terminate'; stress on the second syllable, unmarked because it is where the rule predicts), término ('term'; unpredictable stress as marked), and terminó ('he terminated'; unpredictable stress as marked). The

---

[4] Students familiar with spoken French will realize that this is not quite true; polysyllabic French words take a slight stress on the final syllable. The two essential factors remain: there is no reduction of vowels in other syllables and stress cannot be used to contrast words. Additionally, the speaker may strongly stress a syllable other than the final one for emotional or theatrical effect, but this is not contrastive.

[5] There are exceptions to this general rule as a result of prefixes being perceived as part of the word in some cases and as separate prefixes in other cases. For example, úbersetzen means 'to transfer' or 'to ferry,' whereas übersétzen means 'to translate.' However, the stress is not marked in German spelling as it has been in these examples.

[6] The rule in Spanish is that stress falls on the penultimate (second to last) syllable if the word ends in a vowel, an s, or n; otherwise the stress falls on the final syllable.

characteristic of this type of language is that while stress is predictable in most cases, stress alone can be used to carry meaning differences in the exceptional cases.

In a language such as English, there are few rules for stress. Stress might be placed anywhere in a word, so the stress pattern must be learned separately for each word. This system offers the advantage of allowing meaning contrasts: the same string of phonemes may have different pronunciations and therefore different meanings according to the stress placement.


## 9-4 English Word Stress

As noted, Old English had a stress system in which the placement of primary stress in a word was predictable. This is not true of Modern English; the reason is chiefly that the vocabulary that is borrowed from other languages is usually borrowed with the foreign stress pattern.

The Old English system worked this way: the first syllable of a polysyllabic word took primary stress, unless that syllable was a prefix; in that case the first root syllable took primary stress. Indeed, for those English words that have changed little since the days of King Arthur, this rule remains true. The word "fáthêr," for example, has primary stress on the first syllable. The word "fòrbíd" has primary stress on the first root syllable. (For is in this case a prefix, as it is in the word "fòrgét." But in the word "fórtỳ," the syllable for is the root, and it takes primary stress.) A similar pattern can be found for most other English words of Germanic origin. Over 50 percent of the words in our vocabulary have been borrowed from foreign sources, most from the Romance languages (Latin, French, etc.), and from hundreds of other languages as well. In most of these words, the stress pattern of the original language has been retained or an attempt has been made to imitate the original stress pattern when the word has been adapted to English pronunciation. As a result, we have words like "vocábulary," "pajáma," and "automátic," which have unpredictable stress patterns different from those of original English words like "fáthêr" or "bérrỳ."

While stress placement may be mostly unpredictable in English, stress remains a fundamental part of the phonetic shape of any English word. As stated earlier in the chapter, incorrect stress placement often renders a word completely incomprehensible. This can be demonstrated by taking a few polysyllabic words and pronouncing them with incorrect stress placement. Try for example /ənkɔ́rɛkt/, /ǽnəðɛ̀r/, or /mə̀ntɛ́zə̀mù/.[7] Our understanding of spoken words depends on correct stress; it is unlikely that anyone would understand the words if they were pronounced as suggested above. This should convince one of the necessity of paying attention to stress in correcting speech.

Words in English can be contrasted on the basis of stress alone, without any other phonetic difference signaling the contrast (except, of course, the change in vowel quality that is a direct result of the stress change). Let us look at some examples of this. Noun-verb pairs are often contrasted in English by stress:

---

[7] "Incorrect," "another," and "Montezuma."

| Noun | Verb |
|------|------|
| cónflìct | cônflíct |
| cóntràst | côntrást |
| défèct | dêféct |
| dígèst | dîgést or dìgést |
| éxpòrt | êxpórt |
| ímpòrt | împórt |
| récôrd | rêcórd |
| súbjèct | sûbjéct |

There is considerable dialect difference concerning whether all such pairs are contrasted. You may find that in your own speech you have the two pronunciations of "subject" but only one for "digest" or "import." However, all of us will agree that there are some pairs whose form is distinguished by stress. Thus we can conclude that stress serves a contrastive function. In fact, the effect of stress may be so strong psychologically that we do not even think of the two forms of "defect" as even being the same word. (This can be seen in the expressions "a défèct in materials" and "the spy will dêféct to the other side.")

9-4.1 The Distinguishing Function of Stress

The noun-verb pairs above demonstrate that words can differ on the basis of stress alone in English (vowel quality, of course, is changed as a result of stress). Other words are similarly distinguished. "Personal" and "personnel" are distinguished by stress, as are "plastic" and "plastique" (a kind of explosive), "moral" and "morale," "local" and "locale," and "human" and "humane." [8]

But if stress plays a truly distinctive role in English, pairs of unrelated words should be distinguished this way. Stress differences should not be limited to pairs of related words such as the noun-verb pairs or the doublets above; that is, there should be pairs of words that just happen to be stressed differently. And indeed, such pairs exist; for example, insight/incite, debtor/deter, decade/decayed (in most dialects), bellow/below, demon/demean, desert/dessert, Concord (and Concorde)/conquered,[9] weakened/weekend, and coral/corral.

In all the example words listed in this section—whether or not the words are related—it can be seen that the same sequence of phones can form

---

[8] These pairs of words are examples of what etymologists call **doublets**—they are instances of the same word being borrowed twice. In each pair, the first word was borrowed from French early in the history of English and has become stressed on the first syllable to conform to usual English pronunciation. The second word in each pair was borrowed later in history (for example, the word personal was used in English in the fourteenth century; personnel was not used in English until the nineteenth century). The second of each pair is stressed on the final syllable, in imitation of the French pronunciation and in contrast with its doublet.

[9] The Massachusetts town of Concord is pronounced like "conquered"; most other cities with that name, and the Concorde aircraft, have a contrasting stress pattern.

different words depending upon stress placement and the other phonetic changes (in vowel quality) that result directly from stress placement.

### 9-4.2 Stress and Parts of Speech

Those noun-verb pairs in which stress placement changes have already been noted, such as the noun "défect" and the verb "dêféct." Many other English nouns and verbs follow the same pattern, even when not members of pairs. So "pígeòn," a noun, is stressed on the first syllable, whereas "înfér," a verb, is stressed on the second syllable. But there are so many exceptions that this cannot be said to be a general pattern.

A similar process occurs in some noun-adjective pairs. For example: (1) The pair "ínvâlìd/ìnválîd," as in "he is an invalid as a result of his accident" and "your argument is invalid." (2) The word "learned" may be pronounced as a one- or two-syllable word. It has one syllable when used as a verb ("he learned his lesson"), but when it is an adjective (meaning 'educated' or 'scholarly'), the -ed has secondary or tertiary stress, making it a two-syllable word in the phrase "my learned colleague." Examples of this phenomenon are quite rare.

### 9-4.3 Contrastive Stress

Contrastive stress involves a speaker giving an unusually strong stress to a syllable in order to prevent possible ambiguity or confusion. For example, the words "illusion" and "allusion" would normally be pronounced similarly, since the first syllable of each word carries weak stress and its vowel is reduced to schwa, but if it was thought that a listener misunderstood, one might say, "I said allusion, not illusion," stressing the distinctive syllables. Similarly, "gorilla" and "guerrilla" may be pronounced alike unless contrastive stress is used to differentiate them; the pair "lumbar" and "lumber" would also be subject to such stress for contrastive purposes. Of course, context usually supplies the cue a listener needs to know what is being discussed; only in unusual circumstances is contrastive stress used. One of the most common instances in everyday speech is with numbers: "thirteen" is often confused with "thirty," "fourteen" with "forty," and so on. Here, context is often an inadequate guide to the speaker's intentions since either number may be possible in the context, so contrastive stress is used.

Even when there is considerable phonetic difference between two words, one might still want to give the word contrastive stress to be sure his listener understood. In discussing styles of art, primary stress might be given to the first syllable of "impressionism" to be sure to distinguish it from "expressionism."

In summary, contrastive stress is an unusual stressing of an otherwise weakly stressed syllable in order to prevent confusion with another word.

### 9-4.4 Stress and Spelling

English spelling, for the most part, does not record stress. This lack does not create much of a problem for the native speaker, who has learned the stress pattern and spelling of each word separately, but it does create a problem for two groups in particular, the deaf individual and the foreigner learning English, since the written word offers few clues to the pronunciation.

Stress is reflected in one way in our spelling, however, though for most of us it is simply an additional spelling problem rather than a clear representation of spoken English. When a suffix whose first letter is a vowel—particularly the -ed past tense marker—is added to a word ending in a consonant, the question arises whether to double the final letter of the word. Usually, when the final syllable of the root word is stressed, the consonant is doubled. So we have timber/timbered but infer/inferred (however, note the spelling "inference," a word that is stressed on the first syllable).

## 9-5 Stress and Nonnormal Speech

All the facts presented in this chapter should lead to a serious consideration of the importance of stress in speech correction. An individual may pronounce the individual phones of a word correctly, but if they are stressed incorrectly, the word will be quite unintelligible to the native speaker. This can result in considerable frustration—and even an attitude of defeat and noncommunicativeness on the part of the speaker—if he does not realize the nature of his difficulty. Special word stress problems will be discussed below.

### 9-5.1 The Foreign Speaker

The foreign speaker of English must be taught the importance of stress in contributing both to his intelligibility and to his foreign accent, though the extent of his problem will depend on the use of stress in his native language. Speakers of languages, such as French, that lack contrastive word stress of the sort found in English can be expected to have particular difficulty. Another type of difficulty is created by international words—those that appear in many languages but may have different stress patterns in each language. Or, the individual's native language may make use of borrowed English words whose stress pattern has been modified; a foreign speaker may think he is using an English word, yet it is not recognizable to the native speaker.

The problem of spelling has already been mentioned. A foreign speaker who has learned English by reading (or from teachers who were not fluent) may make stress errors in pronunciation, though he reads or writes without difficulty. The beginning foreign speaker may benefit from an exaggeration of stress by his teacher to emphasize its importance. Furthermore, just as it is necessary to learn the grammatical gender of each new word when one studies Spanish, German, or French, the student of English must learn the correct stress patterns of polysyllabic words along with their spelling and meaning.

### 9-5.2 The Deaf Speaker

The problem facing the deaf speaker is in some ways similar to that of the foreign speaker, though for vastly different reasons. Not having heard words spoken, and not being helped by English spelling, the deaf speaker is likely to make inappropriate use of stress. Indeed, the most typical problem is one of placing too much stress on syllables that ought to contain reduced vowels. One approach to this problem is for the teacher to make use of an instrument that displays amplitude (loudness) on a television-like screen. By this means the deaf speaker receives visual feedback as he attempts to imitate the patterns for words and for sentences.

### 9-5.3 The Stutterer and Others

The stutterer, too, may make inappropriate use of word stress. After blocking on a word, the speaker may finally release the initial consonant very abruptly with great pressure. This gives the impression of heavy stress on the initial syllable. In the case of the stutterer, inappropriate use of stress is tied directly to the main problem of stuttering—it cannot be separated out and dealt with alone as it can in the case of the foreign or deaf speaker (it is true that some approaches to therapy work toward a reduction of subglottal air pressure; this is only one aspect of stress).

Those suffering from other communication disorders—be they voice (laryngeal) disorders, dysphasia, or whatever—may show disruptions of stress patterns in their speech. In dyspraxia disruptions of stress patterns may be caused directly by a lack of muscle coordination; in a voice disorder these disruptions may be caused by difficulty in regulating subglottal air pressure. In any case, the therapist may want to evaluate the situation and decide whether the individual's overall intelligibility can be improved through direct efforts to improve the use of stress, or whether stress anomalies will be corrected automatically through a broader approach to the individual's problem.

## 9-6  The Acoustics of Stress

As shown earlier in the chapter, stress is really a combination of factors, rather than just a single one. Not all these factors need to be present together for stress to be perceived by the listener. Indeed, the acoustic quality of amplitude may be in a specific sense contrary to what has been outlined above, while in a more general sense it is still in agreement. Let us clarify this apparent paradox. The more open vowels (i.e., the low vowels) have greater amplitude than the high vowels, simply because the mouth is more open, allowing more sound energy to escape. An /ɑ/, for example, normally has greater amplitude than an /u/, so an /ɑ/ under **secondary** stress may actually have greater amplitude than an /u/ under **primary** stress. However, the listener would perceive this /u/ as having stronger stress, because it is stronger for an /u/ than the /ɑ/ is for an /ɑ/. In other words, the perceived amplitude is relative to the "normal" amplitude for the vowel in question.

While stress information is carried primarily by the vowels, individual consonants have their own characteristic amplitudes. The release of plosives particularly has a high amplitude, the voiceless ones more than the voiced. The overall amplitude of the syllable may thus be affected by the consonant that begins it. Again, our perceptual mechanism factors this out, since we know the "normal" amplitude of each consonant.

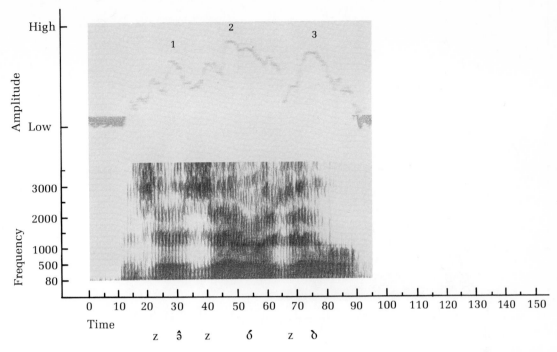

**Figure 9.3.** Stress and amplitude. An instrumental measure of amplitude has replaced the higher frequencies of this spectrogram. The nonsense word <u>zozozo</u> was pronounced with the stress pattern of the word <u>pimento</u> [zᵊzózò].

These two facts imply that we cannot simply build a machine to measure amplitude and use it as an instrumental measure of what we perceive as stress in words. That implication should be borne in mind in looking at spectrograms that show an amplitude analysis (Figures 9.3 and 9.4). In order to avoid introducing complications from different vowels and consonants, we have used nonsense words that repeat the same phones. The nonsense words "zozozo" and "bebeebee" have been pronounced with the intonation pattern of the word "pimento," giving (with normal vowel reduction) [zᵊzózò] and [bᵊbíbì]; they were pronounced as if they were ordinary English words.

In the spectrograms, an amplitude analysis has been added, replacing the higher frequencies. In this type of display, the amplitude is shown as a line moving predominantly from left to right but with many peaks and valleys. The higher the peak, the greater the amplitude. In Figure 9.3 [zᵊzózò], the relative amplitudes of the three vowels can be seen, and they follow the expected pattern: the highest peak is in the primary-stress (second) syllable; the second-highest peak is in the secondary-stress (final) syllable; and the lowest peak is in the weakly stressed (first) syllable. Notice also that the second syllable is longer than the final syllable; length is another acoustic cue to stress. The vowel of the primary-stress second syllable is also more diphthongized than that of the other syllables.

**155**    Word Stress

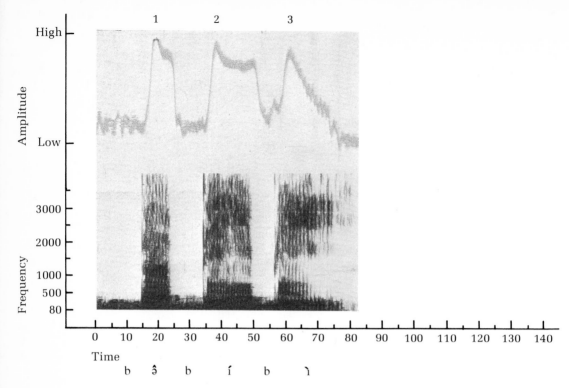

**Figure 9.4.** Stress and amplitude. As in Figure 9.3, the higher frequencies have been replaced by a measure of amplitude. The nonsense word <u>bebeebee</u> was pronounced with the stress pattern of <u>pimento</u> [bɜ̂bíbì].

In Figure 9.4 [bɜ̂bíbì], the situation is complicated; because the plosive release tends to have high amplitude, the different stress of each syllable is not uniquely reflected in the amplitude pattern of that syllable. The initial plosive in a word tends to have greater pressure than one in medial position (section 8-2.6), therefore the first, weakly stressed syllable appears to have great amplitude. Also, the peak amplitude for the second and third syllables does not appear to be very different, so other cues to stress must be perceived. The primary-stress (second) syllable holds its high amplitude for a longer period than the final syllable, whose amplitude level drops quickly. Also, the second syllable shows more diphthongization than the final syllable. The cue that the first syllable is weakly stressed is that it is short; the formant pattern indicates that the vowel is reduced to schwa.

In summary, we can see that the acoustic parameters by which we perceive stress are a combination of any or all of the following: (1) amplitude (relative to the normal amplitude for that vowel or consonant), (2) length, and (3) vowel quality (including reduction and diphthongization).

## Questions for Discussion

1. Find some examples of pairs of words, in addition to those in section 9-4.1, which are distinguished by stress alone.

2. Give some examples of dialect differences in the stress pattern of individual English words. One example given in the chapter is the town of Concord. What about the words controversy, laboratory, and corollary? Find some additional examples.
3. Give some examples from your own experience with foreign speakers, deaf speakers, or individuals with some communication disorder who have pronounced the right word with the wrong stress, causing problems of comprehension.

## Annotated Bibliography

Most introductory books in phonetics discuss word stress to some extent. Some of these books are listed in the References.

Chomsky and Halle [1968] discuss several aspects of stress, including rules for predicting word stress in many English words.

Ladefoged [1967] and Lehiste [1970] both contain long sections on stress. These discussions also include sentence stress, the topic of Chapter 13. Additional references may be found in the bibliographies of these books.

# Chapter 10

## Assimilatory Processes: Sounds in Contact

### 10-1 Introduction

Chapters 7 and 8 illustrated how speech sounds are articulated, and each phone was considered separately, which may have given the impression that speech is made up of a series of static postures with movements in between; this is a false impression. Speech is a dynamic rather than a static phenomenon, and the articulators are in a state of constant movement during speech. Oftentimes we have begun to articulate one phone before completing our articulation of the previous one, and indeed, we are sometimes even one or two full segments ahead in our articulatory preparation for subsequent sounds. The result is that sounds are modified by the context they are in. This chapter will consider a few of the ways in which sounds are modified by their context.

Any attempt to pronounce repeatedly a speech sound identically, irrespective of where it is situated in a word or phrase, will inevitably result in speech that sounds artificial and stilted. If a person tries to take tape recordings of individual phones and splice them together to form words, the results will be incomprehensible. (In fact, even if you try to splice together recordings of whole individual words into sentences, the results will be difficult to understand or at least they will sound strange.) The practical implications of this fact are numerous. For example, a deaf person cannot simply be taught standard articulatory positions for speech sounds and be expected to put these in sequences to produce natural-sounding words. To take another example, the foreign-language learner has to get used to the ways in which sounds are modified by their environment in the language he is learning.

Assimilation and combinatory processes in general have in the past been explained by the notion of "ease of pronunciation," or the so-called "principle of least effort." While this explanation holds a great appeal—

assimilations often reduce the number or extent of articulatory movements—it has certain drawbacks. First, the same combination of sounds does not undergo the same assimilatory process in all languages, so the simple explanation that assimilation is the result of finding the path of least effort is clearly inadequate. And second, the statement that assimilation serves to reduce the muscular effort in speech suggests to many people that assimilations are the result of laziness. While it is true that assimilations are reduced in careful speech, it is not true that assimilations and other combinatory phenomena are necessarily something "bad" or "lazy" that ought to be purged from good speech. They are entirely normal: speech without assimilations would sound terribly stilted and might be incomprehensible. When we say "I mish you" for "I miss you" in conversational speech, we are speaking in a completely normal way; avoiding it does not make our speech any "better." Since assimilation is a normal part of speech, it should be taught along with other aspects of speech; indeed it is often the *lack* of normal assimilations that contributes an unnatural quality and a low intelligibility to the speech of the deaf or the foreign speaker.

There are two general processes at work modifying speech sounds in context. The two are not strictly separate, but overlap considerably. The first is **assimilation,** which refers to the ways in which the primary articulation of speech sounds becomes like that of surrounding sounds; this term is used for gross modifications in sounds. The second is **coarticulation,** which is used for the small modifications, resulting from secondary articulatory gestures that occur to speech sounds in particular contexts.

The concept of **context** or **phonetic environment** must be emphasized. Speech sounds are modified by the speech sounds near them, and the exact nature of the modification is dependent upon the particular sounds in the immediate neighborhood. The terms context or (phonetic) environment, then, simply refer to the speech sounds near the phone in question.


## 10-2 Types of Assimilation

Assimilation refers to the phenomenon of a sound becoming like neighboring sounds; the change is usually a gross one (that is, one that is noticed by untrained listeners). Assimilation can affect the place of articulation, the manner of articulation, voicing, or a combination of these factors. It may result in a **total** change (the two sounds become identical) or a **partial** change (the two sounds become more alike).


### 10-2.1 Progressive Assimilation

One common type of assimilation is **progressive:** a sound affects one that follows. For example, in the word "dogs" the final s is pronounced /z/ while in "cats" the final s is pronounced /s/. The /g/ of "dogs" is voiced and that affects the following sound; the /t/ of "cats" is voiceless, similarly affecting the sound that comes after it. If you were to pronounce "Ridge Street" in a normal conversational way, the first sound of "street" might well be /š/ under the influence of the preceding /ǰ/.

## 10-2.2 Regressive Assimilation

**Regressive** or **anticipatory assimilation** occurs frequently in English. It results in a sound being modified by the sound that *follows*. For example, in pronouncing "noise shield," many speakers would pronounce the final /z/ of "noise" as /ž/ in anticipation of the following /š/. The n of "think" is pronounced /ŋ/ to assimilate in place of articulation the /k/ that follows.

## 10-2.3 Double Assimilation

Double assimilation occurs when a sound is influenced in the same way by the phone preceding and following it. For example, the word "latter" is often pronounced /læɾɚ/. The /t/ has become voiced under the influence of the vowels that come before and after it. But notice that the /t/ of "material" does not become voiced. This is because of the influence of word stress. The effects of stress on assimilation will be dealt with later in this chapter.

## 10-2.4 Total and Partial Assimilation

All the examples we have seen so far show partial assimilation. The n of "think" assimilates in place of articulation only—it keeps its manner of articulation and voicing. The s of "dogs" assimilates in voicing only—it keeps its place and manner of articulation. When the word brother changed historically from having a stop /d/ (it still does in the German equivalent Bruder) to having a fricative /ð/, it was the manner of articulation that changed greatly—the phone retained its voicing and almost the same place of articulation.

By contrast, assimilation may be total—every feature of the assimilated sound comes to be like that of the sound which is causing the assimilation. For example, the /t/ of "nutcracker" may change its place of articulation to that of the /k/ following it and—since the voicing and manner of articulation are already identical—is thus *totally* assimilated. Usually when total assimilation occurs, only one of the two identical sounds is retained.

Often in American English, a /t/ following an /n/ becomes totally assimilated. For example, the word "winter" is often pronounced just like the word "winner." But notice that only one /n/ is pronounced—once totally assimilated, the /t/ disappears altogether.

In the development of German, /d/ following /n/, and /b/ following /m/, were totally assimilated and subsequently lost. So the German Donner corresponds to the English thunder and the German Zimmer corresponds to the English timber.

## 10-3 Coarticulation

Coarticulation refers to articulatory movements for one phone which are carried over into the production of previous or subsequent phones, but which do not affect the primary place of articulation, as occurs when assimilation affects the place of articulation.

For example, consider the syllables /pi/ and /pu/. Notice that before you even begin to say /p/, you already have your jaw, lips, and tongue in position to pronounce the following vowel. It is important to recognize that two distinctly different kinds of /p/ have been produced. While the difference is inaudible, normal articulation of English requires minute adjustments such as this one, and while the production of these different kinds of /p/ is not audible, any attempt to produce the same /p/ in both syllables will definitely be audibly substandard.

## 10-3.1 Primary and Secondary Articulations

In the example given in the last paragraph, it can be seen that for the pronunciation of the /p/ in the syllable /pi/, the important articulation is the bilabial plosion; while it is true that the tongue is in the palatal region and the lips are somewhat more spread in anticipation of the /i/, this is not as important an aspect of the articulation and does not greatly affect the sound of the /p/. We call the main or most important articulatory gesture the **primary** articulation. Other less important articulatory gestures, which may or may not be caused by coarticulation, are called **secondary** articulations. Secondary articulations are not always inaudible, however; important sound contrasts can be accomplished by secondary articulations.

The secondary articulations are generally identified by verbs ending in -ize and nouns ending -ization. Primary articulations can be modified by processes of labialization, palatalization, velarization, nasalization, pharyngealization, or even glottalization.

## 10-3.2 Labialization

If a phone is labialized, there is a secondary articulation involving rounding of the lips. For example, compare the /k/ sounds in the words "kid" and "quid." In the word "kid," the /k/ is pronounced with the lips spread; in "quid," the lips are rounded during the production of the /k/. The /k/ in "quid" can be said to be labialized.

The /t/ of "twenty" is labialized, as is the /d/ of "dwell." Even the /θ/ of "thwart" is labialized. A small raised w is used to indicate a labialized sound in transcription, or a small w is placed below the phone in question: [dʷwɛl] or [dwɛl]. This is usually not done for the transcription of English, since consonants are invariably labialized when followed by /w/ or a rounded vowel.

## 10-3.3 Palatalization

Palatalization occurs when there is a secondary articulation in the region of the palate. Since front vowels are articulated in the region below the palate, palatalization is a common occurrence. For example, when English borrowed the word "position," it was pronounced /pozizion/. The /si/ changed to /š/ because of the influence of the palatal vowel on the alveolar consonant. The glide /j/ is also palatal and causes palatalization. This is why "did you" is often pronounced /diǰə/. The /j/ of "you" palatalizes the /d/. Similarly, historically /sjugɚ/ became /šugɚ/, and /sjɚ/ became /šɚ/. In the cases given here, the secondary articulation has become the primary articulation after the passage of time.

In the earlier example of the syllable /pi/, the /p/ has a secondary palatal articulation. Palatalized consonants are very common in Russian, and a number of other languages. Special symbols for palatalized consonants can be found in Table 4.1.

## 10-3.4 Velarization

Velarization occurs when there is a secondary articulation in the velar region. For example, in English there are two types of /l/ sound. In pronouncing the word "little," it is easy to detect that the first occurrence of the /l/ sound is purely alveolar while the second has a different sound because of raising of the tongue in the velar region. The purely alveolar /l/ is called a **light** or **clear** /l/. The velarized variant is sometimes called **dark.** It may be transcribed as an l with a bar through it: /ł/. Other velarized consonants may similarly be indicated with the bar through them, as indicated in Table 4.1.

Other consonants may be velarized as well, and, while it is not a common phenomenon in English, velarization can be expected to occur in the vicinity of high back vowels: the /t/ of "too," for example, is slightly velarized (as well as being labialized).

## 10-3.5 Nasalization

Nasalization occurs when the secondary articulation involves lowering the velum. Normally, the term is restricted to vowels that are produced with a lowered velum. If there is complete oral closure when the velum is lowered, a nasal *consonant* is produced, and velic position is considered as primary.

Nasalization occurs frequently in most dialects of English. When we say "man," for example, the velum must be lowered for the /m/, raised again for the /æ/, and lowered again for the /n/. Often, the velum does not close for the vowel production, and we pronounce the /æ/ with nasalization. Nasalization of a vowel may be indicated by a tilde over the normal vowel symbol: [mæ̃n].

Some dialects of American English have a pervasive nasalization throughout the speech. This is popularly referred to as a **nasal twang.**

The speech of an individual having a cleft palate or velic deficiency (see section 5-5) will have a nasal quality, but this is a result of the physical condition, and not of a secondary articulation. The individual having a repaired cleft palate and normal velic musculature may not use velic valving in the normal way, resulting in speech with pervasive nasalization.

## 10-3.6 Pharyngealization

Pharyngealization refers to a secondary articulation involving a constriction in the pharynx. The root of the tongue is retracted into the pharyngeal region.

A number of languages have distinctively pharyngealized sounds, and there is some evidence that this may occur nondistinctively in English. For example, the consonant /r/ is normally pronounced with retraction of the tongue root into the pharynx (its primary articulation is partly pharyngeal), and neighboring vowels can be expected to be influenced through coarticulation. The /o/ of "boat" does not have the same quality as the /o/ of "roar"; it is likely that some pharyngealization of the vowel is present and is responsible for the change in vowel quality.

## 10-3.7 Glottalization

Glottalization occurs when an oral plosive is produced simultaneously with a glottal stop. In some languages, the two explosions occur in opposite directions. One plosive is made in the mouth, the other at the glottis. The larynx is pulled downward in the throat with the glottis closed, producing a reduced air pressure between the two points of occlusion. When they are released simultaneously, the glottal plosive is egressive while the oral plosive is ingressive. This is the glottalic airstream mechanism introduced in section 5-4. This manner of articulation is completely foreign to the English language. Again, Table 4.1 provides a symbol to indicate glottalization.

## 10-4 Stress and Assimilation

In general, as shown in Chapter 9, reduced stress is accompanied by a more relaxed articulation. Vowels are articulated closer to the mid-central (/ə/) position, and consonants may be pronounced more quickly and less distinctly in unstressed than in stressed syllables. A direct consequence of reduced stress, then, is to encourage assimilation; and conversely, strong stress tends to block or reduce assimilation and coarticulation.

Look, for example, at these phrases we have seen already: "the White House" and "the white house." In the phrase referring to the president's residence, the word "house" carries less stress than in the other phrase. Note that the /h/ of "house" is much more likely to be elided (dropped) when the word is not stressed. This is a matter of assimilation, since the /h/ is becoming voiced like the vowel that follows it, and for this reason seems to disappear.

Any time that we speak very distinctly we are increasing the stress on each syllable and thus reducing assimilations. This, coupled with the fact that we are speaking more slowly, is what aids the hard-of-hearing person or the foreign speaker when we enunciate well.

Stress patterns within words affect the extent of various types of assimilatory phenomena. For example, we have noted that the intervocalic /t/ in English is frequently voiced and flapped to [ɾ]; "matter" is often pronounced [mæɾɚ]. But notice that the /t/ of "material" is never voiced or flapped. This is because the first syllable of "matter" carries primary stress, whereas in "material" it is the second syllable that carries primary stress. The /t/ is the first sound of the second syllable, and if that second syllable is stressed, voicing assimilation is blocked. A similar pair of words is "pattern," in which the /t/ is often flapped, and "paternal," in which flapping does not occur.

The relation between stress and assimilation has left some permanent changes in our language. At one time, "of" and "off" were the same word. In the meaning "of," the word usually was not stressed; thus in voicing the /f/ sound assimilated with the vowel, and the modern pronunciation has a /v/ sound. On the other hand, when the word meant "off," it usually was stressed. The strong stress prevented assimilation, and the /f/ sound was preserved. This fact, along with historical changes in the phonemic structure of English, gives us the modern words, which most of us do not even realize are related. What is important for us here is the fact that the effect of strong stress is to block assimilations.

Let us look at two more historical changes from the point of view of the effect of stress on assimilation. Of course, this is not a history of English, but sometimes things that appear odd can be understood by looking at their history. In this case we can understand some phonetic peculiarities by looking at their development, as well as finding a good example to illustrate the inter-relatedness of stress and assimilation. The two words in question are "to have" and "to use." Both words change their pronunciation in certain meanings. "Have" is normally pronounced /hæv/ except when it means 'must.' Then it is pronounced /hæf/. This is apparent in the sentences

> You have two cars.        (/hæv/)
> You have to go.           (/hæf/)

The word "use" is pronounced /juz/, and its past tense, "used," is pronounced /juzd/, except when it functions as an auxiliary verb meaning 'did it at one time, but does not any more'; then the past participle is pronounced /just/. The pronunciations can be seen in these contexts:

> I used two teaspoons of sugar in the recipe.     (/juzd/)
> I used to cook a lot, but I don't any more.       (/just/)

In each of these words, the consonant in question was once voiceless and the now-silent final e̲ was pronounced. So, when the words were not stressed, the consonant assimilated in voicing with the surrounding vowels, but the voiceless consonant was preserved when the word was used emphatically. Notice that the emphatic forms are still pronounced with greater stress in most contexts. Once again, stress prevented assimilation. (Another historical change is that the -e̲d past tense suffix has lost its vowel except when following a /t/ or /d/. So the final consonant of "used" has, through progressive assimilation, come to follow the /s/ or /z/ in voicing, giving the modern forms /juzd/ and /just/.)

## 10-5  Variants of English Phones

We have seen a number of ways in which English—and a few foreign—speech sounds that we would have called the same are actually different because of the influence of surrounding sounds. Let us pursue this investigation, concentrating on the common variant forms of English speech sounds.

### 10-5.1  Release of Plosives

We noted in Chapter 8 that plosive sounds may be unreleased at the end of a word, if no other word follows immediately. The /p/ at the end of "top" may be an unreleased stop rather than a released plosive sound. In this case, the assimilation is occurring as a result of the silence following the word. If a word beginning with a vowel follows the word in question, as in the phrase "top of the mountain," the /p/ will be released. It is important to remember that an unreleased plosive may be called a **stop** (see footnote 3 in Chapter 8).

Unfortunately, there is a lack of a standardized means of transcribing unreleased plosives. Among others, these means have been used (an unreleased /p/ is indicated): [p⁻] or [p˹].[1] Note that, in English, unreleased final nasals are also common: "jam" [jǎm⁻] or "can" [kæn⁻].

## 10-5.2 Single Release of Plosives

When two similar plosives come together, there may be only one release. For example, in the phrase, "I bought two," there is usually one release for both /t/'s. Notice that we often compensate for the missing release by holding the /t/ longer before releasing it. A satisfactory means of transcribing this, when necessary, is to indicate that the first plosive is unreleased: [bɔt⁻ tu].

This process may be carried further in that two plosives having different places of articulation but adjacent in the same word or phrase may have just one release. For example, in saying "locked," many of us articulate the /k/, but do not release it separately from the /t/; that is, we say not [lɑkt] but [lɑk⁻t]. This may happen even if the two plosives are in different words. So in the expression "back to nature," the /k/ of "back" may be unreleased.

## 10-5.3 Aspiration of Plosives

Aspiration refers to the puff of air that accompanies some voiceless stops in English. For example, say the word "pin" while holding your hand in front of your mouth and you will feel a puff of air. This is not characteristic of voiced stops, however. There is no puff accompanying the /b/ of "bin," but the voiceless stops are not always aspirated. With your hand in front of your mouth, compare the pronunciation of "pin" with "spin." There is usually considerably less aspiration when the /s/ precedes the stop. The same process is true for /t/ and /k/, although the aspiration is less noticeable since the articulation takes place further back in the oral cavity. The aspiration of a consonant may be indicated by a raised "h." Thus "pin" may be transcribed [pʰɪn], and "spin" [spɪn].

Very few languages have aspirated voiced plosives, but some languages have voiceless plosives that are much more strongly aspirated than those of English. Chinese, for example, has strongly aspirated plosives, and the speaker of English, when he hears words spoken with these consonants, might have the impression that the speaker is angry and is spitting out his words; however, such aspiration is a normal part of the articulation of these sounds in Chinese, and is not a result of the emotional state of the speaker.

## 10-5.4 Nasal Plosion

Plosive sounds, as we have seen, are normally released through the oral cavity, either between the lips (for /p/ and /b/) or over the tongue (for /t/, /d/, /k/, /g/); however, if a nasal sound immediately follows a plosive, the plosive can be

[1] The use of square brackets [ ], as opposed to slash marks /  /, is discussed in Chapter 11.

released through the nose. In the expression "Help me," for instance, the /p/ is released through the nose. The velum is lowered *before* the lips are parted. Nasal plosion occurs most often when the nasal has the same place of articulation as the preceding plosive, but it may occur with nasals having another place of articulation. So a /t/ or a /d/ will be nasally exploded when followed by an /n/ (and sometimes by /m/); /p/ or /b/ when followed by an /m/ (or an /n/). In English, /k/ and /g/ are never followed immediately by /ŋ/ but may be nasally released when followed by other nasals. There is no standard way to transcribe nasally released plosives, but in the event that it were necessary to indicate it, one could use a small raised N: "Help me" [hɛlpᴺ mi].

## 10-5.5 Lateral Plosion

The phones /t/ and /d/ are normally released over the top of the tongue; they are released through the nose when followed by /n/. If /t/ or /d/ is followed by /l/, however, the release is lateral; that is, when we say "little" or the phrase "Bet low," the blade of the tongue is kept against the alveolar ridge when the /t/ is released. Instead of moving the blade of the tongue, the sides of the tongue, which have formed a seal along the upper molar teeth, are pulled inward. The plosive release occurs laterally, over the sides of the tongue.

As with nasal plosion, there is no transcription symbol in general use to indicate this phenomenon. Indeed, there is usually no need to, since lateral plosion can be expected whenever an /l/ follows a /t/ immediately, unless there is a pause between the two sounds. Again, this could be indicated with a small raised L [bɛtᴸ lo].

## 10-5.6 Place of Articulation of /t/ and /d/

The plosives classified as alveolars are normally articulated in English with the blade of the tongue against the alveolar ridge; however, this place of articulation may be further forward under the influence of a dental sound, or further back under the influence of a back vowel or a palatal glide. For example, in the expression "both Tom and me," the /t/ of "Tom" follows a dental sound, /θ/. The articulation of this /t/ may be advanced to the point that it is dental. In the word "doom," because of the influence of the back vowel, some speakers may pronounce the /d/ further back, making it palatoalveolar. This retraction (pulling back) may also occur before /š/, or before a /j/ in those dialects in which a word such as "dupe" is pronounced /djup/.

Further, the /n/ of English is susceptible to a similar change in place of articulation, although usually not to the same extent as /t/ or /d/. In many languages, /t/, /d/, and /n/ may normally be dental; this is the case in Spanish and French, for example, and speakers of these and other languages can be expected to make this substitution when speaking English.

The symbol ˌ is added to any IPA symbol to indicate a dental articulation: "both Tom" [boθ t̪ɑm]. A small plus sign under any IPA symbol indicates that the articulation is unusually far forward, so a dental /t/ could also be written [t̟]. (This plus sign can be added to any IPA symbol to show fronting, and thus can be used for vowels and other consonants as well, but the symbol ˌ is restricted to dental articulations alone.) The symbol ˍ is used to indicate a retracted (further back) articulation, so the /t/ of "meatshop" could be indicated as [ṯ].

### 10-5.7  Place of Articulation of /k/ and /g/

The consonants /k/ and /g/ are velar sounds, according to our classification. But the velum is quite long, and the actual point of articulation may be further forward or further back along the velum. Generally, the influencing factor is the following vowel. So in the word "keep," which has a front vowel, the /k/ is pronounced further forward than in the word "coop," where the /k/ is followed by a back vowel. Pronounce the two words, and you can feel as well as hear the difference. If it is necessary to transcribe the two variants, [k] is used for the front sound, and [q] for the back sound. Or, one can use the same symbols introduced above (section 10-5.6) to mark the front and back varieties of both /k/ and /g/: [k̟], [k̠], [g̟], and [g̠].

### 10-5.8  The Articulation of /h/; Voiceless Phones

The consonant /h/ assimilates in tongue and jaw position to the vowel which follows it. Try saying "heat" and "hoot." Notice that while you are pronouncing the /h/ your mouth is already in the configuration for the following vowel. In fact, the assimilation is total except for voicing, and for this reason we could call /h/ a voiceless vowel having an unusually great airflow. In transcribing unusual speech sounds, we can indicate voicelessness by a little circle under the phone in question. If it became necessary to show the different variant forms of /h/, we could indicate them with the symbol for a voiceless vowel. We could transcribe "heat" as [i̥it], and "hoot" as [u̥ut]. Of course, it is not normally necessary to transcribe /h/ this way; it is done here to show the extent of the assimilation. Normally, these words would be transcribed as /hit/ and /hut/.

Incidentally, the symbol for voicelessness may be used with any IPA symbol for a normally voiced sound, to indicate that that phone is de-voiced in a particular pronunciation, whether it is because of assimilation, foreign accent, or pathological speech. For example, the first vowel in the word "suppose" is often voiceless, because of the surrounding voiceless consonants. One could transcribe this word [sə̥poz]. Or, to take another example, a native speaker of French may have a tendency to de-voice the final /l/ of the word "people," as he would do in his native language. This /l/ could be indicated [l̥]. In the realm of pathological speech, abnormal de-voicing, as is common in stuttering, may also be indicated with this symbol, and Table 4.1 gives a symbol to indicate unusual voicing of otherwise voiced sounds; for example, the /h/ of "hit" in the expression "she hit it" may be voiced because of the influence of the vowels that surround it.

### 10-5.9  Vowels

Vowels, like consonants, are affected by surrounding phones. For example, English vowels are lengthened before voiced consonants. The /i/ of "feed" is temporally longer than the /i/ of "feet." The same is true of all the other vowels and the diphthongs. The /ai/ of "tide," for example, is longer than the /ai/ of "tight." And the diphthong /au/ changes its quality as well as its length before a voiced consonant: compare, for example, the pronunciation of "mouse" and "browse," or "about" and "proud."

Vowels tend to be longer when they occur in word-final position. (A syllable ending in a vowel is known as an **open** syllable, and one ending in a consonant is known as a **closed** syllable.) So /i/ in an open syllable such as "fee" is long as in "feed" rather than short as in "feet." The diphthongs, too, are longer in open syllables than in syllables closed by a voiceless consonant: compare "tide" and "tie" with "tight," for example.

Vowels are also modified by certain consonants. When an /l/ follows a vowel, the vowel often seems longer, with a diphthong-like quality: compare the /o/ of "hope" and "hole" or the /e/ of "bait" and "bail" (dialects differ in the extent of this effect).

Also, r-sounds following vowels tend to modify the vowels and combine with them, such that we have suggested analyzing these sequences as diphthongs. The vowel of the word "or" occurs only preceding an "r." While we transcribe this vowel with the symbol /o/, it is not identical to the vowel in "boat," for example (see also section 10-3.6).


## 10-5.10 Other Assimilations

In the preceding sections, it has been possible to give only a brief selection of common assimilatory processes in English. If section 10-5 were an exhaustive cataloging of all assimilations in English, it would be as long as this entire book. Every sentence spoken provides a multitude of examples of assimilation and coarticulation. By becoming sensitive to this, it is possible to discover the almost endless variety of ways in which phones are modified by their context. We will consider a brief selection of other assimilations not previously mentioned. (Again, it is important to remember what was said in Chapter 1: when words are said self-consciously, they are often pronounced in an unnatural way and assimilations are blocked. The examples discussed here would occur in natural rapid speech.)

Notice that in saying "pine-cone," in normal rapid speech, most of us would pronounce the n of "pine" as /ŋ/. In saying "pine paneling," that same n is likely pronounced /m/. In saying "that place," the /t/ of "that" often becomes an unreleased [p¯]. The /d/ of "bad" in the expression "bad boy" is usually an unreleased [b¯]. The /d/ of "broadcast" is usually pronounced as an unreleased [g¯]. The n of "inferior" is often pronounced as a labiodental nasal (symbolized /ɱ/), as it is in "infer," though stress usually prevents this assimilation in a word such as "infamous" (stressed on the first syllable). This list could be extended indefinitely.

It is true that when all the details of assimilation and coarticulation are transcribed, the transcriptions look rather strange (at least, they are certainly more complicated). Inevitably, the student will want to know whether he will be expected to transcribe all the fine detail.

While this matter will be clearer after the student has read Chapter 11, there are some things that can be said now. Teachers will vary in how much detail they demand in transcriptions; that is up to them; but there is a much more important issue here. We make these assimilations and coarticulations when we speak, and if we did not, our speech would sound very strange indeed. It is natural and normal to make these adjustments in our pronunciation of phones in context. So the practical phonetician—the speech pathologist, second-language teacher, or teacher of the deaf—needs to be sensitive to these phonetic events to be effective in his/her work. Again, it is not enough to say that someone talks funny—you need to know *how* in order to do something about it. The foreigner learning English, the deaf individual, and the individual with an articulation disorder can all be expected to produce speech that either lacks the expected assimilations and coarticulations or contains unexpected assimilations. A sensitivity to this aspect of normal speech will provide one with the resources to analyze and correct these problem areas.

## 10-6 Historical Assimilations

Up to this point, assimilation in Modern English has been the primary consideration. We can say that in the examples given above, assimilation is a *productive* process; it is going on right now, modifying sounds. But sometimes a product of assimilation has occurred historically, and the modern word is shaped by this historical event. Here, the assimilatory process is nonproductive, since it has permanently affected the shape of the word. We will look at a few examples of interesting historical assimilations.

The very word <u>assimilation</u> provides a case in point. It was originally "ad + similation"; the /d/ became totally assimilated to the /s/. Many other examples of historical assimilation can be found by looking at random through an etymological dictionary. By looking at the roots of words, as was done for the word <u>assimilation</u>, you can discover how common assimilatory phenomena are in shaping our modern vocabulary.

You may have noticed that the word "house" is pronounced /haus/ but that its plural is pronounced with a voiced fricative, /hauzəz/. Most nouns in English that end with voiceless fricatives (except many but not all words ending /s/ and /š/) voice the fricative in the plural form. This is shown in the spelling of some words: knife/knives, dwarf/dwarves. Many words do not show the change in their spelling, only in their pronunciation. Note the plurals of these words, and others like them: "moth," "path," "bath," "staff" (the plural can be "staffs" or "staves"). However, the rule is not universal: the plural of "laugh," for example, is /læfs/. This is another example of a historical assimilation that is no longer productive. Subsequent sound changes have obscured the source of the original assimilations, and today there are words whose plurals are—from our modern viewpoint—"irregular."

The English words "brother" and "father" did not always have the fricative consonant /ð/; as already mentioned, they and words like them had instead the plosive consonant /d/. This change can be seen as a process of historical assimilation if we look at another way of classifying speech sounds.

We can divide all speech sounds—vowels and consonants—into *continuants* and *noncontinuants*. The continuants include the vowels, fricatives, liquids, and glides; that is, those sounds produced with no interruption of the airflow out of the mouth. The noncontinuant sounds are those in which there is oral blockage—the plosives and nasals.

The /d/ in the Old English word for 'father' is a noncontinuant. There are vowels before and after the /d/; they are continuant sounds. The change from /d/ in Old English to /ð/ in Modern English is one of assimilation. The /d/ became assimilated to the continuant nature of the surrounding vowels. In the history of English and many other languages, many intervocalic (between vowels) plosives have become fricatives. The new fricatives usually maintain the same (or almost the same) place of articulation as the plosive they replace.

This same argument can be used to show that the Modern English substitution of the flap /ɾ/ for a /d/ or /t/ between vowels is a process of assimilation. A flap, whose occlusion is very brief, is in fact a continuant sound since there is no prolonged blockage of the airflow as there is for a plosive. So, when we say /lærɚ/ for "ladder" and "latter," the consonant is assimilating in that it becomes a continuant like the vowels (and, in the case of "latter," there is the voicing assimilation as well: a flap is too short for us to stop voicing and then start again). Of course, this is not a historical assimilation but one that is currently productive; we have the choice of saying either /lætɚ/ or /lærɚ/. Perhaps eventually, such words will come to be pronounced always with the flap, and then the assimilation will have become a historical rather than an optional one.

## 10-7 Distant Assimilation

Up to now, all the assimilatory processes we have discussed have involved **contact,** or **contiguous,** assimilation. This simply means that the phone causing the assimilation and the phone thus affected are in contact—they are next to one another, like the n of "think," which is next to the /k/ that assimilates it.

By contrast, **distant assimilation** (also called **noncontiguous assimilation,** or **dilation**) involves assimilation in which the two phones are not in contact—there is at least one phone in between.

With consonants, distant assimilation is relatively rare. When it does occur in English, it is often judged to be an error or "slip of the tongue," rather than an acceptable variant form of the word. One might say, "No one answered, sho (/šo/) she knocked at the side door," in which the /s/ of "so" becomes like the /š/ of "she." This is an instance of **regressive** distant assimilation. One word that has been permanently changed in English by distant consonant assimilation is *orang-utang.* Originally borrowed into English as *orang-utan,* whose final consonant is /n/, it has undergone modification such that this final sound is pronounced /ŋ/ under the influence of the /ŋ/ at the end of the first part of the word. Both forms are current in English. In French, the word "jusque" (/žyskə/) is often pronounced /žyškə/ in running speech, without the change being noticed by the speaker. This is an instance of progressive distant assimilation. In neither language is the primary articulation of a consonant often changed by distant assimilation.

Distant *vowel* assimilation is a much more common phenomenon, although not in Modern English. Two specific sorts of distant vowel assimilation bear special mention: **umlaut** and **vowel harmony.**

### 10-7.1 Umlaut

Umlaut is a form of regressive vowel assimilation specific to the Germanic family of languages, including German, English, Swedish, and others. Some plurals in Modern English show the effects of this process. The plural of goose, for example, is geese, and while we may now think of this as an irregular plural, it is typical of what was once a common means of pluralization in English. The singular word once had a back vowel (actually /o/, not the modern /u/). The plural form once had the same vowel but had a high front vowel at the end to indicate plurality. So the singular was something like /gos/ and the plural /gosi/. Through umlauting, the back vowel of the root word assimilated to the front vowel of the plural suffix and became /e/ (notice that /e/ and /o/ have the same height). So now the singular was /gos/ and the plural /gesi/. Then the plural suffix was lost, and the two forms were /gos/ and /ges/. Later, by a totally unrelated historical process, both vowels were raised from upper-mid to high, giving the modern /gus/ and /gis/.

This process is no longer productive in English (that is, we do not pluralize new words this way), but it has left its mark on many words. Note, for example, these pairs: foot/feet; brother/brethren (the more usual plural form brothers is not umlauted); louse/lice; mouse/mice (words like the last two pairs, containing diphthongs, went through a later sound change that obscures the earlier umlaut). Umlauting remains a productive process in German, forming a large part of the plural forms of nouns, as well as affecting the vowels in verbs, adjectives, and adverbs.

## 10-7.2  Vowel Harmony

Vowel harmony is a process unknown in English, but it is an interesting example of the lengths to which an assimilatory process can go. In a language having vowel harmony, all the vowels in a phonetic unit (which may be a word, a phrase, or a whole sentence) must all be of the same type. Just what determines the type depends on the particular language. For example, one language might demand that the vowels in a phonetic unit must be either all high or all be low. Whether they are high or low is determined by the vowel in a certain key word, usually the verb. So, if the verb has a high vowel, the other words in the sentence—subject, object, adverbs, etc.—must all have high vowels, and vice versa. Another language might demand that all the vowels be either front or back: only front vowels go together and only back vowels go together in one phonetic unit. Still another language might make the restriction on the basis of tense and lax.

While this may seem very complicated—and is indeed difficult for the foreigner trying to learn to speak the language—it is no more complex for the native speaker than it is to "remember" that English nouns ending in a voiceless consonant must be made plural with a /s/, and a /z/ must be added to those ending in a voiced consonant.

Turkish is a language having vowel harmony, as are a number of other languages, including several African languages. In Akan, a West African language, the verb, the future tense marker (equivalent to English will), the object (English it, him, her, them, us, or you), and the subject (English I, we, you, he, she, or they), are considered together as one unit. Depending upon the vowel of the verb, all these words must contain a tense vowel or all must contain a lax vowel. Each word, except the verb, has two forms: one that goes with verbs having a tense vowel and one that goes with verbs having a lax vowel. In this language, the equivalent of you is /wʊ/ (lax) or /wu/ (tense), and the equivalent of I is /mɪ/ (lax) or /mi/ (tense), and so on.

## 10-8 Other Combinatory Phenomena

This chapter has dealt with various kinds of assimilation and coarticulation, two of the many phenomena that occur when the segments or phones of speech combine to form words, phrases, and sentences. Next, several of the other phenomena that occur when sounds are in combination will be considered.

### 10-8.1 Dissimilation

If assimilation were carried to its extreme, there would be no phonetic contrasts left by which to carry meaning. One of the countervailing forces is dissimilation. Tongue twisters are difficult to say because they put so many similar phones close together; when we make slips of the tongue it is sometimes because there are too many similar sounds in the same phrase. Languages sometimes change over time in a way that dissimilates sounds. One example is the word marble, which was borrowed from French as marbre. The two r-sounds were too close together and dissimilation resulted. Notice that the substituted sound is a liquid like the sound it replaces. Other examples are purple, which was borrowed as pourpre, which is its form in Modern French, and colonel, in which the first l in the spelling is pronounced as an r-sound. Again, the original l-sound is retained in French.

Notice that in these examples, **dissimilation** affects nonadjacent phones, much as distant assimilation does. It is conceivable, however, that examples of contact dissimilation could be found.

### 10-8.2 Elision

When a phone, or several phones, are left out of a word when it is pronounced, we say that the sounds have been elided. Elision occurs when the word "police" is pronounced /plis/ and in the pronunciations of "forecastle" (/foksl̩/) and "halfpenny" (/hepni/). In Chapter 3, we discussed the influence exerted upon the English language in the United States by such grammarians as Noah Webster. These prescriptive grammarians regarded the then-current pronunciations of words such as interest (2 syllables) and secretary (3 syllables) as substandard elisions. They were not, and still are not, regarded that way in England or other English-speaking countries. This example is given to point out that whether a particular elision is substandard or standard depends upon the opinion of the person you ask, not upon any final authority.

### 10-8.3 Epenthesis

Epenthesis is the addition of a vowel sound, usually to separate a group of consonants. The vowel inserted is called an **epenthetic vowel.** Many people insert an epenthetic vowel into the words "film" (/fɪləm/) and "athlete" (/æθəlit/). Epenthesis is common with foreign speakers of English who find the clusters of consonants difficult (consonant clusters are further discussed in Chapter 12).

## 10-8.4 Haplology

Haplology is like elision in that it involves leaving out certain sounds, with the difference that in haplology an entire syllable is left out. This occurs when two identical or very similar syllables occur next to one another. For example, the adverb probably is not pronounced "probable-ly"; this is because of haplology. Another example is the term for the scientific study of mammals, which is mammalogy and not mammalology. The syllable spelled ol, although not identical to the preceding syllable, is similar enough to be dropped. Another technical term—used by phoneticians and linguists—that has undergone haplology is morphophonemics, also known as morphonemics. Both the form that has undergone haplology and the form not so modified are in use.

## 10-8.5 Metathesis

Metathesis, or inversion, is said to occur when two adjacent phones are reversed. In some English dialects, for example, the word ask is pronounced /æks/; and in fact that is how the word was pronounced in Old English. In English the word burn has a vowel before the r. (The phonetic combination of the vowel u and the r into one sound /ɚ/ occurred later in the development of English.) In Modern German, the equivalent word is brenn(en), reflecting the fact that metathesis occurred in the history of one or the other language.

## 10-8.6 Spoonerism

Spoonerisms are named for the Reverend William A. Spooner, a preacher and lecturer at Oxford University who was renowned for making this type of inversion. It is said that his classes and services were full of people hoping to hear one of the verbal peculiarities for which he was famous. A spoonerism results when the initial sounds or groups of sounds are exchanged between two words, as in "May I sew you to your sheet?" instead of "May I show you to your seat?" The Reverend Spooner is reported to have said to a student, "You have hissed my mystery classes; you have tasted the whole worm." In a sermon he is supposed to have called God "a shoving leopard." One of his favorite activities was to ride around the campus on "a well-boiled icicle."

## 10-8.7 Sandhi

**Sandhi** is the word used to refer to various combinatory phenomena that occur at word boundaries in sentences. Words are not necessarily pronounced the same in sentences as they are in isolation: assimilation can jump word boundaries, as already shown in the example "did you," often pronounced /dɪǰə/.

In French, a sandhi phenomenon called **liaison** occurs. Many words in French have lost their final consonant through historical change, but this lost consonant is pronounced when the following word begins with a vowel. The specifics are relatively complex and vary with the individual word and dialect, but the fact is that the pronunciation of an individual word depends upon the word that follows. For example, the plural article meaning 'the' is les. It is pronounced /lɛ/, except when followed by a word beginning with a vowel, when it is pronounced /lez/. Thus, the French equivalent of 'the courses' is les cours (/lɛ kuʀ/), but that of 'the animals' is les animaux (/lezanimo/).

A similar sort of liaison occurs in "r-less" dialects of English. Those dialects in which final r-sounds are elided (or appear as a schwa or as lengthening of the preceding vowel—see section 7-3.4) may have the r-sound reappear preceding a vowel. So the speaker may pronounce <u>father</u> as /fɑðə:/ before a word beginning with a consonant or when no word follows, but may pronounce the r-sound in an expression such as "father is here," in which a vowel follows the <u>r</u>.

Other forms of sandhi occur in English as well, and some are optional, depending upon the individual speaker or the formality of the speaking situation. Among many others, we could mention contractions (<u>I'll</u> for <u>I will</u>, <u>won't</u> for <u>will not</u>, <u>he's</u> for <u>he is</u> or <u>he has</u>, <u>ain't</u> for <u>am not</u>) and variant forms of the article (<u>a</u> car/<u>an</u> apple; <u>the</u> car [/ðə/]/<u>the</u> apple [/ði/]).

## 10-9 Using Assimilatory Processes in Teaching Speech Sounds

We have already discussed the importance of proper assimilation to normal-sounding speech and why understanding assimilation is so necessary for the practical phonetician (section 10-5.10 above). But there is another way in which assimilatory phenomena are important: they can be used to help teach sounds to individuals having difficulty.

The fact that assimilation occurs at all suggests that certain sounds are easier to pronounce in one environment than in another. Generally, some similarity between the target sound and the sounds in the environment is responsible for this ease of pronunciation. This similarity may be one of voicing, manner of articulation, or place of articulation, as we have seen, or may be caused by some feature that affects both vowels and consonants. The continuant/noncontinuant distinction, for example, applies to both major types of speech sounds, and front vowels are articulated below the palate, and back vowels below the velum, meaning that there can be an articulatory similarity between, for example, a back vowel and a velar consonant.

If a particular target sound is causing difficulties for an individual, the general knowledge of articulation should be put to work and an attempt made to devise a phonetic environment in which the sound is easier to produce.

Let us take a few examples of how this might be done. Further examples will have to come from your own ingenuity. This first example was used successfully by the author.

The target sounds were the dental fricatives, /θ/ and /ð/. The students were native speakers of French learning English, and were having considerable difficulty with these sounds (as is quite common). One particular student, in extreme frustration, asked for some personal guidance during a language lab. He was trying to pronounce "there" without much success; he substituted a /d/ for /ð/. It was suggested that rather than continuing to frustrate himself trying to say "there," he start with words like "father" and "brother" instead. In this phonetic context, with a continuant on either side, the continuant /ð/ is easier to pronounce. A few tries enabled the student to say these words with considerable ease. No miracle was accomplished, but the self-confidence generated by his successful pronunciation of /ð/ in just one context encouraged this student to work on his pronunciation with considerably greater enthusiasm and without an attitude of defeat.

To take another example, if a client were having difficulty pronouncing /s/ or /z/ sounds, what contexts would provide the greatest ease of pronunciation? Would there be any difference in difficulty, for example, in pronouncing the /z/ in "easy" and "ozone"? In the word "easy," the /z/ is surrounded by high front vowels having a similar tongue placement to the /z/. The vowels surrounding the /z/ in "ozone" have a very different tongue position from the /z/ itself, and this disparity complicates the articulation of the difficult consonant.

Would there likely be any difference in the difficulty of pronouncing the /s/ in the words "beets" and "beaks"? Again, notice the similarity of tongue position between /t/ and /s/ (indeed, /ts/ is a common affricate in many languages), and the dissimilarity of tongue position between /k/ and /s/. For an individual having difficulty pronouncing /s/, "beats" would probably be easier to say.

In general, when compiling lists of practice words for those with specific articulation problems (or difficulties resulting from a difference between their native language and the one they are learning), you may generate earlier success and reduce frustrating and self-defeating failure by carefully selecting words that place the difficult sound in helpful environments. Exercises may then be graded in difficulty up to the most troublesome environments for the target sound. In certain cases, of course, there is no getting around a complex group of consonants.

**Questions for Discussion and Review**
1. Give some examples of assimilations from casual speech.
2. Have you noticed any dialect differences in assimilations? If so, give some examples.
3. Many of us find it difficult to hear the modifications to speech sounds brought about by assimilation, and often we are even disbelieving of the assimilatory changes in our own speech. Why do you think that this is so?
4. What is the difference between a labial and a labialized phone, a nasal and a nasalized phone, a laryngeal and a laryngealized phone, etc.

# Chapter 11

## The Phoneme: Contrastive Units of Sound

### 11-1 Contrast in Language

The point was made in Chapter 7 that for spoken language to function effectively, there must be a systematic **contrast** among the sounds of the language and quite a number of such contrasts for efficiency. The study of **phonemics** is the study of the system of contrasts.

In spoken English, the sound /t/ contrasts with other speech sounds in English. It is because of this contrastive role that one is able to perceive the word <u>tin</u> when someone says it and to know that the person meant 'tin' and not 'sin' or 'bin' or 'pin' or 'din' or 'gin' or 'fin.' It is easy to conclude that /t/ is a separate sound in English and that it is **distinct** (that is, *a different sound*) from /d/ or /s/ or other sounds. This seems obvious, hardly worthy of mention.

However, the matter is complicated by the fact that, as shown in Chapter 10, there is not just one kind of /t/ in English, but many. For example, /t/ may be aspirated or nonaspirated, released or unreleased. It may have an alveolar, alveopalatal, or dental place of articulation. When released, it may be centrally released, or it may be nasally or laterally released (depending upon the sound that follows). It may even be pronounced like a "d," as /ɾ/. Indeed, a careful acoustic study would show that virtually every instance of /t/ would be slightly different.

Why is it that we group all these quite different sounds together and call them simply /t/? Is it perhaps because they all sound so much alike that it would be impossible to differentiate them? With some varieties of /t/, this is undoubtedly true, but not for all. For example, it is easy to hear the difference between an aspirated and an unaspirated /t/, and the speakers of some languages make the distinction all the time.

Or perhaps we group them together because of assimilation; that is, since the various kinds of English /t/ are determined mostly by the phonetic environment, could it be that it is simply impossible to produce certain kinds of /t/ in certain environments? This again is only partly true. It would be pretty hard to produce a centrally released /t/ just before an /l/ without putting in any intervening sound. But there is no physical reason why we could not pronounce an unaspirated /t/ where we pronounce an aspirated one, and vice versa.

No, the reason why we, as speakers of English, group these different sounds together as "one" speech sound is not because we could not hear the distinction and not because we could not pronounce the distinction everywhere. Rather, it is because we are speakers of English, and the English language groups these sounds together functionally. This is relatively arbitrary: English happens to work that way. You cannot assume, just because two phones seem to you to be slightly different forms of the "same" sound, that they will seem that way to speakers of every language.

The speakers of some languages distinguish between aspirated and unaspirated /t/: to them, these are different sounds. Speakers of another language may distinguish, at the ends of words, between a released and an unreleased /t/: they do not feel, as you do, that either one can be used without the change being significant.

A group of phones, or sounds, that go together in a certain language to form what the speakers of that language feel to be one sound and that are never used in a contrastive way form what is called a **phoneme** of that language. The various forms of that one sound, such as the aspirated, unaspirated, dental, alveolar, and laterally exploded /t/'s of English, are called **allophones** of that phoneme. We can say, therefore, that /t/ is a phoneme of English, and that its allophones include all the various kinds of /t/ mentioned here and in Chapter 10.


## 11-2 The Phoneme

The idea of the phoneme is somewhat abstract; that is, you cannot put your finger on the phoneme /t/. It is not a single, unchanging entity. Rather, it is an abstraction from the many many different instances of /t/ that are heard in speech, some of which are likely very close to one's idea of what a /t/ should be, and some of which are almost unrecognizable (particularly in rapid speech).

The idea that the phoneme is abstract should not be disconcerting, nor should it make the concept seem terribly complex. Virtually every word we use in everyday conversation is abstract and in the same way that the word phoneme is.

For example, the word tree is quite familiar, and while there are different kinds, a mental picture of a typical tree can be conjured up without much difficulty. It is of no consequence (or it should not be) that every single tree in the whole world is different; they are still trees, even when some of the "typical" characteristics are lacking. For instance, the typical tree may have leaves, but many trees do not. The typical tree may be quite large, but it does not matter that there are dwarf trees that may stand only a foot high although they may be a hundred years old. So, while the mental picture of a typical tree is idealized, it is a recognized fact that there are many varieties of trees, some of them quite unlike the accepted image, and these must be acknowledged as trees.

Just as one's mental picture of a tree is somewhat idealized, the definition of a particular phoneme in a certain language is idealized as well. All instances of the phoneme /t/ in English are different, ranging from those that are almost identical with one's ideas of a typical /t/ to those that are acoustically deviant (a stuttered /t/, for instance, may be highly anomalous).

So, when we speak of a particular phoneme, say the English /t/, we mean a typical /t/, but we also take into consideration all the various forms that that phoneme may have in that language. Also, even the various allophones cover a broad range of possible articulations. In our analogy, the **allophone** may be said to correspond to a species of tree. Pine trees, for example, share a great number of common features that distinguish them from other types of trees, but each pine tree is different. Similarly, if we speak of the laterally released allophone of /t/, each instance will be a little different, but the term is still useful for grouping together speech sounds that share many common features.

Of course, one can be specific or general with his terminology. Just as one can distinguish trees as ponderosa pine or southern pine or western pine, one can distinguish heavily aspirated, moderately aspirated, and lightly aspirated /t/'s. Or, they can all be grouped together as /t/'s and referred to, for example, as the "aspirated allophone of /t/."

## 11-2.1 Some Allophones of Some English Phonemes

Let us reinforce the notions of phoneme and allophone by reviewing some of the material from Chapter 10, using the new terminology. In the examples, note that we place the symbols for phonemes between slash marks (/t/), and the symbols for the allophones between square brackets ([tʰ]).

1. The phoneme /t/ in English has many allophones:

| [t] | unaspirated /t/ | stop |
| [tʰ] | aspirated /t/ | top |
| [t˺] | unreleased /t/ | bough<u>t</u> two |
| [ɾ] | flapped /t/ | butter |
| [tᴺ] | nasally released /t/ | button |
| [tᴸ] | laterally released /t/ | little |
| [t̪] | dental /t/ | both Tom and I |
| [t̠] | back (alveopalatal) /t/ | meatshop |

2. The phoneme /p/ in English has many allophones:

| [p] | unaspirated /p/ | spot |
| [pʰ] | aspirated /p/ | pot |
| [p˺] | unreleased /p/ | stop (optional) |

3. The phoneme /l/ in English has three main allophones:

| | | |
|---|---|---|
| [l] | "light" (nonvelarized) /l/ | limb |
| [ɫ] | "dark" (velarized) /l/ | mole |
| [l̩] | syllabic /l/ (usually velarized in English, but for clarity, not indicated) | little |

4. The phoneme /e/ in English has a number of allophones:

| | | |
|---|---|---|
| [e͜i] | diphthongized /e/, when fully stressed | fate |
| [e] | shorter, nondiphthongized /e/, secondary stress | gradation |
| [ə] | schwa (unstressed) | Canada |

Note also that /e/ may have long or short allophones, depending upon the voicing of the following consonant:

| | | |
|---|---|---|
| [e:] | long | made |
| [e] | short | mate |

Both of these are diphthongized, but for clarity this is not indicated.

This listing is given to show only a few examples; it is by no means exhaustive. An important point can be made about these examples. Not all information is necessarily given all at once if it is not relevant. For example, one may have a /t/ that is both aspirated and dental. Many combinations are possible, and one may record only what is necessary for clarity. A second point to note is that the allophones, while phonetically more specific, are still abstractions. For example, each instance of a laterally released /t/ will be a little different from every other one.

## 11-3 The Predictability and Contrastiveness of the Phoneme

A phoneme is made up of a group of allophones, representing the main types of phones (speech sounds) that go together to make it up. In a list of allophones of some English phonemes, it is evident that the various different types of /t/, for example, properly belong together. However, the *feeling* that they belong together does not constitute a definition, and that feeling is likely to cause difficulties when studying a language other than one's own. What are the criteria for deciding that a certain group of phones should be grouped together as allophones of a certain phoneme?

The first criterion is **phonetic similarity.** The allophones of a phoneme are generally quite similar: that is, their place of articulation is the same or nearly the same, and their manner of articulation is usually the same or similar (the phoneme /t/ may have /ɾ/ as an allophone, but flaps and plosives are similar). One would not expect a bilabial nasal to have a velar fricative as an allophone.

The second criterion has to do with the **functioning** of sounds in a particular language. It is reflected in the **predictability** of a sound or its **contrastiveness.** While these two notions may seem quite distinct, they are actually two sides of the same coin. Let us look at each aspect in turn.

## 11-3.1 Contrastiveness of the Phoneme

Why do we group [p] and [pʰ] together as one phoneme, and count [b] as a separate phoneme? (Of course, it is perfectly obvious to the English speaker that we do this; here we are trying to answer the question *why* we are doing it.) The most obvious reason that [p] and [b] are considered to be separate is that the difference between them alone can be used to signal the difference between two words: "pit" has a different meaning from "bit." These two words form what we call a **minimal pair**; that is, a pair of words whose sounds (not necessarily spelling) differ by *one* phone only. In this case, the sound difference between the words /pɪt/ and /bɪt/ lies in the difference between /p/ and /b/.

The existence of this minimal pair tells us that the difference between these two sounds can *signal a meaning difference* in English: it is **contrastive.** We can confirm this by finding other minimal pairs: putter/butter; lap/lab; pan/ban; rapid/rabid; post/boast. Of course, not every word will have such a mate; there is a word "prairie" but no word "*brairie" (the asterisk is used to indicate a nonexistent word). With some pairs of sounds, it may be quite difficult to find minimal pairs, and sometimes they do not exist at all, because of an accidental gap in the language or because of phonotactic restrictions (the subject of Chapter 12). If a minimal pair can be found, an important discovery has been made about the functioning of the phones under question: they are contrastive. "Pan" has a different pronunciation and meaning from "ban," and therefore /p/ contrasts with /b/. We may therefore say that they are separate phonemes.

Let us now try the test of contrastiveness on [p] and [pʰ]. The first thing noticed is that no minimal pairs can be found; that is, there may be a word [pʰɪt] but no word [pɪt]. There may be a word [spɪt] but no word [spʰɪt]. It will not be possible to find a pair of words whose only sound difference is the difference between [p] and [pʰ]. Let us try substituting one sound for the other: say [pɪt] instead of [pʰɪt]. There is no difference in meaning. It may sound a little strange, but it is still the same word. Try saying [spʰɪt] instead of [spɪt]. Again, it may sound a little odd, but the word has not changed.

Since substituting one for the other does not change the meaning, *the two sounds are not contrastive.* We conclude that they are **allophones** of the same phoneme.

In summary, the test of contrastiveness reveals whether two sounds are separate phonemes or allophones of one phoneme. When the substitution of one sound for the other can totally change the meaning of the word, one is dealing with two separate phonemes; when it cannot, one is dealing with allophones of the same phoneme.

At this point, it must be stressed that the *absence* of a mate to form a minimal pair does not *prove* that one is dealing with allophones. Positive evidence is conclusive; negative evidence is not. For example, in trying to determine the status of /t/ and /d/ in English, one might check to see if there were a word "*dask" to go with "task." The absence of this word is an accidental gap in English and proves nothing. Even if one found twenty other words with no mates, it would not have been *proved* that these were allophones. Only *one* contrastive pair is needed to prove that the two sounds are separate phonemes: "tot" and "dot." For some sounds, particularly among the vowels, the clear-cut evidence of minimal pairs may be difficult or impossible to find. In such cases, other tests may be applied.

## 11-3.2 Predictability and the Phoneme

The second way the function of a sound is revealed is through its **predictability.** An example will demonstrate how one might test for predictability.

Imagine being presented with this transcription with one symbol replaced by a hyphen: [-æt]. If the choice were given of replacing the hyphen with either [p] or [pʰ], could it be predicted which would go into the space? Yes, the correct answer must be [pʰ], as long as we know it is an English word. This must be the case, since the word-initial /p/ is aspirated in English. Notice that this prediction could be made even without knowing the word. Try the same exercise with the nonsense word *[s-æš]. Is the hyphen replaced by [p] or [pʰ]? This time the answer must be [p]. You can make this prediction whether or not you know what the word means and whether it has any meaning at all.

Now try the same test with [p] and [b]. Given the transcription [læ-] with one symbol left out, can you predict which of the two sounds belongs? No. The answer will be that it depends upon the meaning of the word. If you are given a nonsense syllable and asked to perform the same task, as with *[stɪ-] you will see that there is no way at all to predict which sound is the correct one.

In summary, the choice between two allophones is normally predictable while the choice between two phonemes is not (except, as will be shown, as a result of phonotactic restrictions).

The various allophones of a phoneme are normally found each in its own environment and not in the environments of the other allophones. The environments, therefore, are for the most part mutually exclusive; this idea is expressed by saying that the allophones are in **complementary distribution.** Things that are **complementary** go together to make a coherent whole,[1] and indeed the environments of each of the allophones go together to make up the environment for the entire phoneme. As an example, we could say dark and light /l/ are in complementary distribution in English. Another way this idea is often expressed is by stating that the allophones are **conditioned variants, variants** because they are variant forms of the same phoneme and **conditioned** because they are conditioned (determined) by their particular phonetic environment.

Certain allophones, it should be noted, are in so-called **free variation.** For example, if asked to predict whether a word will end with a released or a nonreleased /p/, you will have to admit that you cannot, that either one is acceptable. But this does not mean that the two are separate phonemes. Here

[1] Don't confuse *complimentary,* meaning 'flattering,' with *complementary,* suggesting 'completeness.'

the test of contrastiveness would provide the answer: [stɑp] and [stɑp⁻] both have the same meaning, and are both perfectly acceptable pronunciations of this word.

## 11-4 Functional Units in Language

Languages, as we said before, depend upon sound contrasts in order to carry or convey meaning. But what languages contrast is not phones (individual speech sounds) but phonemes. In English, /t/ is contrasted with /p/. The choice between /t/ and /p/ depends upon whether a particular word happens to have one or the other; a substitution of one for the other is not usually tolerated.

If a particular word contains a /t/, however, the particular type of /t/ is selected on the basis of the sounds around the phonetic environment. One may say that the major selection between phonemes is based on a criterion dependent upon meaning; the small choice among allophones depends upon the surrounding sounds.

Unfortunately, this simple picture is made a little more complex by some situations that do not fit neatly into it. Let us consider a few of these.

### 11-4.1 Morphophonemics

The first problem we come across in a phonemic analysis is that sounds that appear to be contrastive sometimes are not. For example, we can use the test of minimal pairs to demonstrate that /s/ and /z/ are contrastive in English: sip/zip; bus/buzz. But then we note that the English plural ending, usually spelled -s or -es, is pronounced according to the surrounding sounds; [s] in the word "cats," [z] in the word "dogs" (and [əz] in the word "buses," but we will ignore this for the moment). Now, "cats" cannot contrast with *[kætz], nor can "dogs" contrast with *[dɑgs] (or *[dɔgs]).

This is a case where phonetic considerations are mixed with other aspects of the grammar. A **morpheme,** you will recall, is the smallest **meaningful** unit of language. The word cats, for example, contains two morphemes: cat, which means what you think it does, and -s which means 'more than one' (plural). Some morphemes, like cat, can stand alone. Others, like -s, must be attached to another morpheme. Some morphemes, like -s, have several common pronunciations, whereas others have one usual pronunciation. (Those that can stand alone are **unbound** morphemes; **bound** morphemes must be attached. Both types may have one pronunciation or several.)

The morpheme -s must be attached to a word, and its pronunciation depends on the phonetic shape of the word to which it is attached. The change in pronunciation is not a small one—that is, the choice of one or another allophone—but is between two phonemes. Normally, a change from one phoneme to another changes the meaning of the word, but not here.

The solution to this problem is to propose the existence of the **morphophoneme,** a morpheme having more than one different phonemic realization. Elsewhere, the difference between /s/ and /z/ is a **phonemic** or **contrastive** difference, but in this specific morphophoneme, the difference between [s] and [z] depends upon the phonetic environment (as is usually the case for allophones of one phoneme).

Another example would be the negative prefix, spelled <u>in</u>- or <u>im</u>-, and pronounced [ɪn], [ɪm], or [ɪŋ]. Since two variants are reflected in the spelling, these tend to be thought of as different prefixes, but they are actually different pronunciations of the same morphophoneme. Three of the main variants can be seen in these words:

| | |
|---|---|
| indistinguishable, inordinate | [ɪn] |
| impossible | [ɪm] |
| incredible | [ɪŋ] |

## 11-4.2 Neutralization

The second problem we find in phonemic analysis is that certain pairs of phonemes lose their phonetic contrastiveness in some environments. As an example, the difference between /t/ and /d/ in English is phonemic or contrastive. Minimal pairs such as tin/din and mitt/mid show this to be true.

When the sounds /t/ and /d/ are in intervocalic position, however, and the preceding vowel is short and stressed, it is often difficult to make the distinction in speech. For example, the words "betting" and "bedding" are often both pronounced [bɛɾɪŋ], with the voiced flap [ɾ] replacing both /t/ and /d/. In this case, two sounds that are normally contrastive are *no longer* contrastive and are not used to signal a meaning distinction. Of course, context supplies the clue to meaning, and no confusion for the listener generally results.

How do we analyze this situation *phonemically*? We say that /t/ and /d/ are separate phonemes and are contrastive but that this contrastiveness may be **neutralized** in one phonetic environment. There are two points to notice in this example. First, neutralizations may be optional or obligatory. In this example, the neutralization is optional; "bedding" may be pronounced [bɛɾɪŋ] or [bɛdɪŋ]; "betting" may be pronounced [bɛɾɪŋ] or [bɛtɪŋ]. Other neutralizations may be obligatory.

The second point is an important, though somewhat abstract, one. While the word "betting" may be *phonetically* pronounced [bɛɾɪŋ], it is still *phonemically* /bɛtɪŋ/; that is, even when the word is pronounced with the flap [ɾ], the speaker of English knows that the basic sound is /t/; in fact he probably thinks he *hears* [t]. One reason for this is that the neutralization is restricted to the one phonetic environment; in the related words "bet" and "bed," for example, the contrastiveness between /t/ and /d/ remains.

## 11-4.3 Variant Pronunciations

Another problem for phonemic analysis is optional pronunciations. The word "either" may be pronounced as /aiðɚ/ or as /iðɚ/, and the first sound in "economics" may be /i/ or /ɛ/. The problem here is that since /i/, /ai/, and /ɛ/ are different phonemes, a change from one to another should change the meaning. "Might" and "meet" (/mait/ and /mit/) are different words with different meanings, but /aiðɚ/ and /iðɚ/ are not.

This is really not a great problem, since the number of words in this category is small. Certain words have more than one acceptable pronunciation, and /ai/ and /i/ are still separate phonemes, which are contrastive despite the two pronunciations of "either."

## 11-4.4 Dialects

The fourth problem found in phonemic analysis is that different dialects of the same language make different phonemic contrasts. For example, we have noted that some dialects distinguish /ɑ/ and /ɔ/, where others do not. Thus, some speakers distinguish "caught" and "cot," while these words are homophonous to speakers of other dialects. Not only is the exact phonetic shape of the phones different, but the *contrasts* made are different as well. Some dialects have two separate phonemes corresponding to /ɑ/ and /ɔ/; others have but one phoneme (which may have the two phones as allophones). Small phonemic differences such as this generally do not cause communication problems.

To take another example, the Cockney dialect of English has leveled the distinction between /f/ and /θ/ and between /v/ and /ð/. Just the sounds [f] and [v] are pronounced. The words "thought" and "fought" are pronounced with an initial [f] sound; the words "that" and "vat" are pronounced with a [v] sound. Thus, Cockney lacks two *phones* of standard English, and correspondingly lacks two standard English *phonemes*.

Two dialects may differ in their inventory of speech sounds *without* differing in phonemic structure. Let us take the example of Cajun English, a dialect spoken in Louisiana, in which aspiration of initial voiceless plosives is reduced or not present at all. Thus /p/ does not have the aspirated allophone of Standard English. Cajun thus has one less *phone* but the same number of *phonemes* (with respect to this point).

Two dialects may differ in having phonetically different realizations of the same phoneme. For example, the consonant /r/ (not in postvocalic position) is quite different in North American English as compared to upper-class British English. The North American /r/ tends to be more of a liquid type sound; the British /r/ is generally closer to a flap than a liquid in articulation. The two dialects have different *phones* but the same *phonemic* structure (with respect to this point).

## 11-5 Stress Is Phonemic

In Chapter 9 we noted that English words are often contrasted on the basis of differences in stress and the concomitant changes in vowel quality. So, a pair of words such as "ínvalid" and "inválid" are contrasted by stress alone.

We can therefore conclude that stress in English is *phonemic*; that is, stress plays a *contrastive* role in English speech. (Occasionally, the term **prosodeme** is used, but the idea can be expressed by the terms *phonemic* or *contrastive*.)

Chapter 9 noted that Spanish uses stress contrastively, so it can be said that stress is phonemic in that language as well, though it is not used as extensively as in English. In French, stress is not contrastive and therefore not phonemic. This is not to say that all syllables in French carry the same degree of stress but that words are not changed by a change in stress alone. (Of course, if a French word is pronounced with the stress sufficiently misplaced, the listener might not understand; but a slight misuse of stress would not have as serious consequences as it does in English.)

## 11-6 Languages and the Phoneme

We will next examine a few examples from languages other than English and examine their phonemic structure. The purpose of these examples is to see how the phonemic systems of languages can vary; the specific details of these particular languages are not the point of the examples. Rather, non-English examples are used to emphasize the principle of phonemics, which may be obscured by our intuitive knowledge of our native tongue.

### 11-6.1 Some Examples

In Spanish, [d] and [ð] are allophones. They are in complementary distribution; [ð] occurs intervocalically, and [d] occurs everywhere else. Both are spelled with the letter d in the Spanish spelling system. The word nada, for example, is pronounced [naða]. The Spanish-speaking person has both sounds in his phonetic repertoire but does not contrast them. There could not be a pair of words whose only difference was that one had the sound [d] where the other had the sound [ð]. The speaker of Spanish who is learning English would have difficulty learning to distinguish "other" and "udder," or "den" and "then," even though he can pronounce both sounds. He would distribute the two sounds as they are distributed in Spanish: he would say "other" for both other and udder, and "den" for both then and den, and would have difficulty recognizing his error.

The French or German speaker learning English would also usually have difficulty with [ð] but for a different reason. This phone is lacking in these languages.

Thai provides us with an example of a language that contrasts aspirated and unaspirated voiceless plosives. Both English and Thai have the phones [p], [pʰ], and [b], but the two languages differ in their phonemic structure. Fromkin and Rodman [1974] give the example of these three contrasting Thai words:

|       |          |
|-------|----------|
| /paa/  | forest   |
| /pʰaa/ | to split |
| /baa/  | shoulder |

The example demonstrates that [p] and [pʰ] are contrastive in Thai, since we have found a minimal pair. We know that [p] and [pʰ] are in complementary distribution in English and are not contrastive, so the same three phones must function as two phonemes in English but as three in Thai:

| Thai phonemes | Phones | English phonemes |
|---------------|--------|------------------|
| /p/ ——————— [p] ———————➤ /p/ | | |
| /pʰ/ ——————— [pʰ]↗ | | |
| /b/ ——————— [b] ——————— /b/ | | |

To take another example, Japanese has a sound very similar to English /l/ and a sound very similar to English /r/. These are not separate phonemes, however; they are allophones of the same phoneme. The l-like sound occurs with certain vowels; the r-like sound with other vowels. The Japanese speaker can produce both sounds but only in certain environments. English speakers often say that the Japanese reverse the r and l when they speak English, but this is not true. The correct or incorrect variant may be used, in accordance with the distribution in Japanese.

Other examples could be given. In Russian, the difference between dark and light /l/ is phonemic. In Old English, [f] and [v] were allophones, as were [s] and [z].

## 11-6.2 Phones and Phonemes

When speakers of English hear [t], [t˺], [t̪], [tʰ], or another variant of the /t/ phoneme, they "hear" the sound /t/. The difference between the variants, when appropriately used, is not significant for communication (though it may be significant to the practical phonetician). Even in the case of neutralization, the phone uttered will correspond specifically to one or another phoneme. So [bɛrɪŋ] is interpreted as /bɛtɪŋ/ or as /bɛdɪŋ/, depending on context; we will "hear" [bɛtɪŋ], even when the speaker *said* [bɛrɪŋ] if that is what makes sense in the context. The question of whether [bɛrɪŋ] or /bɛtɪŋ/ is *transcribed* is a matter of how much need for detail there is; this question will be dealt with in section 11-8. Here we must realize that there is a basic phoneme /t/ that is perceived by the listener even if it is not pronounced differently from a /d/ by the speaker.[2] The word "betting" contains the phoneme /t/, even if its pronunciation is indistinguishable from that of "bedding."

One phone that exists in three different languages will illustrate how one phone may correspond to different phonemes. The affricate [t͡s] exists as a phone in German, one dialect of French, and English, but its status as a phoneme differs. In German, the affricate [t͡s] has a separate status as a phoneme. This can be demonstrated by minimal pairs (pay attention to the phonetic transcription, not the standard spelling):

| Ziegel | [t͡sigəl] | tile |
| Tiegel | [tigəl] | saucepan |
| Zank | [t͡saŋk] | quarrel |
| Tank | [taŋk] | tank |

These examples prove that /t͡s/ is not a variant of /t/. Could it be a variant of /s/? No, since /s/ does not occur in word-initial position in German. Could it be a variant of /z/ (as its spelling might suggest)? No, there is a minimal pair:

| Zank | [t͡saŋk] | quarrel |
| sank | [zaŋk] | sank |

[2] This is true, however, only where neutralization normally occurs. If /d/ were said for /t/ elsewhere, the listener would either recognize the error or would misunderstand the message.

In a similar way, the possibility that /ts/ is a variant of any other phoneme in German can be eliminated, so it must have its own status. The word Z̲ank, for example, must have /ts/ as its basic first sound.

Next, the phone [ts] will be considered as it occurs in the French spoken in North America. In Canadian French, the phoneme /t/ is pronounced [ts] when preceding a high front vowel, /i/ or /y/. So a word such as t̲ype, pronounced [tip] in standard French, is pronounced [tsip] in Canadian French, but a word such as t̲out is pronounced [tu] in all dialects. In Canadian French, /t/ has two allophones, [t] and [ts], which are conditioned by their environment. We cannot find a minimal pair as we could in German. So, when a speaker of Canadian French says [tsip], the basic sound is /tip/. The two phones do not have separate phonemic status.

In English, the sequence of /t/ followed by /s/ is often pronounced as an affricate when we speak quickly. So, "bits and pieces" may be pronounced [bitsən. . . ], but while, *phonetically*, an affricate may be pronounced, from the point of view of *phonemics* or basic sounds it is simply a /t/ followed by an /s/. The English speaker, hearing [ts], interprets it as /ts/.

Consequently, while each of these three languages has the same phone, its function is very different in each, and the same phone in each of these languages will be heard differently by the native speaker, in view of the different contrasts made in each language:

| Language | Phone | Sample word (usual spelling) | Basic sound or phoneme |
|---|---|---|---|
| German | [ts] | Z̲ank | /ts/ |
| Canadian French | [ts] | t̲ype | /t/ |
| English | [ts] | bit̲s̲ and pieces | /ts/ |

## 11-6.3 Phonemics and Phonetics

Phonetics has as one of its objectives a universal system of classifying speech sounds on an articulatory basis. Phonemics, on the other hand, devises a simpler classification system that captures only the distinctions necessary for a particular language. One result of this is that there are occasional misunderstandings as to what is meant by certain transcriptions or statements. Sometimes students are confused by statements that appear to be contradictory; often it is found that the apparent contradiction results from a confusion over whether one is talking phonetically or phonemically.

The vowel [ʌ], for example, is described as a **central** vowel in many phonetics textbooks. Chapter 7 stressed that it is a **back** vowel. However, the contradiction is not as serious as first appears. In Chapter 7, the details of the articulation were stressed since it was felt that the articulation is of primary importance to the practical phonetician.

For one who is interested only in the *distinctiveness* of English phonemes, there is economy in classifying [ʌ] as a central vowel. As noted, rounding (labialization) is a redundant feature of all English vowels with the exception of the pair [ʌ]-[ɔ]. That is, for all other *English* vowels, rounding is predictable from other articulatory information: no high front vowel is rounded; no high back vowel is spread; no low vowel is rounded (in most dialects); and so on. This is an aspect of the overall phonemic system of English, and this generalization can be captured by calling [ʌ] a central vowel (which is not far from the articulatory truth). One can then generalize that front vowels are unrounded and back vowels are rounded ([ʊ] is an exception because it is lax, and the only remaining exception, [ɑ], can be explained by the fact that its rounded counterpart, [ɒ], is rare in all languages). Such a classification does not cause any problems among central vowels, since most English dialects have [ə] only in unstressed (weak) syllables and have [ʌ] only in syllables with primary or secondary stress.

Thus, in an analysis of the phonemic system of English, [ʌ] may be classed as central. The only problem arises when a person mistakenly assumes that the phonemic analysis is supposed to be a precise articulatory description, which it is not.

Another case where the two types of analysis are in apparent conflict is in the case of [ɚ]. Many transcription systems will transcribe the word "bird," for example, as /bərd/, where this book has suggested /bɚd/ (but see footnotes 3 and 6 in Chapter 7). Again, the contradiction is not one of substance. From a purely phonetic point of view, English has one rhotacized, nondiphthongized vowel in the word "bird": the vowel cannot be separated from the /r/ in the articulation (of course, these remarks do not apply to the so-called r-less dialects, or to certain British dialects with flapped r̲'s).

From the point of view of a phonemic analysis, the transcription /bərd/ may best indicate the contrastive system of English. Historically, schwar developed from the sequence of a vowel plus the consonant /r/. Schwar makes no phonemic contrast with the consonant /r/, and our intuition as speakers of English is that "bird" contains a sequence of vowel plus consonant /r/.

Again, the phonemic analysis serves us well, and the instructor may use the transcription system in which "bird" is transcribed as /bərd/. We have stressed the existence of schwar in English because it is important for the practical phonetician to realize that a word like "bird" will sound odd if an attempt is made to pronounce a sequence of vowel plus consonant /r/.

## 11-7 Practical Implications of Phonemics

The study of the phonemic structure of language has practical implications for the teaching and correction of speech. This is so, because, while the phoneme may be an abstract notion, it has a certain degree of reality in the mind of the speaker.

Let us take the example of the Spanish speaker learning English. To him, [d] and [ð] are allophones, and the choice of one or the other will be based purely on the surrounding phones. He will tend to pronounce both udder and other the same, with [ð], and he will tend to pronounce both den and then the same, with [d]. He does not need to be taught to pronounce [ð] (a problem many learners of English face); rather, he needs to learn to *distinguish* them and to produce them at appropriate places. The problem is *not* in the mouth, it is in the mind, at the level of perception and interpretation.

Let us take another example. Most children go through a stage where they pronounce /r/ and /w/ alike, as [w]. Most of them, however, learn at a certain stage to *perceive* the difference and to recognize its contrastive significance, before their articulatory competence has had a chance to catch up. So the child will say "wabbit" for <u>rabbit</u> but will reject an adult's pronunciation "wabbit." The child distinguishes the *phoneme* /r/ from /w/, but both are realized (pronounced) the same, as [w]. Most children will naturally grow out of this as their skill at articulation improves, but if a child not only persisted in pronouncing the two alike but also went on failing to distinguish the two sounds as pronounced by an adult, this would be a matter of a faulty phonemic system. This defect would be particularly evident if the child produced both [r] and [w] but produced them in complementary distribution. That is a different problem from not being able to pronounce [r], and the remedial technique should reflect this.

Phonemic theory is important because this abstract notion corresponds to something that "exists" in the mind of the speaker. If two sounds are noncontrastive in the internal system of an individual, this fact must be taken into consideration in teaching the sound. For example, a common articulation error is to fail to distinguish /t/ from /k/. Performing a phonemic analysis on the speech of an individual with this problem is important for revealing his phonemic system, which may be different from that of someone else with what at first appears to be a similar problem. For example, we may find any of these (or other) systems:

1. The individual may have one or the other phoneme missing entirely. Articulation therapy is needed to help him pronounce the missing sound, but the exercise is meaningless to him without ensuring that he can perceive the difference in the speech of others and that he perceives the contrastive role that the difference plays. (Does he confuse "cap" and "tap"?)
2. The individual's system may involve using both sounds but in a noncontrastive way: /t/ and /k/ may be in allophonic variation. Here he needs less articulation therapy, since he can pronounce both sounds, but needs help (as in paragraph 1) in perceiving the contrastive role of the sounds. He may need guidance in articulating the sounds in all environments, when the two are in complementary distribution.
3. He may have the correct phonemic system. He perceives the difference between /t/ and /k/ without difficulty, and while he attempts to articulate the two sounds distinctly, he has difficulty in pronouncing one or the other sound. Here the pathologist needs to provide pure articulation therapy; the individual does not need guidance in the contrastive role of the sounds.

A phonemic analysis of an individual's speech is helpful to the pathologist or language teacher in performing his job, but perhaps this does not yet seem very real. Let us consider the case of an English-speaking person trying to learn a foreign language, which is quite analogous to the person with a communication disorder learning his native language. From this comparison, it is evident that there are two separate and distinct aspects: (1) the physical articulation (phonetics) of the new sounds, and (2) the mental realization of the contrastive role of foreign sounds (the phonemics).

In Spanish, for example, there is the problem of the two kinds of "r."

In learning the language well, it is necessary to produce *and* to perceive the two consistently, so that not only is <u>pero</u> pronounced differently from <u>perro</u>, but when you hear them you know, from the pronunciation, whether the speaker said 'dog' or 'but.'

An individual who has studied French rather than Spanish, may have a problem distinguishing /y/ and /u/, as in <u>tu</u> (/ty/; 'you') and <u>tout</u> (/tu/; 'all'). An equivalent problem for the English speaker learning German would be the distinction between /k/ and /x/,[3] as in <u>Lachen</u> (/lɑxən/; 'laughter') and <u>Laken</u> (/lɑkən/; 'sheet' or 'shroud').

Charles Van Riper, in his classic text *Speech Correction* [1972], argues for what he calls a phonetic analysis of the speech of those with articulation errors and cites the following case:

> One of our student speech therapists gave an articulation test to a boy of seven and came out with the astounding summary that although he had thirty-two defective sounds, his speech was perfectly intelligible. When we checked her findings we found that the child actually was doing only one thing incorrectly: He was *forming* the final sounds of every word, but was not pronouncing them audibly. The student therapist had been right in finding that thirty-two sounds were defective, but this actually had no significance or importance. Our therapeutic task was clearly to teach the child to strengthen his terminal sounds [p. 189].

In this child's speech, every phoneme had a nonaudible allophone in word-final position. The same process existed for forming the nonnormal allophone of each phoneme. In this case, it is quite obvious that the therapist should attack the problem not as a case of thirty-two misarticulations but as *one* articulation defect.[4]

## 11-8  Transcription and the Phoneme

The notion of the phoneme plays a role, whether we are aware of it or not, in how we transcribe "phonetically." This section will describe how the phoneme relates to transcription and some specific aspects of transcription as they relate to nonnormal speech.

### 11-8.1  Phonemic and Phonetic Transcription

As noted in Chapter 10, sometimes we want our transcriptions to contain more detail, sometimes less. The more detailed type is called a **phonetic**, or **narrow**, transcription, whereas the less detailed type is called **phonemic**, or **broad**, transcription.

We put a **phonemic** or **broad** transcription between slash marks (/    /). Each symbol represents a phoneme. So the symbol /p/ represents the unaspirated allophone, the aspirated allophone, and the unreleased allophone. We do not use a separate symbol for each type of /p/ since all types are just

---

[3] The symbol [x] represents a voiceless velar fricative, such as occurs in the Scottish pronunciation of the word <u>Loch</u>. It does *not* represent the sequence [ks].

[4] Chapter 14 will show how such a substitution can be indicated by *one* phonological rule.

instances of the same phoneme, /p/. Similarly, the effects of coarticulation are not marked, and the effects of assimilation are marked only when a segment crosses a phoneme boundary. Therefore, we would not indicate that the /d/ in the word "handle" is laterally released, since laterally released /d/ is not a separate phoneme; but we would mark the fact that someone pronounced the first /s/ of "street" as /š/ in the expression "Goodge Street," since /s/ and /š/ are separate phonemes.

This is the most common form of transcription. But what happens when someone reads it? Does he make errors in reading since so much phonetic information is left out? Generally not, since most of the information left out is predictable. For example, it is not necessary to tell a person to release the /t/ of "little" laterally; he does that automatically. If that information were left out of a transcription, he would supply it unconsciously when reading the transcription. Similarly, in reading a transcription, he would aspirate the plosives when appropriate, if the speech that was recorded was normal speech. What if a speech pathologist wants to record some nonnormal speech and indicate that the plosives are not appropriately aspirated? If the therapist uses a broad, phonemic transcription, it will not accurately record what is unusual about the speech since the error being recorded is not phonemic but subphonemic: the wrong allophone is being used. In this case, we would need the other type of transcription, in which these details are marked.

We put a **narrow** or **phonetic** transcription between brackets ([    ]). Here each different allophone has a different symbol, and we carefully mark the effects of coarticulation and assimilation. We mark every relevant phonetic detail.

Suppose we are recording speech in which aspiration is not used as it usually is in English. If *all* voiceless plosives were aspirated, we could simply use a broad transcription and write a note to this effect. If *none* of the plosives was aspirated, a note would suffice as well. But if some plosives were aspirated, and some were not, in a pattern differing from standard English, our transcription would have to show this. In a narrow transcription, aspirated and unaspirated /p/ would be marked: [pʰ] and [p]. Similarly, we would use different symbols for dark and light /l/, and so on.

The narrow transcription is not useful to the speech pathologist alone. We may also want to use a narrow transcription in recording a dialect other than our own or to record the way a foreigner speaks English.

You will note that as a result of combinatory processes (assimilation, coarticulation) certain epenthetic or **intrusive** sounds appear, and you may wonder whether you ought to transcribe these. For example, let us take the word "buy." This word would be transcribed /bai/ in the system introduced in earlier chapters. But what about the word "buying"? The student with a good ear for sounds will note that there is an intrusive /j/ approximant inserted between the /ai/ of buy and the /ɪ/ of -ing in most people's speech. If recorded, this would give the transcription [baijɪŋ]. Does one record this intrusive sound? In a very narrow phonetic transcription, it should be included since it is, after all, a sound that is articulated. But for the purpose of a broad phonemic transcription, there is no need because the insertion of /j/ is *predictable* and does not represent a separate and distinct phoneme. Whenever the -ing suffix is added to a word whose final sound is /i/, /e/, /ai/ or /ɔi/ (that is, a high or upper-mid front vowel), the /j/ is automatically and unconsciously inserted, as in the words "being," "baying," "buying," and "annoying." Otherwise, it is not; notice the words "testing," "teasing," and "jawing," as well as others like them. (You may also have noted that if the word ends with a high or upper-mid *back* vowel, the approximant /w/ is inserted.) Since the insertion of this sound is predictable, there is no more need to indicate it in a broad transcription than there is to indicate the aspiration or nonaspiration of /t/. However, the same caution applies here as elsewhere: if you are recording speech that is not typical, be it a foreign accent, an unusual dialect, or the speech of someone with an articulation problem, the use of such intrusive sounds may not be predictable and should be recorded carefully.

In summary, slash marks enclose a broad, phonemic transcription while brackets enclose a narrow, phonetic transcription. It is important to use these symbols correctly, since the meaning of the letters of the phonetic alphabet changes depending on the enclosing marks. For example, the symbol /p/ means *both* aspirated and unaspirated variants, but [p] means *only* the unaspirated variant. (Some books do not follow this convention, but you will find that it is widely accepted. By carefully maintaining the use of slash marks and brackets in your own professional use of transcription, you will avoid errors and misunderstandings.)

It should be noted that there is not a simple two-way choice between narrow and broad transcriptions. There is a continuum running all the way from very broad transcription to transcription containing extremely detailed information about the articulation of each and every phone. Generally, our transcriptions are somewhere in the middle, with our broad transcriptions tending toward less detail, and our narrow transcriptions tending toward more detail. Also, we often include a narrow transcription of certain sounds under discussion, while letting other sounds be represented in broad transcription. Almost never do we achieve a completely phonemic transcription; almost always some subphonemic distinctions are recorded.

One particularly important aspect to remember about broad transcription is that it lumps together under one symbol sounds that are different (the allophones). There may be a tendency to think that sounds that are represented with the same symbol are in all important respects the "same." However, as we have seen, the various allophones of one phoneme may be, from a phonetic and articulatory viewpoint, quite different.

## 11-8.2 Specialized Transcription for Speech Therapists

There are a number of conventions used in the recording of nonnormal speech that are not in general use by phoneticians and so are not usually included in books on phonetics. A few important ones will be mentioned here.

If an individual substitutes one phoneme for another, this can be recorded with a broad transcription, thus: /wæbət/ for "rabbit." If an individual makes subphonemic substitutions—that is, if he substitutes one allophone for another—a narrow transcription is needed, at least with respect to the affected sound, thus: [spʰɪt] for "spit," if the /p/ is aspirated. This sort of transcription can be employed to show these types of substitution and indeed must be used when the individual is inconsistent in his substitutions.

When the individual consistently makes the same substitution or distortion in the same phonetic environment, however, a kind of shorthand employing abbreviations is used. The letters (I), (M), and (F) in parentheses refer, respectively, to initial, medial, and final position in a word. This marks the position at which the distortion usually occurs. If the distortion occurs in all positions, all positions are marked. The minus sign (−) is used to indicate that a sound has been omitted; the plus sign (+) is used to indicate that a sound has been inserted; and the diagonal or slash (/) is used to indicate a substitution or distortion. Let us look at several examples:

t/s (I, M, F) means [t] substituted for /s/ in all positions.

θ/s (I) means [θ] substituted for /s/ in initial position.

−l (F) means that the final /l/ is omitted.

+ə (M) means that the vowel [ə] is inserted medially where it is not appropriate (though a more complete indication of the context of the insertion would be useful).

A familiarity with some of the less common IPA symbols can also be useful to the speech pathologist or second-language teacher recording unusual substitutions. If, for example, an individual substitutes a dark or velarized /l/ for the light /l/, the appropriate symbol, [ɫ], may be used. Or, if an individual has a certain type of bilateral lisp that is similar to the voiceless lateral fricative [ɬ], one can indicate this substitution without complicated explanation. For example, "ɬ/s (I, M, F)" would indicate a bilateral lisp in all positions.

Some therapists employ the usual English spelling to indicate substitutions, but there are disadvantages to this. For example, if one writes "th" for /θ/, there is considerable ambiguity; "th" may indicate either the voiced or the voiceless dental fricative, whereas /θ/ is specific. And using "th" for /θ/ makes it difficult to distinguish an aspirated from an unaspirated /t/, which may be important in some cases. It is a good idea to avoid transcribing speech with English spelling. As more and more speech pathologists have training in the IPA, there should be more consistency in the use of symbols.

## Questions for Discussion

1. Make a phonemic analysis of English; that is, make a list of all the phonemes of English. Compare your list with that of your classmates. Discuss the reasons for any differences.
2. Take the list you have made for question 1, and beside each phoneme indicate the conditioned variants it has, and the environments in which they appear.
3. What *phonemic* differences have you noted among various dialects of English? Leave out any phonetic differences which do not reflect phonemic differences; also ignore differences in stress, rhythm, or intonation.
4. Make a phonemic analysis of a sample of misarticulated speech, or a sample of English as spoken by someone learning it as a second language.
5. Discuss the phonemic system of a foreign language which a substantial number of the students in the class are familiar with. Note similarities and differences with English, both in phonemic and phonetic inventories. What allophonic variants does each phoneme have? If you cannot find a language with which enough students are

familiar, use data from the exercises in Gleason [1955] and Pike [1947] for this question.

6. We sometimes say, when a spelling error such as <u>nite</u> for <u>night</u> is made, that the person spelled the word "phonetically." Is this true? Should an ideal spelling system for a language be phonetic? or phonemic? Discuss.

## Annotated Bibliography

A set of exercises in determining the phonemic status of phones in a number of languages can be found in Gleason's *Workbook* [1955]. Pike's volume [1947] contains theory and useful exercises on phonemics as well. Both are highly recommended for practice.

Jones [1967], Twaddell [1966], and Bloomfield [1933] give classic accounts of phoneme theory. Discussions can also be found in Abercrombie [1967], Brosnahan [1970], Fromkin and Rodman [1974], Lyons [1968], and O'Connor [1973].

# Chapter 12

# Phonotactics

## 12-1 Introduction

As shown in Chapter 11, a particular language may be characterized by its phonemic structure. English, for example, counts /θ/ and /ð/ among its phonemes, whereas French and German do not. Also, the phonemic inventory of a language may differ from its phonetic inventory. The overall phonetic structure of a language or dialect, however, cannot be summarized in a phonemic or phonetic inventory alone. Another important factor plays a role: the combining and ordering of these sounds, the domain of **phonotactics.** An example follows:

Both English and Spanish have the phonemes /s/, /t/, /r/, and /e/ (the differences in phonetic quality between the English and Spanish phonemes will be ignored for the moment). In both languages, these phonemes could be ordered /tres/ to form a word (English <u>trace</u>, Spanish <u>tres</u>). In English, these phonemes can be combined in this pattern: /stret/, but in Spanish such a sequence is not permitted. No Spanish word begins /str-/, so, while /stret/ is made up of Spanish phonemes, they are not combined according to Spanish phonotactic rules.

Phonotactics is the study of how phonemes are combined and ordered in a particular language or dialect. Chapter 10 showed how people who have speech difficulties (foreign speakers, those with speech dysfunctions, the hearing-impaired) may be able to pronounce individual phonemes well but have difficulty with modifications that take place in context as a result of assimilation. Here it will be shown that sometimes it is the *combination* of phonemes that causes problems even when the individual phonemes can be pronounced in isolation or in other combinations. It is for this reason that the study of phonotactics is important to us.

But first, a brief look at the syllable will be in order, since much of our discussion of phonotactics will involve the idea of the syllable.

## 12-2  The Syllable

In school one learns how to divide words into syllables and how to divide a word at the end of a line between syllables, as indicated in a standard dictionary. Yet it is difficult to decide upon a satisfactory definition of the syllable. It is clear, however, that the idea of the syllable cannot be abandoned; we have an intuitive notion of what a syllable is, and most of the time we would agree about how many syllables a word has (although we might sometimes divide them at different places). If there is so much agreement among people, there must be something real about the concept of the syllable. Without giving a specific definition, let us see what constitutes the syllable.

Some of what will be said about the phonetics of the syllable may contradict what the student knows about dividing words for spelling purposes. For this reason it should be noted that the dictionary is still the authority when it comes to finding the correct place to divide a word at the end of a line of writing. Just as in spelling, even when it does not make sense there are still conventions that must be followed. But here syllables will be considered from the phonetic point of view: how they are characterized, and how they function.

A good place to begin is to note that there is normally a vowel (or vowel-like sound) acting as the *nucleus* of a syllable. In fact, this is where the word **consonant** comes from: it always *goes with* (con) a *vowel* (sonant). Every syllable has one vowel or diphthong, which may be preceded and/or followed by one or more consonants. These English words are one syllable in length: I, to, up, sit, site, straight. A more extensive list is given in the next section on the English syllable.

It is important to note that a syllable may contain not a vowel or diphthong but a vowel-like or **vocalic** sound. Certain sounds that are usually thought of as consonants—"l," "r," "n," "m," for example—can function as vocalic elements in the syllable. For example, many of us say [bʌtn̩] and not [bʌtən] for "button," with the [n̩] acting as the full second syllable. Consonants acting this way are called syllabic, as already mentioned. Indeed, even a voiceless fricative such as [s] can act syllabically, as it does in the interjection "Pssst!" Among the consonants, the liquids and nasals most commonly act as a syllable nucleus, both in English and in other languages. The fricatives, such as [s], much less commonly act this way—again, this is also true of languages other than English. The plosives do not act syllabically in English or any other language. Of course the glides are never syllabic in themselves, since they become vowels when syllabic.

There have been a number of attempts to correlate the notion of the syllable to articulatory or acoustic events, that is, to see whether an analysis of the sound patterns of speech will show recognizable syllabic boundaries. This effort has not been particularly successful. From the articulatory point of view, there have been attempts to link the syllable with patterns of respiration. This has not been very successful either. Also, any attempt to define a syllable by pauses in speech is doomed to failure, because in running speech we simply do not pause between syllables.

Perhaps the best characterization of the syllable relies on the notion of degree of openness of individual phones, and calls the most open phone the syllable nucleus. Briefly, it works like this. All phones are rated according to the degree of openness of the vocal tract. The low vowels are the most open, followed by high vowels, then liquids, then nasals, glides, fricatives, trills, flaps, and plosives, in that order. A syllable is characterized by a more open segment surrounded by less open segments (or by nothing at all). The word "button" (pronounced [bʌtn̩]) provides an example. [ʌ] is a syllable nucleus, being surrounded by less open segments. [n̩] has a less open segment on one side and nothing on the other. The word is defined as having two syllables, since the [t] is between two segments more open than itself, that is, the oral tract is quite open for [ʌ], becomes less open, and then becomes more open again, indicating that one has crossed a syllable boundary.

While this means of defining the syllable is better than most others, it is not without its problems. For example, by this definition, a word like "beats" would be defined as having two syllables, since there is an open segment ([i]) followed by a less open segment ([t]), followed in turn by a segment more open than the [t], namely [s]. This difficulty can be avoided by a rule that states that a fricative may act as a syllable nucleus only when surrounded by plosives or other segments that rate very low on the scale of openness, as in the English expression "Pssst!" Any definition, apparently, will have to be qualified with such riders and conditions.

So there is left the intuitive notion of the syllable and the one concrete fact that each syllable contains one vowel or diphthong (or nonplosive consonant acting vocalically). As in other areas, however, intuition should not be the only criterion. For example, if asked to divide the phrase "not at all" into syllables, most people would divide it between the words, but many do not pronounce it that way. Often the /t/ of "at" is attached to the word "all," so that the three syllables are "not-a-tall." Other speakers go even further, attaching the /t/ of "not" (pronounced as a flap [ɾ], since it comes at the beginning of a weakly stressed syllable) to the following word, giving [nɑ-ɾə-tɑl] (syllable breaks are marked with hyphens).

This process of dividing an expression into syllables, ignoring the word divisions as we speak, has even permanently changed some words in our language. For example, the word "napkin" used to be "apkin" but was changed through the influence of the indefinite article. Thus "an apkin" came to be pronounced "a napkin," and the change became permanent. Interestingly, the word "apron" is related to the word "napkin" but did not undergo the same change. The words "newt" and "nickname" underwent a similar process.

At this point it is necessary to introduce a few new terms, in order to have labels for some important concepts. Sometimes it is necessary to distinguish between syllables that end with a consonant and those that do not. If a syllable ends with a consonant, it is called a **closed** syllable; the words "up," "hut," "asks," and "treat" are examples of closed syllables in English. If a syllable ends in a vowel with no consonant following, it is called an **open** syllable. Examples in English would be such words as "I," "tree," "through," "oh," and "straw." Remember that whether or not a syllable is closed depends upon how it is pronounced, not upon how it is spelled.

The consonant that begins a syllable is often called the **releasing** consonant. The letter t represents the releasing consonant in each of these English one-syllable words: "to," "top," "tree," and "town." Of course, despite the spelling, the releasing consonant of the word "through" is [θ] and not [t]. The consonant that closes a syllable is called the **arresting** consonant; /t/ is the arresting consonant in these words: "best," "passed" ([pæst]), "put," and "hut."[1]

One other term is necessary before we proceed to examine the English syllable. A group of consonants together in the same syllable without vowels in between is called a **cluster** (or sometimes a **blend**). For example, there is a cluster at the beginning of the word "tree" and one at the end of the word "eats." There are no clusters in the word "thought" since it is sound, not spelling, that counts. There is no cluster in the word "handy" since the /n/ is the arresting consonant of the first syllable and the /d/ is the releasing consonant of the second syllable.

## 12-2.1 Importance of the Syllable as a Phonetic Unit

Before making a study of the phonotactics of the English syllable, we should take a moment to consider the role of the syllable in the phonetic structure of a language. Clearly it is a basic unit, as shown by a number of phenomena. (1) Phonotactic rules are based mostly on the syllable rather than on the word; that is, there are restrictions on the combinations and ordering of phonemes in the syllable, but few further restrictions are needed to describe the word. (2) The syllable is considered a basic unit for spelling in those languages using syllabic writing systems (Chapter 4); there is even evidence that reading is faster with such a writing system. (3) As Chapter 13 will show, the rhythm of many languages (English not among them) is based on the syllable. (4) Word stress (Chapter 9) is a syllable-level phenomenon.

(5) Also, there is some psycholinguistic support for the notion that the syllable is the basic unit of spoken language. Some experimental evidence for this follows. As stated by Lieberman [1975],

> The coding and decoding of speech in terms of syllables is an essential aspect of human linguistic ability. Children who have severe reading "disabilities" can, for example, be taught to read with 3 to 6 hours of tutoring by making use of a syllabic notation [Rozin et al., 1971]. Traditional methods of teaching reading essentially assume that the phonemic level of language is basic (roughly the alphabetic level). Much of the difficulty in teaching children to read can be overcome if intermediate units, representing syllables, are used to introduce reading [p. 9].

In an experiment by Schumsky [1977], children with reading deficiencies were taught "pig latin," which, as every child knows, is a coded form of English based on moving the first consonant phoneme in a word. Little success was achieved, but when such children were taught so-called "syl-

---

[1] A word of caution regarding these terms is necessary. Vowels are sometimes classified as **close** (meaning 'high') and **open** (meaning 'low'). It is important to keep those concepts separate from the idea of **closed** and **open** syllables. It is also important to remember what it means to **release** a plosive consonant (see sections 8-2.6 and 10-5.1) and to keep this notion separate from the **releasing** consonant of a syllable. For example, one could say that, in the speech of a certain individual, "the arresting consonant was released." This is not a contradiction in terms. The confusing similarity of terms having very different meanings results from the haphazard way that terminology develops in any science over the years. All that can be done is to take precautions where confusion is likely to result.

latin," in which the whole first syllable was moved to the end of the word, much more success was obtained.

(6) Finally, as indicated in section 8-8.1, a syllable such as [pæt] cannot be segmented *acoustically*. Of course, the speaker or listener will *feel* that the word can be segmented, and the phonetician might want to segment the articulatory gestures involved in producing the syllable. But acoustically, the plosive consonants in such a syllable are not independent from the vowel. Our perception of speech must therefore take into account the syllable as a whole.

These facts and others underline the degree to which the syllable, rather than the phone or phoneme, is a basic phonetic unit in speech.

## 12-3 The Phonotactics of the English Syllable

In Chapter 4, we mentioned syllable structure briefly in introducing syllabic writing. Let us now look more closely at the English syllable.

In Table 12.1, examples of the various possible forms for English syllables are given. Each English syllable has a vowel or diphthong, and the list is arranged by the number of consonants preceding and following the vowel. However, before looking at the list, it is important to realize that your dialect of

**Table 12.1.** Phonotactics of the English Syllable

| Number of Consonants Before Vowel | Number of Consonants After Vowel | Some Sample Words |
|---|---|---|
| 0 | 0 | oh, ah, I, eye |
| 0 | 1 | at, up, ought, in |
| 0 | 2 | ask, oust, eighth, elf, apt |
| 0 | 3 | asks, ousts |
| 1 | 0 | to, how, pea, though |
| 1 | 1 | tot, hut, thought |
| 1 | 2 | task, takes, rats |
| 1 | 3 | tasks, pests |
| 1 | 4 | sixths |
| 2 | 0 | tree, spy, through, schwa |
| 2 | 1 | stick, stop, steak, trap |
| 2 | 2 | stops, steaks, trust |
| 2 | 3 | trusts, tramps |
| 2 | 4 | twelfths |
| 3 | 0 | spry, squaw, straw |
| 3 | 1 | streak, squeak, straight |
| 3 | 2 | strains, squeaks, scrapes |
| 3 | 3 | sprints, splints |
| 3 | 4 | strengths [strɛŋkθs] |

Note: These one-syllable words are arranged in order by the number of consonants preceding and following the nucleus (vowel or diphthong). As always, it is pronunciation and not spelling that matters. The final word ("strengths") might not be counted because the [k] is epenthetic rather than phonemic. Note that polysyllabic words may contain some syllables not found in any one-syllable word; for example, schwa does not occur in one-syllable words when stressed but may be contained in one or more syllables of a polysyllabic word.

English might simplify some of the more complex syllables. For example, in a word such as "sixths" (/sɪksθs/), there is a cluster of four consonants following the vowel. Most of us do not usually pronounce all four final consonants; rather, we simplify the cluster to /sɪks/. The list shows the most complex possible English syllables, which may be subject to simplification in some or many dialects; it is not intended to indicate the "correct" pronunciation.

Table 12.1 shows that the form of the English syllable can be summarized in the formula (CCC)V(CCCC). This simply means that the English syllable can have from zero to three consonants, C, followed by a mandatory vowel or diphthong, V, followed by zero to four consonants. (In the formula, parentheses indicate optional phonemes.)

The number of consonants one counts will depend on several theoretical issues. (1) Are affricates one or two consonants? Does the word "plunged" have three or four consonants following the vowel? Because of the way affricates behave in English, we are counting them as one unit. (2) How does one count the plosive that often intervenes between a nasal and a homorganic fricative? Is "fence" /fɛns/ or /fɛnts/? Phonetically, [t] should be counted if it is pronounced, but it is questionable whether the **phoneme** /t/ is present, and since phonotactics deals with the phonemes, it may be best not counted. (3) Does one count a sequence such as that found in the English word "or" as a diphthong or a sequence of vowel plus consonant? As pointed out in section 7-5.1, either may be satisfactory. Once again, phonetically, it is more accurate to speak of a diphthong, but phonemically we are dealing with a sequence of vowel plus consonant.

The formula given above, indicating the number of consonants in an English syllable, is one aspect of phonotactics. It is clear that a syllable of the form CCVCCCCC could not be an English syllable (but may be possible in another language). There is more to phonotactics: not any phoneme can go in any place in the formula. There are never two plosive consonants in a cluster before a vowel; /pti/ could not be an English word, even though it is made up of English phonemes.[2] If the releasing cluster contains two consonants, one of which is a plosive, the cluster must take one of these two forms: (1) /s/ followed by a voiceless plosive: "speed," "stop," "skate"; or (2) a plosive followed by an approximant: "please," "blue," "pray," "brat," "beauty" /bjuti/, "gray" (/w/ only in borrowed words such as "bwana"; and /j/ following /t/ or /d/ only in some dialects: "tube," "duty").

In all cases where three consonants precede the vowel, the first must be /s/, the second a voiceless plosive, and the third an approximant: "streak," "squeeze," "spleen," "spew," "skew," "scrape," etc.

A cluster may be formed of a fricative and certain approximants: "thwart," "slip," "flip," "friction." Notice that most, if not all, releasing fricatives that form part of a cluster are voiceless: we have "slip," but not "*zlip."

Nasals also form releasing clusters, either following a fricative or preceding /j/: "small" and "mew" ("new" may have a cluster /nj/ or a single consonant /n/, depending on the dialect).

Alveopalatal fricatives cannot enter into releasing clusters as can

---

[2] Once again we should note that it is sound and not spelling that counts. There is no initial cluster in the word pterodactyl, for example.

other fricatives: we have "flip" and "slip," but no "*shlip." German and Yiddish permit /š/ in releasing clusters, and some words have been borrowed into American English in this form, though these are mostly restricted to certain dialects. Notice that the word "strafe," which comes from the German strafen (/štʀɑfən/; 'to punish'), has been modified to suit English phonotactic restrictions.

Almost any consonant can release a syllable singly. The exceptions are /ŋ/, which never precedes a vowel in the same syllable, and /ž/, which normally only releases a syllable other than the first syllable of a word (of course, it can be argued that the /ž/ of "measure" is the arresting consonant of the first syllable and not the releasing consonant of the second). Some people will pronounce a borrowed French word such as genre with a /ž/ in initial position, but this is not typical of English pronunciation. Also, in some dialects, /ž/ is not an arresting consonant in word-final position. "Measure" may be pronounced /mɛžɚ/, but "garage" is /gəræǰ/. A speaker of this dialect can, of course, pronounce /ž/, as he does in "measure," but there is a phonotactic restriction against pronouncing it in word-final position.

In English, only tense vowels occur in open syllables. So, there are words like "beet," "bean," and "bee," but with the lax vowel only "bit" and "bin," never a word like /bɪ/. It is not just that this word does not happen to exist but that the vowel /ɪ/ never occurs in a word-final open syllable. Similarly, one can examine the other lax vowels /ʊ/ and /ɛ/ from this point of view.

## 12-3.1 The Syllable in Phonotactic Restrictions

Many of the phonotactic restrictions mentioned are in reference to the syllable (this is why the syllable was discussed at some length). For instance, the restrictions noted on clusters apply within single syllables: consonants that happen to be juxtaposed across syllable boundaries do not have the same restrictions;[3] for example, /stv/ is not a permissible cluster in English, but these consonants can come together in an English word when a syllable boundary intervenes, as in the word "postvocalic."

However, there seem to be some restrictions on the combinations that can occur even across syllable boundaries. Many individuals avoid the sequence of two fricatives (/fθ/) in such words as "diphthong" and "diphtheria," replacing the first with the stop /p/. The word diphthong provides an interesting example of a different phonotactic restriction in another language. It comes from the Greek and can be analyzed as di ('two') phthong ('sound')—note the related words monophthong and triphthong. The releasing cluster of the second part of this word has had two forms in Greek, neither of which is phonotactically acceptable in English. Classical Greek pronunciation would have had /pt/ as its releasing cluster. Modern Greek permits /fθ/ as a releasing cluster. But notice that in English we divide this word into syllables thus: diph-thong. Such a division is consistent with English phonotactics, not with the origin of this word, since phthong could stand alone.

But not all phonotactic restrictions relate to the syllable. As shown

---

[3] **Cluster** is defined as a group of consonants *within the same syllable* and having no intervening vowel.

above, the phone [ž] in English is restricted as to its place in a word, not only as to its place in a syllable, and restrictions on lax vowels affect only **word-final** open syllables, not all open syllables.

## 12-4  Dialect Differences in Phonotactic Restrictions

A few dialect differences in phonotactic patterns have already been mentioned, particularly with respect to the phone [ž]. A few others follow.

Not everyone pronounces some of the consonant clusters as indicated in Table 12.1. The reduction of various consonant clusters is characteristic of many dialects, while the specifics of this reduction will vary from dialect to dialect. To take one example, Black English of the United States has a tendency to reduce consonant clusters in word-final position. Clusters of two phonemes are often reduced to one, and clusters of three phonemes are often reduced to two or even one. Thus, "tests" and "test" may both be pronounced /tɛs/, and similar changes occur in other words. This reduction is more common with homorganic clusters (e.g., "tend" becomes [tɛn]) and with final clusters made up of plosives (e.g., "act" becomes [æk]).

It is important for the speech pathologist to be familiar with dialects other than his/her own, in order that dialect features are not diagnosed as misarticulations. In the example given above, it is clear that a person pronouncing "test" as [tɛs] does not have any difficulty articulating the phone [t], and should not be diagnosed as such; it is merely a dialect feature of the *distribution* of the sounds. (The "missing" /t/ reappears in the form "testing.")

Of course, it may well be that a person who is interested in acting, announcing, or running for public office may wish to have speech training in order to lose some of the distinctive characteristics of his native dialect. There is nothing automatically right or wrong about trying to eliminate dialect characteristics—phonotactic or others—from an individual's speech. What is important is not to diagnose dialect features as misarticulations and to attempt to eliminate these from your client's speech when it is not desired. The problem is small if your client is an adult, but with children much time could be wasted trying to achieve an unwanted goal.

## 12-5  Some Practical Implications of Phonotactics

The most significant aspects of phonotactics for our purposes are twofold: first, one should see that the patterning of phonemes is regular and systematic, governed by phonotactic rules; and second, as a consequence of this, an individual may be quite able to pronounce a sound in one context but not in another.

One proof that the phonetic structure of a language (including its phonotactic restrictions) is regular is that when we make up a nonsense word—for a children's story, or to name a new invention or product—it is never *phonetic* nonsense; that is, such a word will use English phonemes, and will order them according to English phonotactic restrictions (they will also be subject to normal English patterns of stress and assimilation). An English-speaking person would not invent a nonsense word that conformed to French phonetic patterns, and a consumer product would not be likely to sell if its name were unpronounceable. Sometimes nonsense words or product names break English spelling rules—like the company name Exxon with its double x—but the *pronunciation* is not nonsense; it could be an English word. Sometimes science fiction writers make up unpronounceable names for alien beings, but such stories are usually read silently. We would never put unpronounceable nonsense in a play, movie, or children's story, and certainly not on a new product we wished to sell.

The individual speaker's grammar contains rules describing the phonotactic patterning, and these rules may or may not be the same as yours or those of "standard" English. The consequences for teaching the articulation of sounds are enormous. There is a world of difference between not being able to pronounce a certain sound and not being used to pronouncing it in certain contexts or combinations.

As an example of *context,* the English speaker learning French may have trouble with words like je, jamais, and genre, which have [ž] as their initial sound. It is not that the English speaker is unused to saying [ž]—all but a few dialects have this sound in words such as "vision" and "leisure"—but that the English speaker is not used to saying it *in word-initial position.* The experienced teacher of French will use the familiar contexts in introducing the French sound, and it will not seem so difficult to the learner.

Also, it may be the *combinations* that are difficult. In learning German, it may be difficult for some to pronounce a word like Knabe (/knɑbə/) very well—they may insert an epenthetic /ə/ between the /k/ and the /n/ to break up the unfamiliar cluster. Of course, it would not be correct to conclude that they cannot pronounce /k/ or /n/, since they can, perfectly well. It would not even be correct to say that they have difficulty pronouncing /k/ and /n/ when they are adjacent—they can in a word like "breakneck." It is when they are adjacent *in the same syllable* that there may be difficulty. It would not be very helpful for a German teacher to drill students on pronouncing these phones individually, since it is the combination that needs practice.

But in studying either German or French, there would be trouble with the vowel /y/ for a different reason: this sound does not occur in English in *any* combination or position. Learning it is quite a different matter from learning to say [ž] in an unusual context.

The foreign speaker learning English is likely to speak in a way that conforms to the phonotactic structure of his native language. A speaker of Spanish, for example, is likely to pronounce school as /ɛskul/, since Spanish does not begin any words with the /sk/ cluster. When the /k/ follows /s/ in Spanish, the phonemes are in different syllables. Thus, the addition of the initial vowel sound makes school into a two-syllable word that can be pronounced easily by the Spanish speaker. Here is another example of the speaker having difficulty not with individual sounds but with their combination and ordering.

As noted in Chapter 4, the phonotactic structure of Japanese requires that every syllable be either of the form V or of the form CV (that is, either a vowel alone or a consonant followed by a vowel). When a Japanese speaker pronounces an English word, consonant clusters are broken up and arresting consonants are followed by an extra vowel. A Japanese would likely pronounce club as /kurubu/, knife as /naifu/, and tranquilizer as /turɑnkuaizɑ/ (/n/ being vocalic in Japanese). In fact, these words have been borrowed into Japanese in these forms.

This process of adding epenthetic vowels to break up consonant clusters is quite common to foreign speakers of English whose native language does not have the complex clusters of English.

All of us make articulation errors of a phonotactic variety when we try to pronounce tongue twisters quickly. It is the phonotactic structure of the phrase that leads us astray: the frequent repetitions and the combinations of sounds.

Pronunciation errors besides those made in tongue twisters may be phonotactic as well. The word "statistics" is one that causes problems for many individuals whom we would not describe as having an articulation disorder. One of my friends has difficulty with words that contain /m/ and /n/ in adjacent syllables, such as "women," "cinnamon," and "minimum." This particular problem is subclinical and does not reflect any articulation difficulty with either /m/ or /n/. Words with repetitions of either nasal cause no difficulty; "banana," for example, presents no problem for this individual.

Thus, in analyzing the errors made by an individual with an articulation difficulty, it may be useful to determine whether the problem is phonotactic in nature. Does the individual make the error everywhere or only in certain combinations? If everywhere, then the approach will be one of articulatory therapy. But if the error is made only in certain combinations, exercises should aim at expanding the environments in which the sound is correctly pronounced. When the individual can pronounce a phone in isolation but not in certain combinations, graded pronunciation exercises may be helpful. Start with simple clusters (using some of the principles outlined in section 10-9) and work up to the more complex ones found in the everyday spoken language.

The phonotactic approach is useful because, whenever a context can be found in which the troublesome sound is correctly pronounced, one already has a foot in the door toward expanding the contexts in which proper articulation occurs.

## Questions for Discussion

1. How do you use your intuitive knowledge of English phonotactics in solving crossword puzzles?
2. Comment on the phonotactic patterning of consonants in these words: sphere, thwart, spleen.
3. Analyze phonotactic regularities in arresting clusters as was done for releasing clusters in section 12-3.
4. What is indicated about changes in phonotactic patterns by the spelling of these words: bdellium, mnemonic, knight, limb, sing, pneumonia, pterodactyl, ptomaine, psychology, gnat, xenon?
5. Find other words like those in question 4.
6. For the words in question 4, consult an etymological dictionary and find out which words reflect a change in English phonotactic patterns and which reflect foreign phonotactic patterns that were modified when the words were borrowed into English. Include the words agnostic and diagnosis on the list.
7. What phonotactic patterns, foreign to English, are used in these foreign words: Knabe (German); psychologie, trois (French); Nguyen (Vietnamese name)?

8. An interesting historical phonotactic change has taken place in English. Note the spelling and pronunciation of the following sets of words:

| | |
|---|---|
| limb | limp |
| jamb | camp |
| comb | tramp |
| | |
| sing | sink |
| sang | sank |
| fling | frank |
| | |
| pinned | pint |
| wind | hint |
| hind | went |

a. What overall pattern do you see? What exceptions are there?
b. There is a dialect in which the following words (and words like them) are pronounced as indicated. How does this fit the pattern established above?

| | |
|---|---|
| wind | [wɪn] |
| went | [wɛnt] |
| hind | [hain] |
| pint | [paint] |

**Annotated Bibliography**

A discussion of phonotactics is not found in most introductory phonetics textbooks. There is a good discussion found in O'Connor [1973], and a thorough study of the question is reported in Schole's *Phonotactic Grammaticality* [1966]. Chapter 6 of Hill [1958] contains a concise discussion of the phonotactic structure of English, including final clusters (which may be helpful in answering question 3).

# Chapter 13

## Sentence Stress, Timing, and Intonation

### 13-1 Introduction

Previous chapters have dealt mostly with the individual **phonemes** or **segments** of which speech is composed. Here we will look at a group of phenomena whose effect crosses the boundaries between individual segments and that are thus appropriately called **suprasegmentals.** These include stress, timing, and intonation.

Once again, we must caution against the vague use of terms. Terms such as **accent** or **intonation** are frequently used loosely for a variety of aspects of speech. Here, however, these various terms will be used with precise meanings. The term **accent** has so many different meanings that it will be avoided in the present discussion.

### 13-2 Stress

In section 9-3 three types of stress were distinguished: word, phrase, and sentence stress. Here, the latter two kinds will be dealt with. The terms **word stress** and **sentence stress** may be misleading at first. As shown in Chapter 9, word stress operates phonetically on the **syllable**—for example, "cónvict" and "convíct" are distinguished by the differing degrees of stress on the individual syllables. This is called *word* stress, however, since, functionally, this type of stress serves to distinguish *words* (in those languages where it is used). In a similar way, sentence stress results from the stressing of certain *words*. Again, this is called *sentence* stress because it affects the meaning of the *sentence*. If a person says "I didn't break it" as opposed to "I didn't <u>break</u> it," certain individual words are stressed differently, but this does not change the meaning of the individual words <u>I</u> or <u>break</u>; rather, it affects the interpretation of the sentence *as a whole*.

In this discussion of stress, whether it is stress of syllables or whole words, the acoustic effect is similar to that discussed in Chapter 9. Stressed syllables or words are spoken more loudly, more slowly, and more distinctly, and assimilations with surrounding sounds are reduced.

## 13-2.1 Phrase Stress

Many short phrases take a distinctive stress pattern in English, determined by the syntactic (grammatical) or semantic relationship of the words in the phrase. In an adjective-noun combination, the adjective usually takes secondary stress while the noun takes primary stress:

> Ìt's â whìte hoúse.
>
> Ìt's â blàck boárd.

(The stress marks were explained in section 9-1.) This pattern is in contrast to compound nouns made up of an adjective plus a noun or two nouns:

> Ìt's thê Whíte Hoùse (or Whíte Hoùse).
>
> Ìt's â bláckboàrd.

The second element of the compound may take tertiary or secondary stress. Note that a compound noun does not need to be *spelled* as one word in order to be *pronounced* as a compound and to function as one. The term White House is pronounced as a compound noun, as are the underlined words in the sentences below:

> He's reached middle age.
>
> He's just a lame duck (a helpless, ineffectual person).

Contrast the stress pattern of these phrases with the following ones:

> It happened in the Middle Ages.
>
> It's a lame duck (duck with a broken leg).

Just a word stress provides a means for signaling meaning differences, so too phrase stress allows a distinction in speech between a blackbird and a black bird, between a hot dog (frankfurter) and a hot dog (overheated canine), an English teacher (teacher of English literature or language) and an English teacher (teacher whose nationality is English), and between a German shepherd (kind of dog) and a German shepherd (German sheepherder).

## 13-2.2 Sentence Stress

Within the English sentence, certain words carry heavier stress than others. Let us look at one sentence to see that this is so:

> The couple came to the party.

We see (or hear), barring contrastive or emphatic use of stress, that the words couple, came, and party are more heavily stressed than the other words in the sentence. Notice that these are the so-called content words (those containing the greatest semantic or meaningful information—usually nouns, verbs, adjectives, and adverbs) as opposed to the weakly stressed **function** words (articles, prepositions, and so on, necessary for syntactic completeness, but usually low in meaning content). Note that words often change their syntactic or semantic role, so it would not be correct to say that a certain word, such as to, is never stressed. In the sentence

> The (unconscious) man came to.

the word to carries heavier stress than it did in the first example. In this latter sentence to is part of the verb and plays a greater role in carrying the meaning of the sentence than it did in the previous example (note the effect of leaving out the word to in each sentence).

As a result of the varying degrees of stress on words in a sentence, the pronunciation of individual words may be very different in a sentence from their pronunciation in isolation. For example, if asked to transcribe phonetically the word to, it might be written [tʰu], but in the sentence "The couple came to the party," to may be reduced to a [t] (forming an affricate with the [ð] of the). In the sentence "The couple went to the party," to may disappear except as a slightly prolonged occlusion of the [t] of went. In either of these sentences, the word to may be pronounced as [tə] because of its reduced stress. In the sentence "The man came to," to is more heavily stressed, with a full vowel. In the sentence "The children came too," too may be heavily stressed, having a full, slightly diphthongized vowel.

From this example, it is evident that stress (and vowel reduction resulting from stress) depends in large measure on the sentence in which a word is situated. In a sentence, the various syllables of a polysyllabic word generally retain their *relative* degree of stress (the weakest syllable is still the weakest and the strongest, strongest), but the *absolute* degree of stress may be changed in a sentence. For example, the word pimento will still show three levels of stress if heavily stressed in a sentence, but may be more heavily stressed than when pronounced in isolation.

It is for this reason that in analyzing the stress of sentences, generally *four* levels of stress are distinguished (as mentioned in Chapter 9), called primary, secondary, tertiary, and weak. In Chapter 9, however, we did not distinguish **tertiary** and **weak** since we were dealing with only three levels. In discussing sentences, some authors make a careful distinction between tertiary and weak stress; the marks ´, `, and ˆ are used for primary, secondary, and tertiary, respectively; and weakly stressed syllables are left unmarked. The details of this are beyond our present needs. We should, however, note the interaction between word stress and sentence stress.

13-2.3 Contrastive and Emphatic Stress

Just as word stress can be used contrastively (íllusion, not állusion), so too sentence stress can be used this way. For example, if speaking about someone named Bill who might be confused with another person named Bill, we might say

Bill Báker is bringing the soft drinks.

stressing the family name for **contrastive** purposes.

We may wish to stress certain individual words in a sentence in order to change the emphasis. Compare:

| | |
|---|---|
| I'm not a member of the party. | (statement of fact) |
| <u>I</u>'m not a member of the party. | (emphatic or contrastive: 'someone else is') |
| I'm <u>not</u> a member of the party. | (emphatic or denial) |
| I'm not a <u>member</u> of the party. | ('I may be associated with the party in other ways') |
| I'm not a member of <u>the</u> party. | (contrastive: 'I'm a member of a party but not the one being discussed') |
| I'm not a member of the <u>party</u>. | (contrastive: 'I'm a member of something, but not the party') |

Also, contrastive stress may be used when one feels that the listener may have expected hearing something else. For example:

The <u>consumer</u> is responsible for the oil shortage.

might be said if the speaker thought the listener would expect an accusing finger being pointed at the oil companies or the government.

In **emphatic** stress, we stress a particular word or phrase, not because it might be confused with something else, but because we wish to emphasize it. This may be because the term is a new one to the listener or may be a result of other factors, some noted in the examples above.

Today we will talk about <u>photosynthesis</u>. <u>Photosynthesis</u> is the process by which plants change light energy into chemical energy.

Here the stress is on a new term. In most textbooks one finds new terms underlined or in italics (the printed equivalents of verbal emphasis).

He's an <u>atheist</u>, you know.

Here the stress may be a result of the speaker's emotional reaction to the subject or because he wishes to draw attention to some aspect of the subject that he feels his listener will understand with a little prodding.

## 13-3 Timing

There are three main aspects to timing. The first concerns the overall rate of speech; the second aspect concerns the use of pauses; and the third aspect concerns the rhythm or cadence of the syllables.

### 13-3.1 Rate

The overall rate or speed of speech is determined by several factors. Some languages tend to be more rapidly spoken than others (but do not confuse the fact that foreign languages in which we are not fluent always sound terribly fast).

Within a certain language, speed may be determined in part by the emotional state of the speaker or the urgency of the message. As we become upset or excited, we speed up our rate. And of course warnings, whose content is very urgent, are spoken quickly.

The social situation, and its formality, affect the speed as well. A formal address, or a lecture, is generally delivered more slowly. One effect of this reduced rate is the reduction of sandhi (assimilation across word boundaries) and other assimilatory phenomena.

### 13-3.2 Pauses

Because of the influence of writing—in which words are separated by spaces—we tend to overestimate the number of pauses in speech. Normal speech is surprisingly fluent, with few pauses. What we may want to call pauses are often rather the *prolongation* of a preceding sound. Often, pauses are filled by "um" or "ah" or "er," particularly by nervous speakers.

Pauses (as we shall call them, even if they are in fact prolongations) do occur, and—frequently in combination with stress—help to make meaning distinctions. Examine these sentences (as spoken normally):

He came to.

He came, too.

In the first sentence, the words He and to are more heavily stressed than He and too in the second, and conversely, the word came is more heavily stressed in the second than in the first, but in combination with this, there is a slight pause or prolongation corresponding to the comma in the second sentence.

Compare these two sentences:

| | |
|---|---|
| He didn't stay because I was there. | ('He stayed, and my being there wasn't the reason for his staying.') |
| He didn't stay, because I was there. | ('He left because I was there.') |

These sentences, whose meaning is almost opposite, are distinguished by different stress, intonation (as will be shown later in the chapter), and a short pause or prolongation corresponding to the comma in the second sentence.

Pauses in speech may also be caused by the speaker's searching for the right word. Certainly this may be the case with dysphasic individuals or people with poor memory. Sometimes, though, speakers may use the pause even when they know what they are about to say, for dramatic or emphatic effect:

What this country needs is . . . morality in government!

Who knows? . . . The Shadow knows!

A series of dots is the usual way of indicating a pause, and while it is not an official phonetic symbol, it could be used in transcriptions for this purpose.

Another case in which pauses appear to occur is in the speech of stutterers. Foreign speakers also may pause to consider their choice of words or syntactic construction.

It is a curious fact that a great percentage of fluent speakers have great difficulty reading aloud. When asked to do so, they put pauses (as well as stress) in all the wrong places, despite the fact that when speaking normally they put pauses and stress at the appropriate places.

13-3.3 Rhythm

The rhythm of speech is related to the frequency of syllables; this is of course partly dependent on rate (section 13-3.1). Languages also differ in the criteria for timing syllables.

As shown earlier (section 13-2), not every syllable is stressed in an English sentence; strongly stressed syllables occur at intervals depending on syntactic, semantic, and emphatic considerations. It is these strongly stressed syllables, and not the total number of syllables, that determine the rhythm of an English sentence. For example, O'Connor [1973] cites this pair of sentences:

The man laughed.

The manager laughed.

In each sentence there are two strongly stressed syllables: <u>man</u> and <u>laughed</u>. The length of these sentences is very close to being the same; the *length of time between strongly stressed syllables is very nearly constant*. In the first sentence, there is a compensatory lengthening of the word <u>man</u>.

Similarly, the phrases below have a different number of syllables:

The big man.

The violent man.

They are about the same length when spoken, however, since each has two main stressed syllables.

If it is difficult to believe that this is so, try saying the expressions in time with a metronome whose beats synchronize with the stressed syllables, or beat the rhythm with your knuckles on the desk. This should work not only with the examples above but with virtually any English sentence spoken in a normal conversational way (it is of course possible to disrupt the usual rhythm intentionally).

This type of rhythm, which is determined by stressed syllables, is called **stress-timed rhythm.** It is the rhythm of English and numerous other languages. It has a particularly staccato pattern since there is an uneven and changing number of syllables between successive beats (strongly stressed syllables).

Many languages, such as French, have a type of rhythm based on the total number of syllables. Each syllable takes approximately the same amount of time, so the overall length of a spoken sentence depends on the number of syllables in it. Such a system is called **syllable-timed rhythm.**

If English is spoken with syllable-timed rhythm, it will sound unnatural and stilted. The hearing-impaired have a tendency toward such a rhythm, giving equal weight and time to all syllables. Of course, the foreign speaker whose native language has syllable-timed rhythm can be expected to carry this pattern over inappropriately when learning English. For teaching purposes, a dramatic demonstration of the appropriate rhythm can be made by speaking with a metronome.

## 13-4 Intonation

As has been demonstrated, stress and timing are related in the English sentence; these two suprasegmentals are combined to produce a desired slant on a sentence. Intonation patterns are also often combined to give the overall pattern, and they contribute to the meaning of the sentence almost as much as the words. Although stress, timing, and intonation are usually combined in speech, let us examine intonation separately.

### 13-4.1 The Mechanism of Intonation

The fundamental frequency of the voice is the frequency (speed of vibration) of the vocal folds. The normal frequency is dependent upon the age and sex of the individual but may be varied within a certain range at will by the speaker. This is effected by a change in tension on certain muscles associated with the vocal folds. For instance, one adult male may have a normal fundamental of 125 Hz and a range of 80 to 200 Hz. A certain adult female may have a normal fundamental of 225 Hz and a range of 150 to 300 Hz.

This fundamental frequency is for the most part independent of the formant (resonant) frequencies of the vocalic sounds. What this means is that one can change the fundamental frequency of the voice *without* changing the speech sounds themselves. This is exactly what happens in singing. The vowel /ɑ/, for example, can be sung or spoken on a high note, a middle note, or a low note, but *it is still the vowel* /ɑ/: the phone stays the same while the fundamental frequency changes.[1]

---

[1] Singers become unintelligible when drowned out by the music or when singing very loudly or at the extremes of their range. And when a singer hits a particularly high note, there may be so much distance between the harmonics of the fundamental that there is little energy to excite resonance at the frequencies of the first and second formants.

From the viewpoint of the listener, what is heard is the same vowel /ɑ/ said at a different musical pitch. **Pitch** is a term reserved for our perception of frequency—as the frequency increases, we say that the pitch is higher. If we heard an individual saying /ɑ/ on a high and a low note, we would perceive a change in pitch. If the individual said a sentence with different *patterns of pitch changes*, this would have linguistic significance. It would affect the *meaning* of the sentence, as in this example:

You're going.

You're going?

The two sentences contain the same words and the same phones but different patterns of pitch. Such patterns or contours of pitch change, carrying meaningful information, are called **intonation.** (A spectrogram showing graphically the mechanism of intonation can be seen in Figure 8.16.)

## 13-4.2 The Role of Intonation

Intonation plays a role in carrying the meaning of an English sentence. The two sentences listed above both have the very same words, yet their meanings are quite different. This difference is signaled by the intonation patterns (which are indicated—inadequately—in writing by certain punctuation marks: the period, exclamation mark, and question mark).

Let us examine some intonation contours common to a number of types of sentences. The number of possible different contours is very large, so we will look only at certain basic types.

In a statement, there is usually a relatively level intonation, with a slight rise near the end and a fall at the end:

That is my house.

In a question, the opposite pattern is normally found: a slight fall near the end followed by a rise at the end:

Where are you going?

The exclamation has a pattern similar to that of the statement but with a sharper fall in pitch at the end (and generally a louder voice than in the statement):

You can't go!

If a sentence is very short, one or two words long, the full intonation pattern of a longer sentence occurs but is compressed:

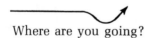

"May I go?"    "No."    "No?"    "No!"

If a sentence is long, there may be variations in intonation corresponding to phrases, clauses, or other syntactic divisions:

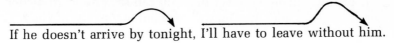

If he doesn't arrive by tonight, I'll have to leave without him.

Lists have a distinctive intonation pattern that separates the individual items and indicates the last item:

I have to buy butter, eggs, cheese, and milk.

In each of the cases above, note that it is the **syntactic structure** of the sentences that determines the appropriate intonation pattern. For this reason, intonation patterns will distinguish between otherwise phonetically similar sentences when their grammatical structure is different. For example, re-examine the following sentences, which we have already noted as having different timing:

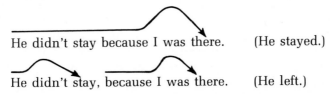

He didn't stay because I was there.     (He stayed.)

He didn't stay, because I was there.     (He left.)

It should be noted that it is the **relative** pitch of the voice (not the absolute frequency) that is used in intonation. Since a male's voice is generally lower than a female's, he will start lower and end lower than the female but will have rises and falls of pitch relative to his normal frequency. The female's voice will rise and fall around *her* normal frequency. Her *lows* may be higher than the average male's *highs*, but this poses no problem for comprehension, since it is the changes relative to normal pitch, and not the absolute frequency, that we pay attention to in speech.

Interestingly, the first aspect of language that a child learns is the general patterns of intonation and rhythm. It seems likely that the first part of the speech signal that the child picks out of his environment is the fundamental frequency of vocal fold vibration. He attends to the way these patterns are modulated long before he hears or attempts to produce individual phonemes. There may be some survival benefit in attending to a parent's voice, and certainly the voice of the mother will comfort a child and relax him. Lullabies have a calming effect on children before they learn to understand the individual words, more so than the effect of music alone.

Infants learn the intonation patterns of the language that they are exposed to. Before they have begun to speak, it is common for children to engage in what is called **jargoning**: the child hums and babbles syllables in recognizable intonation patterns typical of the language to which he is exposed.

It is also interesting to note how dogs respond to human speech. If you have a dog that will respond appropriately to several verbal commands, try this: give one command in the tone of voice (with the loudness, rhythm, and intonation) of a different command. For example, say "Stay" the way that you usually say "Sit" (and be careful not to give visual commands, such as hand signals). You will likely discover that you can say *any* word having the right number of syllables, and the dog will respond to the tone of voice. To the dog, the message is primarily in the suprasegmental pattern of speech and not in the phonemes that make up the word.

The use of intonation in adult speech will be considered in more detail. When two or three people are having a conversation, they rarely interrupt one another (unless they are arguing or are particularly aggressive). There must be some kind of signal we give when we are finished speaking. One aspect of this signal is in *what* we say, but *how* we say it (the suprasegmentals) contributes as well. The last sentence of a discourse generally has a greater drop in pitch than that of an ordinary declarative sentence. This signals to our listener that we have finished talking. If we had just finished talking about one subject, but wished to continue talking, we would not let the pitch fall so far. That signals to our listener not to interrupt. In this way, pitch may be manipulated by an aggressive or argumentative person so as to prevent others from expressing their views. Pauses, too, would be short. Most of us are surprisingly meek about accepting and respecting these subtle signals from the person we are talking with. Intonation is one of those things that is a constant source of information that people respond to, yet few are consciously aware of it. In a case such as that just described, the suprasegmentals are not only operating as part of the sentence, but as part of the **discourse,** or unit of conversation.

It is interesting to note just how automatic the use of intonation is. In acting or dramatic reading, it is difficult to imitate the intonation pattern of an individual who is being interrupted. There is a strong tendency, when an individual *knows* he is going to be interrupted, to let the pitch fall just before the interruption. Of course, this is not done when there is a real interruption, so it is a dead giveaway of the anticipation and a sign of poor acting.

In sarcasm, irony, and dry humor, the intonation patterns are slightly different from those of normal sentences. Intonation can also be used for oratorical or argumentative effect. Quaverings in fundamental frequency signal nervousness, and conversely a firm control over pitch will inspire confidence in our listeners. It will also lend weight to what we say, whether or not there is any justification. Confidence men live up to their reputation as artists by manipulating intonation to good (or bad, depending on your point of view) effect. Also, individuals use very different intonation patterns when they read as compared to when they speak extemporaneously. That is why it is hard to sound relaxed and natural delivering a prepared speech that one is not familiar with. Public speakers need this talent. News announcers tend to compromise between a reading and a talking intonation: if they use the intonation of reading, they sound too dull; if they use a conversational intonation, they do not seem authoritative enough.

## 13-4.3 Suprasegmentals Are Used Together

Finally, let us note that stress, timing, and intonation are used together. In the sentence

I didn't do it.

the stressing of the word I is combined with modifications of the intonation pattern for the statement. And in the sentence,

> He didn't stay, because I was there.

a pause may be combined with the appropriate intonation pattern and stress on certain words. Excited speech is often betrayed by changes in rate, stress, and intonation.

## 13-5  Tone Languages

A language such as English, which uses the intonation patterns in the sentence to carry certain aspects of meaning, is often classed as an **intonation language.** By contrast, some languages, such as Chinese, many AmerIndian languages, and even Swedish, use pitch as a distinctive and inherent part of the *word.* Such languages may be referred to as **tone languages.**[2]

The first point to recognize in understanding the principle of tone languages is that the physiological mechanism of adjusting the vocal fold tension to achieve pitch changes is exactly the same in a tone and an intonation language. The only difference is the way in which the language *makes use of pitch to signal meaning differences.* Language, as we noted before, is an arbitrary system. One type of phonetic cue is used differently in different languages, just as the difference between two phones may be phonemic in one language, but not in another.

In an intonation language like English, as we saw, pitch plays a role at the level of the sentence (and also at the level of the discourse). In that sense, pitch plays a role in the syntax of the language. We distinguish "We're going" from "We're going?" by intonation, that is, patterns of pitch changes.

In a tone language such as Chinese, pitch is not a part of the sentence; it is part of the word. In English, we do not expect ban and pan to be related in meaning just because there is some phonetic similarity between them. In Chinese, do not expect má and mǎ to be related in meaning just because there is some phonetic similarity (the arrows indicate rising and falling pitch). To a person who speaks Chinese, the words má and mǎ sound like different words; they are completely unrelated words to a speaker of Chinese.

To demonstrate this principle, we will take an example from the so-called common tongue of China, known to most Westerners as the Mandarin dialect. For the purpose of this example, imagine a scale of pitch running from 1 to 5: 1 is the lowest pitch, and 5 is the highest pitch, with 3 being the middle point, close to the person's natural fundamental frequency. We cannot give absolute musical values to these pitch levels since, like intonation in English, the levels are relative to one another; a woman's level 1 would be higher than a man's. Also, there might be small differences in the extent of the range; one person's high and low might be closer together than another's in an absolute musical (pitch) sense.

Also in the example shown in Table 13.1 you will note that there is a difference in the speed of change of pitch. The two rising tones (tone 2 and tone

---

[2] Some authors make a finer division than this. For example, Lehiste [1970] divides languages into four types with respect to this point, but this is more detail than we need for our present purpose.

**Table 13.1.** Tones of the Common Tongue Dialect of Chinese

| Tone Number | Tone Name | Pitch at Start and End* | Quick or Slow Change | Example Word | English Meaning |
|---|---|---|---|---|---|
| 1 | High level | $4 \rightarrow 4$ | Not applicable | má | 'Mama' (mother) |
| 2 | High rising | $3 \rightarrow 5$ | Quick | má | 'Hemp' |
| 3 | Low rising | $2 \rightarrow 1 \rightarrow 4$ or 5 | Slow | mǎ | 'Horse' |
| 4 | Falling | $5 \rightarrow 1$ | Quick | mà | 'To scold' |
| — | Neutral | Depends on preceding tone | Not applicable | ma | Question marker |

*A pitch of 3 corresponds to the speaker's normal fundamental frequency; 5 is the highest pitch, 1 the lowest. Do not confuse the tone number, used as a name, with the pitch.

3) are different in this regard, and it is likely that this is important perceptually in distinguishing the tones in speech. Examine Table 13.1, which gives the tone patterns applied to the phoneme string /ma/ in the common tongue dialect.

In a Chinese sentence, the situation is complicated by the fact that there is a kind of sandhi between successive tones. The tone for the word <u>horse</u> would be different from that given in Table 13.1 in the context of the sentence "[The] horse runs." This is similar to phoneme assimilation and sandhi in English; words are not always pronounced in context the same as they are in isolation.

The tone differences in Chinese words make them phonetically distinct and therefore allow the different meanings to be attached to the otherwise same string of phonemes. We can therefore say that tone is **phonemic** in Chinese and other tone languages, whereas it is not in English.

In English, a one-word sentence has the intonation pattern of a longer sentence compressed into one word. So the sentence "No?" has a rising intonation, and the sentence "No." has a falling intonation. What is the difference between this and the Chinese word <u>ma</u> said with rising and falling intonation? Phonetically, there may be no difference, but functionally there is a very large difference in the use of pitch. If you ask the English speaker whether "No." and "No?" are the same word, he will answer that of course they are. The two have basically the same meaning and will have the same definition in the dictionary. It is true that there will be some difference in meaning, but this is relatively abstract. The <u>no</u> with falling pitch means something like, "The answer to the question is 'No.' " The <u>no</u> with rising pitch means something like, "Is the answer to the question really 'No'?" But there is a high proportion of common meaning between the two, and the differences become clear in the context of the conversation.[3]

[3] The importance of context is shown by the fact that there are variations in meaning depending on who is speaking to whom, and about what. Thus, "No?" could mean, (1) "I'm annoyed that you've said 'No' "; (2) "I'm very surprised you've said 'No'; you never have before." (3) "Secretly I'm happy that you've said 'No' because I wanted an excuse not to do it." You can imagine others; the point is that there is no one definition of the English word <u>no</u> spoken with rising pitch.

On the other hand, if you asked a Chinese speaker whether má and mǎ were the same word, he would answer that of course they are not. That would be like a Spanish-speaking person asking you whether "other" and "udder" were the same word. There is nothing common in meaning to such pairs, unless by coincidence.

Swedish uses the principle of tone in a different way; it has both tone and intonation. Most polysyllabic words are pronounced with a rise-fall tone pattern. This tone pattern, the unmarked or normal tone, called tone 1, is used for the vast majority of Swedish words. But certain words, which would otherwise be homophonous, have a fall-rise-fall tone pattern. This is tone 2, the marked or distinctive tone. Certain otherwise homophonous pairs are distinguished in pronunciation by the two tones. For example tanken pronounced with tone 1 means 'the tank'; with tone 2 it means 'the thought.' With tone 1 komma means 'comma'; with tone 2, it means 'to come.' The tone and intonation of Swedish combine in ways similar to word stress and sentence stress in English.

## 13-6 Practical Implications of Suprasegmentals

The suprasegmentals make a major contribution to speech. Inappropriate use of stress, timing, or intonation will lead to speech which is at worst unintelligible and at best stilted and unnatural. Thus in working in speech correction, deaf education, or second-language teaching, one must pay attention to these aspects of speech.

The rhythm of the sentence is one of the areas most susceptible to anomalies. The individual who is hearing-impaired, as we have noted, may tend to give equal stress to all syllables and thus to speak with syllable-timed rhythm rather than stress-timed rhythm. Similarly, an individual learning English as a second language may use syllable-timed rhythm if it is appropriate in his native language. The use of a metronome or knuckles on the desk, as already described, may make this point clear. Emphatic or contrastive stress does not usually present problems, particularly to second-language learners, since its use is probably universal, but the stressing of content words and reduction of function words may not be handled appropriately by the second-language learner or the hearing-impaired.

Intonation patterns present problems to the hearing-impaired for the obvious reason that they cannot hear them. However, individuals whose hearing loss is not profound may, with the help of amplification, be able to pick out the intonation contours of speech. Since the fundamental frequency is generally below 300 Hz, many hearing-impaired individuals with high-frequency hearing loss can pick out the fundamental while missing many of the individual phones.

Intonation patterns may be inappropriately used by the learner of English when the patterns are different from those of his native language. The intonation patterns of most European languages are generally similar in the main to those of English but often differ in detail. Many second-language teachers do not pay much attention to their students' use of intonation. There are several reasons for this. (1) Language courses often stress the written word at the expense of any significant training in speech. (2) Many language teachers lack training in phonetics and cannot put their finger on just what is wrong with their students' pronunciation. (3) Since it is often difficult to correct intonation patterns, the teacher prefers to bear with the students' errors rather than correct them.

But since intonation is so important a part of natural-sounding speech, some effort should be put into teaching it. One method that has been used successfully is having students practice saying sentences following a model. Sentences are chosen as exemplifying various intonation patterns. Some teachers make use of numbers (much as we did in the example of Chinese tones) in teaching intonation. If both teacher and students are musically inclined, musical notes may be used to demonstrate intonation contours.

The second-language learner whose native language is a tone language can be expected to have particular difficulties with intonational contours. This is because to him pitch is an inherent part of the word, not of the sentence.

The laryngectomee (section 5-4.1) who uses esophageal speech can be expected to have difficulties both with stress and intonation. This is because esophageal speech generally does not have much pitch range or dynamic (loudness) range. While these qualities of esophageal speech may be somewhat improved through practice, the laryngectomee is still likely not to be able to make full use of these devices to signal meaning. Phrasing may circumvent the problem. For example, while the laryngectomee may have difficulty producing the contours needed to distinguish "You're going." from "You're going?" there will be no problem differentiating "You're going." from "Are you going?" or "You're going, eh?" Similarly, while the stress necessary for "John did it" may be lacking, the emphasis may be indicated by saying "It's John that did it."

In the past, prosthetic voice devices (buzzers) for laryngectomees were purely monotone, allowing no use of intonation, but devices are now available whose fundamental frequency is adjustable with a hand-held control.


## Questions for Discussion

1. "What?" is often heard as the response to a statement. How does the speaker signal that <u>what</u> means 'I don't believe it'; 'I am shocked'; or 'Please repeat; I didn't hear you'? Say the word such that it has each meaning, and describe the phonetic devices used which signal the various meanings.

*2. Speech has certain resources for conveying meaning that writing can represent imperfectly at best. Say this sentence aloud in a way that will convey each of the meanings indicated below: "He's a very enthusiastic person."

I am simply giving you the fact.
I like him; his enthusiasm is to his credit.
I dislike him; his enthusiasm is depressing.
I am hesitant or reluctant to describe him.
I mean him, not her.
I am asking you, not telling you.

Is that what you said? I can hardly believe it.

The degree of his enthusiasm is quite remarkable.

Enthusiasm is the only good thing about him, and it isn't much; I could say more, but I won't.

Describe as precisely as you can how the various meanings are signaled. Can any of these meanings be shown in writing by punctuation or typographical devices?

3. Take another sentence that you make up, and give it a variety of meanings through the use of stress, pause, and intonation. Paraphrase the meanings, and describe the devices used to achieve the meanings.

4. Do different dialects use suprasegmental features differently? Try to find an example.

5. What special problems are involved in suprasegmental remediation of the laryngectomee, the hearing-impaired, or the student of English as a second language?

6. Suggest ways of dealing with or overcoming the problems brought up in question 5.

*7. Can these pairs be distinguished in speech? If so, how?

| | |
|---|---|
| blue blood (aristocrat) | blue blood (cyanotic condition) |
| red eye (cheap whiskey) | red eye (bloodshot eye) |
| hot line (direct telephone line to Moscow) | hot line (heated cord) |
| New Year (January 1) | new year (fresh year) |
| long shot (kind of bet) | long shot (shot-putting at a far distance) |
| short order (quickly cooked food) | short order (brief command) |
| big head (conceit) | big head (large skull) |
| a man's store (store selling men's clothing) | a man's store (store owned by a man) |
| a fishing pole (rod for fishing) | a fishing Pole (Polish fisherman) |
| a bull's-eye (center of a target) | a bull's eye (eye of a bull) |

*8. Can these pairs be distinguished in speech? If so, how does the distinction differ from that of the pairs in the preceding list [question 7]?

| | |
|---|---|
| New Jersey (the state) | new jersey (blouse purchased recently) |
| old maid (spinster) | old maid (serving-woman of advanced years) |
| little woman (wife) | little woman (small female) |
| Long Island (the place) | long island (any elongated island) |
| good and hot (very hot) | good and hot (hot and good) |

*9. Each of these sentences is ambiguous in writing. Say each sentence in two different ways to make the potential meanings clear. Describe the means you use to make the spoken sentences unambiguous.

Old men and women should be the first to abandon ship.

The doorman asked her quietly to telephone the police.

She gave him an order to leave.

They went by the old highway.

He painted the picture in the hall.

*10. Are these sentences usually distinguished in speech? Can they be distinguished?

He came to.
He came too.

He found a pear.
He found a pair.

The straight way is best.
The strait way is best.

The mathematics department is teaching plane geometry.
The mathematics department is teaching plain geometry.

The directions read, "Leave address with Miss Jones."
The directions read, "Leave a dress with Miss Jones."

11. What problems are there in writing a tone language alphabetically? Do you think this had anything to do with the fact that Chinese uses a primarily ideographic system? Are there any tone languages written alphabetically? How do they cope with the problem?

## Annotated Bibliography

The suprasegmentals are discussed in most introductory phonetics books, a selection of which are mentioned in the References.

Lehiste's book *Suprasegmentals* [1970] is a thorough technical study of these aspects of speech, including an attempt to integrate suprasegmentals into linguistic theory.

Lieberman's study of intonation [1967] discusses the perception and production of intonation, its linguistic significance, and the extent to which it is a central part of speech.

Pike's book [1945] discusses intonation, both from the point of view of analysis as well from the point of view of the utilization of intonation in the teaching of speech.

There are many books available which contain exercises in sentence stress and intonation. Many are designed for the learner of English as a second language; others are designed for the more general goal of speech improvement. A selection includes: Drills [1967], Gordon [1974], Lado and Fries [1954], and Prator [1957].

# Part III

# Introduction to
## Advanced Phonetics

# Chapter 14

## Phonological Analysis of Standard and Nonstandard Speech

### 14-1 Phonology and Phonetics

In studying the sounds of speech in greater depth, it will be found that there are really two areas. The first, properly called **phonetics**, deals with speech sounds in a rather concrete, physical way: their articulation, acoustics, and other measurable properties. The second area, aspects of which have already been considered under other names in Chapters 10 through 13, is called **phonology**, and it deals on a more abstract level with the **system** of sounds in a particular language.

Ideally, phonetics may be studied without reference to any particular language. By contrast, phonology is studied with reference to individual languages. But the distinction between phonetics and phonology is by no means a clear-cut one. We are all native speakers of some language, and so we approach phonetics from the point of view of the phonological[1] system of our particular language. Also, the sound system of a language could not be studied successfully without reference to the physical properties—articulatory or acoustic—of the speech sounds themselves (although some scholars are guilty of trying to divorce the two).

Phonetics and phonology are two ends of a continuum, and are never completely separate. This book, like other books on phonetics, contains a combination of phonetics and phonology. Being written from the point of view of the English language, it has stressed matters of phonological significance in English, and has left aside many matters—equally interesting phonetically—which have no phonological significance in English.

---

[1] **Phonological** is a broader term than **phonemic**, denoting a particular theoretical approach to phonemics, as well as phonotactics, and aspects of stress and intonation.

Although the domains of phonetics and phonology overlap considerably, and no absolute line of demarcation can be drawn, it is true that the emphasis is different. A number of matters are seen differently by the phonologist and the phonetician; a comparison of the two points of view will be made here.

The phonetician, purely speaking, is interested in what one says and hears, as compared to the phonologist, who is interested in what one intends to say and understands. So the word [bɛɾɪŋ] can be described phonetically as having an alveolar flap, but a phonological analysis would depend upon whether the speaker intended to say "betting" or "bedding" and upon what the listener understood or thought he heard. The context would be important here.

Phonetics (again, purely speaking) concerns itself with **differences** among phones, and a good phonetician can detect very fine acoustic or articulatory differences. Phonology, by contrast, is concerned with **oppositions** or **distinctions** of the type we discussed in Chapter 11. For example, the phonetician is interested in the slight differences among a number of different types of /t/ used by speakers of English (and other languages as well). But what is important to the phonologist is that there exists a unit, which may be called /t/, that is *in opposition to,* or *distinct from,* other units, called /p/, /k/, etc.

The phonetician studies sounds for their own sake, whereas the phonologist is interested in the way the sounds **carry meaning** (that is, how sounds *distinguish words*). To the pure phonetician, all phones are of equal value or importance, whereas the phonologist will set up an order or a hierarchy. [t] and [tʰ] are equally interesting phonetically, whereas phonologically /t/ plays a significant role in the *system* of English; its allophones, being merely variants or realizations of /t/, are less important.

One of the more telling differences is in the way that phoneticians talk about the **degree** or amount of a particular phonetic feature while the phonologist talks about its **presence** or **absence.** As an example, the phone [t] can be articulated in a range of positions, from dental, through alveolar, to the front part of the palatal region. The phonetician researching articulation will view this continuum with interest and will study the various articulations. He will view the production of [t] as something that is infinitely variable: the point of articulation may change, the part of the tongue making contact may be the apex, blade, or front; there will be varying degrees of labialization, aspiration, and even velarization (and, in other languages, retroflexion, glottalization, etc.).

By contrast, the phonologist will look at the various [t]'s and see them as varying realizations of the one English speech sound (phoneme) /t/. He will see that it is necessary to distinguish /t/ from /k/ and /p/, since this distinction is a carrier of meaning in English, but will be much less interested in the various types, and he is certainly not interested in the fine differences that are so intriguing to the phonetician. *To him, either it is a /t/ or it is not a /t/.* The extent of his interest in small phonetic differences depends on the distinctions made in a particular language. Thus, for the reasons discussed in Chapter 11, the difference between an aspirated and an unaspirated [t] is much more relevant, *phonologically,* in Thai than in English.

This question of the relevance of certain phonetic features has led to a different system of classification of speech sounds, used by phonologists, a system called **distinctive feature** analysis.

In this book, a system for classifying speech sounds has been introduced, one that phoneticians have used for years. In this system, phones are classified according to their articulation: a voiceless bilabial plosive; a voiced interdental fricative; a high back tense vowel, and so on. Various modifying terms, such as **rounded, velarized, aspirated,** etc., can be added to make the descriptions very precise. We can give a precise articulatory description of any phone in any language.

The very precision of this system, which makes it so useful to the phonetician, makes it more cumbersome for the phonologist. As noted in Chapter 11, when the language being discussed is known, much of the phonetic detail becomes redundant. For example, in English there are no high front rounded (labialized) vowels. Rounding is usually redundant or unnecessary information in specifying English speech sounds, not because we do not have rounded phones—which we do—but because that information is **predictable** from other information. Similarly, aspiration of voiceless plosives in English can be predicted from information concerning the phonetic environment (as shown in Chapter 10), so this information may also be omitted.

The phonologist wants a system of classification of speech sounds that, rather than giving a complete articulatory description, gives the *minimum information necessary* to *distinguish* every distinctive sound from every other distinctive sound in that language. The system of distinctive features meets this need.

A distinctive feature is a feature of a speech sound that normally has some phonetic base, either articulatory or acoustic. But the overall number of these features is carefully reduced until very little redundant information is specified. The reason for this is that when too much detail is given, the phonologist may not be able to see the forest for the trees; that is, the detail may prevent the phonologist from seeing the overall *pattern,* and it is the patterning of speech sounds that interests him.

In all sciences, simplicity is an overriding concern. If two theories or explanations, one complex and the other simple, equally well explain the phenomenon at hand, it is the simpler one which is accepted (in the absence of any compelling reason to do otherwise). The phonologist, looking for the patterning of speech sounds in a language, is looking for the simplest description that adequately explains the phonological processes in that language; to this end he ignores irrelevant or redundant phonetic detail.

Another reason for the use of the distinctive features is that it allows one to compare the similarities and differences among phones. The traditional classification system uses completely different terms for consonants as compared to vowels, making it difficult to compare their articulation, even though we know that vowels and consonants can share many aspects of their articulation (for example /ž/ and /i/ are both voiced, and have similar tongue placement). Also, even within one major group, for example, the consonants, there are similarities among speech sounds that are not indicated by the old terminology. Clearly, the terminology allows us to say that all *voiced* sounds have something in common, all *plosives* have something in common, or all *velars* have something in common. But there are types of commonality not indicated by the terminology. For example, the plosives, affricates, and nasals make up a group based on the fact that oral closure is necessary for their production.

Bilabials, labiodentals, dentals, and alveolars make a natural group in that they are all produced in the front (anterior) part of the mouth. All the speech sounds fall into many different overlapping groups that are natural from the point of view of some aspect (feature) of their articulation or sound; this fact can be best expressed by analyzing each sound into its constituent features. This has been done in Table 14.1 for the speech sounds of English.

A few words of caution are necessary before proceeding to explain what the feature names mean. Experts disagree on the exact features that should be used and how many are necessary; other books may give a slightly different listing. Here we are using a set of features derived ultimately from a pioneering work by Noam Chomsky and Morris Halle [1968].

One other factor concerning distinctive features is particularly relevant for the practical phonetician. Since the features intentionally leave out redundant detail, and since some have an acoustic basis, they *cannot be considered as giving an adequate articulatory description of the various phones.* That is why the traditional articulatory descriptions have been used in this book. The set of distinctive features for [i] will not provide a detailed guide to its articulation, whereas the traditional phonetic description, if detailed, will provide such a guide.

## 14-2.1 What the Features Mean

First, note that all features are given in terms of **plus** or **minus,** indicating whether the phone in question possesses or does not possess that quality or feature. For this reason, they are sometimes called **binary features.** Occasionally, there is a feature that has no applicability to a certain class of sounds (e.g., **tense** as applied to the consonants in Table 14.1) and is thus marked neither plus nor minus. Note also that some of the features have a primarily acoustic basis, while others have a primarily articulatory basis.

Briefly, this is what the terms mean:

**consonantal:** obstruction at some point in the vocal tract; low degree of acoustic energy (abbreviated **cons**).

**vocalic:** free passage through the vocal tract (except at the glottis, where there is vibration); acoustically, presence of formant structure (abbreviated **voc**).

**continuant:** continuant sounds are produced *without* a total blockage of the *oral* cavity at any point (that is, **non**continuant or interrupted sounds are produced with total blockage of the oral cavity) (abbreviated **cont**).

**nasal:** lowered velum, introducing the nasal cavity as a resonator; acoustically, a lowered intensity in the formants (abbreviated **nas**).

**anterior:** produced in the front part of the oral cavity, the alveopalatal region being the dividing line (/s/ is anterior, /š/ is not) (abbreviated **ant**).

**coronal:** produced with the tongue blade arched above its neutral position (abbreviated **coron**).

**Table 14.1.** The Features of English Phones

| | p | b | t | d | k | g | č | ǰ | f | v | θ | ð | s | z | š | ž | m | n | ŋ | r | l | h | j | w | i | ɪ | e | ɛ | æ | u | ʊ | o | ɔ | ʌ | ɑ |
|---|---|---|---|---|---|---|---|---|---|---|---|---|---|---|---|---|---|---|---|---|---|---|---|---|---|---|---|---|---|---|---|---|---|---|---|
| Consonantal | + | + | + | + | + | + | + | + | + | + | + | + | + | + | + | + | + | + | + | + | + | − | − | − | − | − | − | − | − | − | − | − | − | − | − |
| Vocalic | − | − | − | − | − | − | − | − | − | − | − | − | − | − | − | − | − | − | − | + | + | − | − | − | + | + | + | + | + | + | + | + | + | + | + |
| Continuant | − | − | − | − | − | − | − | − | + | + | + | + | + | + | + | + | − | − | − | + | + | + | + | + | + | + | + | + | + | + | + | + | + | + | + |
| Nasal | − | − | − | − | − | − | − | − | − | − | − | − | − | − | − | − | + | + | + | − | − | − | − | − | − | − | − | − | − | − | − | − | − | − | − |
| Anterior | + | + | + | + | − | − | − | − | + | + | + | + | + | + | − | − | + | + | − | − | + | − | − | − | − | − | − | − | − | − | − | − | − | − | − |
| Coronal | − | − | + | + | − | − | + | + | − | − | + | + | + | + | + | + | − | + | − | + | + | − | − | − | − | − | − | − | − | − | − | − | − | − | − |
| High | − | − | − | − | + | + | + | + | − | − | − | − | − | − | + | + | − | − | + | − | − | − | + | + | + | + | − | − | − | + | + | − | − | − | − |
| Low | − | − | − | − | − | − | − | − | − | − | − | − | − | − | − | − | − | − | − | − | − | + | − | − | − | − | − | − | + | − | − | − | + | − | + |
| Back | − | − | − | − | + | + | − | − | − | − | − | − | − | − | − | − | − | − | + | − | − | − | − | + | − | − | − | − | − | + | + | + | + | + | + |
| Voice | − | + | − | + | − | + | − | + | − | + | − | + | − | + | − | + | + | + | + | + | + | − | + | + | + | + | + | + | + | + | + | + | + | + | + |
| Strident | − | − | − | − | − | − | + | + | + | + | − | − | + | + | + | + | − | − | − | − | − | − | − | − | − | − | − | − | − | − | − | − | − | − | − |
| Sonorant | − | − | − | − | − | − | − | − | − | − | − | − | − | − | − | − | + | + | + | + | + | − | + | + | + | + | + | + | + | + | + | + | + | + | + |
| Tense | − | − | − | − | − | − | − | − | − | − | − | − | − | − | − | − | − | − | − | − | − | − | − | − | + | − | + | − | − | + | − | + | + | − | − |

**high:** the body (not the tip) of the tongue is raised (written **high** or **hi**).

**low:** the tongue is lowered below the neutral position, as for low vowels, but not for any consonant except /h/ (written **low** or **lo**).

**back:** produced with a retraction of the body of the tongue (written **back**).

**voice:** produced with vocal fold vibration (written **voice** or **vc**).

**tense:** produced with a greater movement of the articulators away from the rest position, tongue-root advancement; acoustically, a greater energy spread (written **tense** or **tns**).

**strident:** acoustically, a higher intensity of noise (aperiodic sound) (abbreviated **stri**).

**sonorant:** produced with a relatively free passage of air through the mouth or the nose (abbreviated **son**).

By the use of these features it is possible to distinguish among the phones of English (or other languages as well). Each phone has a unique set of features that cannot be confused with that of any other phone. Each phone may be seen as a "bundle" of features. /s/, for example, is really:

$$
\begin{bmatrix}
+\text{cons} \\
-\text{voc} \\
+\text{cont} \\
-\text{nas} \\
+\text{ant} \\
+\text{coron} \\
-\text{high} \\
-\text{low} \\
-\text{back} \\
-\text{voice} \\
+\text{stri} \\
-\text{son}
\end{bmatrix}
$$

The symbol /s/ is simply a shorthand way of representing this bundle of features.

The feature **matrix,** or set of features, for English phones is given in Table 14.1. One can see that it contains some redundant information; that is, some of the specifications could be left out and it still would be possible to distinguish the phones. For example, find all the phones that are *both* [−cons] and [+voc] (these you will recognize as the vowels). Notice that every one of these English speech sounds that is [−cons] and [+voc] is also [+son, +cont, −nasal, −ant, −coron, +voice, −stri].[2] This fact could be stated in the form of what is called a **redundancy rule,** as follows:

---

[2] This is not necessarily true for non-English sounds; for example, some French vowels are [+nasal].

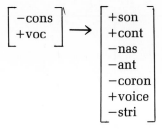

$$\begin{bmatrix} -\text{cons} \\ +\text{voc} \end{bmatrix} \rightarrow \begin{bmatrix} +\text{son} \\ +\text{cont} \\ -\text{nas} \\ -\text{ant} \\ -\text{coron} \\ +\text{voice} \\ -\text{stri} \end{bmatrix}$$

The arrow means 'can be written as,' and this rule simply says that *any* English phone that is [−cons] and [+voc] is assumed to be [+son, +cont, −nasal, . . .]. Because of this fact, one can specify the vowels much more economically, leaving out any mention of the features sonorant, continuant, nasal, anterior, coronal, voice, or strident.

In a similar way, other redundancies can be eliminated. Note that all sounds in Table 14.1 that are [+nasal] have certain other features in common ([+cons, −voc, −cont, −low, +voice, −stri, +son]); all sounds that are both [−cons] and [−voc] share certain features ([+cont, −nas, −ant, −coron, −stri, +son, . . .]). Indeed, if we were to go through the table phone by phone we would find that we could eliminate the specification for many of the features for all of the phones (but notice that only one feature is eliminated altogether). These facts are summarized in Table 14.2, in which all feature specifications have been eliminated except those that are absolutely essential to distinguish the phones. These are the truly *distinctive* features. Note that no two phones have the same combination of features.

The most obvious question at this point is, what good are distinctive features? Since the same features apply to all speech sounds, they allow one to get at similarities and differences that are obscured by the old terminology.

As an example, the plural marker for most English nouns is an ending that is spelled -s or -es and pronounced three ways: /s/, /z/, and /əz/, as in the words "cats," "dogs," and "churches." In Chapter 10, we discussed the reason for the choice between /s/ and /z/: it depends upon whether the preceding phone is voiced or voiceless. But on what basis do we know whether to put a schwa in the plural marker, adding another syllable to the word? One might start by compiling a list; you would find that words like "bus," "fuse," "church," "judge," "bush," and "garage" take the /əz/ ending. Indeed, all words (except perhaps a few irregular or foreign words) that end with the consonants /s, z, č, ǰ, š, ž/ take plurals in /əz/. What do these sounds have in common?

In the old terminology, there is no point of commonality. Four of these sounds are fricatives, but two are not; and there are four other fricatives that do not add an extra syllable in the plural (lathe/lathes, laugh/laughs, for example). These six consonants do not have the same place of articulation or voicing. There is nothing that distinguishes these sounds and these alone.

But now let us examine the feature matrix for some feature or combination of features specific to this group of phones that sets them apart from all others. These six sounds are all [+coron, +stri]. All six have this combination of features, and no other phone does. The features, then, point out what is

**Table 14.2.** The Distinctive Features of English Phonemes

| | p | b | t | d | k | g | č | ǰ | f | v | θ | ð | s | z | š | ž | m | n | ŋ | r | l | h | j | w | i | ɪ | e | ɛ | æ | u | ʊ | o | ɔ | ʌ | ɑ |
|---|---|---|---|---|---|---|---|---|---|---|---|---|---|---|---|---|---|---|---|---|---|---|---|---|---|---|---|---|---|---|---|---|---|---|---|
| Consonantal | + | + | + | + | + | + | + | + | + | + | + | + | + | + | + | + | + | + | + | + | + | − | − | − | − | − | − | − | − | − | − | − | − | − | − |
| Vocalic | − | − | − | − | − | − | − | − | − | − | − | − | − | − | − | − | − | − | − | + | + | − | − | − | + | + | + | + | + | + | + | + | + | + | + |
| Continuant | − | − | − | − | − | − | − | − | + | + | + | + | + | + | + | + | − | − | − | + | + | + | | | + | + | + | + | + | + | + | + | + | + | + |
| Nasal | − | − | − | − | − | − | − | − | − | − | − | − | − | − | − | − | + | + | + | | | | | | | | | | | | | | | | |
| Anterior | + | + | + | + | − | − | − | − | + | + | + | + | + | + | − | − | + | + | − | − | + | | | | | | | | | | | | | | |
| Coronal | − | − | + | + | − | − | + | + | − | − | + | + | + | + | + | + | − | + | − | + | + | | | | | | | | | | | | | | |
| High | − | − | − | − | + | + | + | + | − | − | − | − | − | − | + | + | − | − | + | − | − | | + | + | + | + | − | − | − | + | + | − | − | − | − |
| Low | | | | | | | | | | | | | | | | | | | | | | | | | − | − | − | − | + | − | − | − | + | − | + |
| Back | − | − | − | − | + | + | − | − | − | − | − | − | − | − | − | − | − | − | + | − | − | | − | + | − | − | − | − | − | + | + | + | + | + | + |
| Voice | − | + | − | + | − | + | − | + | − | + | − | + | − | + | − | + | | | | | | | | + | | | | | | | | | | | |
| Strident | | | | | | | + | + | + | + | − | − | + | + | + | + | | | | | | | | | | | | | | | | | | | |
| Sonorant | | | | | | | | | | | | | | | | | + | + | + | + | + | | + | + | | | | | | | | | | | |
| Tense | | | | | | | | | | | | | | | | | | | | | | | | | + | − | + | − | − | + | − | + | + | − | − |

common to phones that group together naturally and that show a common pattern of behavior.[3]

## 14-3 Phonological Rules

Let us review for a moment what was said in earlier chapters about *rules*. As the term is used here, a rule is not a declaration by a teacher of grammar that you should not say "doin' " instead of "doing." Rather, a rule is a statement about some small aspect of the workings of language. Put together, rules make up the **grammar** or knowledge of the language that we carry around in our heads whether or not we ever went to school.

Phonological rules are a way of stating aspects of the pronunciation of language in a formal way so that they are not ambiguous or open to misunderstanding. These rules contain a few simple conventions that must be agreed upon by the users of the system so that they do not get confused, just as in arithmetic we agree on the meaning of the symbol $\times$ (as in $6 \times 4 = 24$).

In phonological rules, an arrow indicates a change, and it may be read as "becomes" or "is realized as." A long oblique line indicates the specification of the environment in which the change takes place and may be read as "in the environment of. . . ." A horizontal line on the environment side refers to the sound in question, to prevent unnecessary repetition. Note also, that we use only the *distinctive* features (those in Table 14.2) in writing rules. For example, let us look at rule 1:

$$
1. \quad
\begin{bmatrix}
-\text{cont} \\
-\text{nas} \\
+\text{ant} \\
+\text{coron} \\
+\text{voice}
\end{bmatrix}
\rightarrow
\begin{bmatrix}
-\text{ant} \\
+\text{stri}
\end{bmatrix}
\Bigg/
\underline{\quad\quad}
\begin{bmatrix}
-\text{cons} \\
-\text{voc} \\
+\text{high} \\
-\text{back}
\end{bmatrix}
$$

This means that the phoneme /d/ (specified by its distinctive features) *becomes* /ǰ/ in the environment before the glide /j/. (The dash, representing the sound undergoing the change, precedes the /j/.) This rule indicates the process affecting the consonant which occurs when we pronounce "Did you" as /dɪǰə/ and "Would you" as /wuǰə/. Since this change is up to the speaker, we may say that the rule is an **optional** one.

Notice, by the way, that to the right of the arrow we did not completely specify the phone /ǰ/. We only stated those features that are *different* from those to the left of the arrow. If no change is indicated, the assumption is

---

[3] It is not surprising that the way information is formalized and written down should have theoretical implications or help to make aspects of the problem clearer. Most people are familiar with Roman numerals. We know that these numerals are quite useless for performing mathematical calculations: it is simply impossible to multiply LVII by XXIX without converting to Arabic (even a person accustomed to the Roman system would have to use very long, roundabout means for solving this problem). The Arabic numerals do not represent simply another means of recording the same information as Roman numerals: built into Arabic numerals are certain sophisticated conventions that allow the user to gain insights into the properties and workings of numbers. Higher mathematics is made possible through this system of recording numerical values. Likewise, the distinctive feature notation system allows us to gain insight into phonological processes that might escape our attention if the traditional phonetic classification were used.

made that no change has occurred: the phone specified to the left of the arrow is [−cont, −nas, +coron, +voice], and since no change is indicated, one assumes that these apply to the phone at the right of the arrow. We save time and space and make the rules simpler by leaving out repetitious detail.

The first reaction to this system is usually that it seems unnecessarily complicated; however, this is not so. In fact, it allows many circumstances that seem complicated to be stated quite simply and allows one to tie together seemingly unrelated processes.

For example, a companion to the change from "would you" to /wúǰə/ is the change from "can't you" to /kǽnčə/. This is obviously a related phenomenon; it is not a coincidence that /t/ and /d/ undergo similar changes in similar situations. We state formally that the two processes are in fact two examples of the same process by writing them with one rule:

$$
2. \quad
\begin{bmatrix} -\text{cont} \\ -\text{nas} \\ +\text{ant} \\ +\text{coron} \end{bmatrix}
\rightarrow
\begin{bmatrix} -\text{ant} \\ +\text{stri} \end{bmatrix}
\Big/
\underline{\phantom{xxx}}
\begin{bmatrix} -\text{cons} \\ -\text{voc} \\ +\text{high} \\ -\text{back} \end{bmatrix}
$$

All we have done in converting rule 1 to rule 2 is to leave out the specification for voicing in the phone represented at the left. As a result, both /č/ and /ǰ/ are specified equally, and the rule applies to them both. Since we have only to write one rule, we can state that there is only one process at work.

Redundancy rules can also express phonotactic restrictions on the forms of words in a language. For example, we know that if a word begins with three consonants, the first must be /s/ and the second a voiceless plosive, as expressed in this rule:

$$
3. \quad
\# \ [+\text{cons}] \ [+\text{cons}] \ [+\text{cons}] \longrightarrow
\#
\begin{bmatrix} +\text{ant} \\ +\text{coron} \\ -\text{voice} \\ +\text{stri} \end{bmatrix}
\begin{bmatrix} -\text{cont} \\ -\text{nas} \\ -\text{voice} \\ -\text{stri} \end{bmatrix}
\begin{bmatrix} +\text{cons} \\ +\text{voc} \\ (-\text{ant}) \end{bmatrix}
$$

The crosshatch symbol (#) indicates a word boundary, so this rule applies at the beginnings of words. It specifies the first of three consonants at the beginning of a word to be /s/, the second a voiceless plosive, and the third a liquid, either /r/ or /l/. If the third phoneme is specified as [−ant] (as indicated in parentheses), it can only be /r/, not /l/. /l/ occurs regularly only after /p/ in three-consonant releasing clusters. Further specification would be necessary in the rule to indicate this explicitly. Note that in distinctive feature terms, /j/ is [−cons], so clusters like the /#spj-/ in "spew" are not covered by this rule.

The study of phonology, the system of sounds in language, is fascinating, and it is filled with many issues of a theoretical nature. One cannot escape a good deal of abstraction, considerably greater than (but similar in nature to) what is encountered in the study of the phoneme. Sources for further reading in this area are given in the Annotated Bibliography. Even without getting into the controversial or highly abstract areas of this field, one can make use of its principles and methods in the analysis of speech that is defective or nonstandard in some way. That is what will be covered in the next section.

## 14-4 Phonological Analysis of Nonnormal Speech

The use of phonological rules and distinctive feature analysis can bring dividends in understanding the structure of nonnormal speech. This is an important issue, since, as we have tried to indicate throughout the book, the sound system of speech, while often complicated, is highly regular and organized. Similarly, nonnormal speech (that of the foreign speaker, deaf speaker, language-delayed child, individual with an articulation disorder, etc.) is also highly structured. It is structured *differently* from standard speech, but it *is* structured. An understanding of the ways it is structured, revealed through analysis, will lead one in the right direction toward finding a solution.

In this section, we will consider a few examples of speech that is in some way nonstandard, and try to show the ways in which it displays regularity. One note: in one case we will use the example of a nonstandard dialect. No suggestion is being made that such speech is "abnormal." Quite the contrary, people often mistakenly believe that dialects other than their own are full of haphazard errors, whereas they are actually highly regular and systematic, as all speech is.

For our first example, let us look again at the case we saw first in Chapter 11, from Van Riper [1972]. There, a student speech therapist analyzed the speech of a child and found 32 defective sounds. The problem with this analysis was that it did not take into account the environments of the sounds in question. The student therapist presumably found some defective /t/'s, but not every /t/ was defective; similarly 31 other phonemes were defective but not everywhere. In this child's speech, all sounds were incompletely articulated in word-final position. This could be stated formally as follows:

4. $$\left[ \quad \right] \rightarrow \emptyset \, / \underline{\hspace{2cm}} \#$$

The empty brackets indicate no specification for features, so the reference is to any and all phonemes. The symbol $\emptyset$ is taken from mathematics; it is the null sign and means 'nothing.' The crosshatch symbol (#), again, refers to a word boundary, so this process takes place just before the word boundary, or at the end of the word. This rule can be read: "All phonemes are realized as nothing (or "are not realized," or "are deleted") in word-final position." What is important here is that *one rule describes all 32 defective sounds*, so there is one abnormal process at work. This suggests the therapeutic approach, which was, as stated by Van Riper, "to teach the child to strengthen his terminal sounds" (p. 189).

In the case of the foreign speaker who has difficulty with /θ/ and /ð/, one speaker may make the substitution of a plosive in all places:

5. $$\begin{bmatrix} +\text{cont} \\ +\text{ant} \\ -\text{stri} \end{bmatrix} \rightarrow [-\text{cont}]$$

This rule indicates that /t/ is substituted for /θ/ and /d/ for /ð/. Here, and in subsequent rules, the sound specified to the left of the arrow indicates the desired or standard sound. In this rule, no environment is specified, so it applies everywhere. But let us, for comparison, consider the case of another individual having difficulty with the same sounds:

$$6. \quad \begin{bmatrix} +\text{cont} \\ +\text{ant} \\ -\text{stri} \end{bmatrix} \longrightarrow [-\text{cont}] \Big/ \underline{\hspace{2cm}} \#$$

This indicates a substitution of a plosive (/t/ and /d/) for a fricative (/θ/ and /ð/) in word-final position only. In this instance, the student would require exercises in pronouncing the difficult sounds only when they appear in this environment.

What about this case:

$$7. \quad \begin{bmatrix} +\text{cont} \\ +\text{ant} \\ -\text{stri} \end{bmatrix} \longrightarrow [-\text{cont}] \Big/ \begin{Bmatrix} \# \underline{\hspace{1.5cm}} \\ \underline{\hspace{1.5cm}} \# \end{Bmatrix}$$

Here we see another symbol used in writing rules: the brace. This indicates an option and is read as "and." In this case, the student substitutes a plosive for a fricative in word-initial and word-final position. Apparently this student has no trouble when the difficult sounds appear in medial position, which makes sense, since medial occurrences are usually intervocalic, an easier environment in which to pronounce them.

As these three cases suggest, it is usually not enough to say that the student in question "has trouble with his th's." Which ones? voiced or voiceless? in which environments? Once this has been determined, one's knowledge of articulatory phonetics and one's ingenuity can be combined in producing drills and exercises that aim at the problem. Some general strategies have been outlined in previous chapters, and others will have to come from the individual problem faced. The phonological rules are useful because they summarize the problem in an unambiguous way and thereby clarify the nature of the problem.

Let us look at an example of a substitution made by a child with delayed phonological development. This particular case, a typical one, was reported by Oller [1973]. This child substituted /ž/ for /ǰ/ and /š/ for /č/ in word-initial position. These substitutions can be summarized as follows:

$$8. \quad \begin{bmatrix} +\text{stri} \\ +\text{coron} \end{bmatrix} \longrightarrow [+\text{cont}] \Big/ \# \underline{\hspace{2cm}}$$

Notice that once again two substitutions can be neatly expressed in one simple rule, indicating that the two are related processes.

Using letters rather than feature bundles, one might write this process in two separate statements:

9. (a)    [č] → [š] / #____

    (b)    [ǰ] → [ž] / #____

Since two statements are used, there is no formal way of indicating (or of discovering) the relatedness of these two substitutions (though in this particular case, the relatedness is quite apparent). It is just as simple to indicate two unrelated substitutions as two related ones, when using the letters rather than the feature bundles, as in this hypothetical example:

10. (a)    [č]  →  [š] / #_____

(b)    [v]  →  [b] / #_____

Notice that rules in 10a and 10b reflect two quite *unrelated* processes and rules 9a and 9b are closely related, *but they are equally simple to express on paper.* The form of the rules gives no clue as to the complexity of the substitution.

Rules 9a and 9b can, however, be collapsed into *one* phonological rule using distinctive features, rule 8:

8.  $$\begin{bmatrix} +\text{stri} \\ +\text{coron} \end{bmatrix} \longrightarrow [+\text{cont}] \Big/ \# \ \underline{\hspace{2cm}}$$

Rules 10a and 10b must remain two separate rules when written using distinctive features; they cannot be collapsed into one:

11. (a)  $$\begin{bmatrix} +\text{stri} \\ +\text{coron} \\ -\text{voice} \end{bmatrix} \longrightarrow [+\text{cont}] \Big/ \# \ \underline{\hspace{2cm}}$$

(b)  $$\begin{bmatrix} +\text{ant} \\ -\text{coron} \\ +\text{voice} \\ +\text{stri} \end{bmatrix} \longrightarrow [-\text{cont}] \Big/ \# \ \underline{\hspace{2cm}}$$

Since the two substitutions shown in rule 10 *cannot* be indicated by one rule, they must be two unrelated processes. This would tip off the language teacher or pathologist to approach the two separately, and probably differently.

In short, the formalized system for writing rules helps one to discover the processes underlying the system of speech, whether it is standard speech, or speech that is in some way nonstandard.

As a corollary to this, the formalizations of distinctive feature phonology can even indicate which types of substitutions are most likely. This is because the system has been designed and modified such that *the simpler the rule is to write, the more natural the process it expresses.*[4]

Some examples will illustrate how this works. Imagine two hypothetical substitutions. The first is the substitution of /p/ for /f/, the second,

---

[4] There is some dispute on this, however, some experts claiming that certain unrelated or unnatural processes can be expressed in a single, simple rule. A brief clear discussion of this as it relates to nonnormal speech can be found in the Oller article [1973] cited earlier. For the most part, this danger can be ignored for our purposes here, since the dispute generally involves rather abstract, sophisticated phonological processes outside the realm of our discussion.

of /g/ for /f/ in word-initial position. Each of these would be expressed in distinctive-feature terms as shown below:

12. (/p/ for /f/)

$$\begin{bmatrix} +ant \\ -coron \\ -voice \\ +stri \end{bmatrix} \longrightarrow [-cont] \Big/ \# \underline{\hspace{2cm}}$$

13. (/g/ for /f/)

$$\begin{bmatrix} +ant \\ -coron \\ -voice \\ +stri \end{bmatrix} \longrightarrow \begin{bmatrix} -cont \\ -ant \\ +voice \end{bmatrix} \Big/ \# \underline{\hspace{2cm}}$$

(In rule 12, there is no need to specify [−stri] to the right of the arrow since all sounds that are [−cont] and [−coron] are also [−stri].)

Notice that rule 13 is more complicated than rule 12, in that more features must be specified to the right of the arrow. Since it is more complex to state the substitution, one can conclude that it is less likely to occur. This agrees both with our intuition and with observed fact. When the substitutions are stated with rules using letters, they appear to be equally complex, and nothing is learned.

Another case shows that simpler rules correspond to more natural processes. Let us compare the case of one child who substitutes /š/ for /č/ in word-initial position, and another child who substitutes both /š/ for /č/ and /ž/ for /ǰ/. We have seen these already in rules 8 and 11a:

11. (a) (/š/ for /č/)

$$\begin{bmatrix} +stri \\ +coron \\ -voice \end{bmatrix} \longrightarrow [+cont] \Big/ \# \underline{\hspace{2cm}}$$

8. (/š/ for /č/ and /ž/ for /ǰ/)

$$\begin{bmatrix} +stri \\ +coron \end{bmatrix} \longrightarrow [+cont] \Big/ \# \underline{\hspace{2cm}}$$

When letters are used to express the substitutions, it appears that the process in rule 11a is the simpler of the two, since only one substitution occurs, but note that it is rule 8 that is the simpler to express in features: it requires one less feature to state. Indeed, the process expressed in rule 8 *is* the simpler, since the same modification occurs to *all* sounds of the same natural class. It is more likely to occur in the speech of a language-delayed child, or in the substitutions of a foreign speaker or the hearing-impaired speaker, than is the substitution indicated in rule 11a.

Next to be considered is the use of phonological rules to describe differences among dialects. The case mentioned in the exercises of Chapter 12, namely the dialect of American English in which word-final /d/ is dropped following /n/, is a good example; "wind" and "win" are homophonous. When the standard English form is placed to the left of the arrow, this process can be expressed as follows:

$$
14. \quad
\begin{bmatrix}
-\text{cont} \\
-\text{nas} \\
+\text{ant} \\
+\text{coron} \\
+\text{voice}
\end{bmatrix}
\longrightarrow \emptyset
\left/
\begin{bmatrix}
+\text{nas} \\
+\text{ant} \\
+\text{coron}
\end{bmatrix}
\right. \underline{\qquad} \#
$$

Notice that standard English has a similar process affecting the other voiced plosives in word-final position following homorganic nasals. For example, the /b/ of "crumb" is not pronounced, though it is in the related word "crumble." The /g/ of "strong" is not pronounced, though it is in the related word "stronger."[5] The dropping of word-final /b/ following /m/ can be expressed in this rule:

$$
15. \quad
\begin{bmatrix}
-\text{cont} \\
-\text{nas} \\
+\text{ant} \\
-\text{coron} \\
+\text{voice}
\end{bmatrix}
\longrightarrow \emptyset
\left/
\begin{bmatrix}
+\text{nas} \\
+\text{ant} \\
-\text{cor}
\end{bmatrix}
\right. \underline{\qquad} \#
$$

The dropping of word-final /g/ following /ŋ/ can be expressed in this rule (which would have to include additional conditions accounting for the problem brought up in footnote 5):

$$
16. \quad
\begin{bmatrix}
-\text{cont} \\
-\text{nas} \\
-\text{ant} \\
-\text{coron} \\
+\text{voice}
\end{bmatrix}
\longrightarrow \emptyset
\left/
\begin{bmatrix}
+\text{nas} \\
-\text{ant}
\end{bmatrix}
\right. \underline{\qquad} \#
$$

For standard English, we have two rules (15 and 16) that express certain elisions, but we can see that these are two instances of the same process: word-final voiced plosives being elided after homorganic nasals. If they are two instances of one process, we should be able to express them with one rule:

$$
17. \quad
\begin{bmatrix}
-\text{cont} \\
-\text{nas} \\
\alpha\,\text{ant} \\
-\text{coron} \\
+\text{voice}
\end{bmatrix}
\longrightarrow \emptyset
\left/
\begin{bmatrix}
+\text{nas} \\
\alpha\,\text{ant} \\
-\text{coron}
\end{bmatrix}
\right. \underline{\qquad} \#
$$

[5] The situation is complicated by the fact that the elided /g/ of "sing" stays elided in "singer." In fact, the -er agentive suffix added to verbs causes different changes as compared to the -er comparative suffix added to adjectives. This complication is beyond our present purposes and may be ignored.

Rule 17 contains another convention used in rule-writing, called the **alpha convention.** It is commonly used in assimilation rules. The symbol alpha ($\alpha$) (and beta, gamma, etc., as needed for more complex rules) is used as a substitute for "+ and −." It may take *either* the value plus *or* the value minus, but it must be *consistent for each reading of the rule.* So rule 17 is really a shorthand way of writing these two rules:

17. (a)

$$\begin{bmatrix} -\text{cont} \\ -\text{nas} \\ -\text{ant} \\ -\text{coron} \\ +\text{voice} \end{bmatrix} \longrightarrow \emptyset \left/ \begin{bmatrix} +\text{nas} \\ -\text{ant} \\ -\text{coron} \end{bmatrix} \underline{\hspace{2cm}} \# \right.$$

(b)

$$\begin{bmatrix} -\text{cont} \\ -\text{nas} \\ +\text{ant} \\ -\text{coron} \\ +\text{voice} \end{bmatrix} \longrightarrow \emptyset \left/ \begin{bmatrix} +\text{nas} \\ +\text{ant} \\ -\text{coron} \end{bmatrix} \underline{\hspace{2cm}} \# \right.$$

As always, the fact that they can be collapsed into one rule means that they are one process.

What about the dialect that drops final /d/ after /n/, as expressed in rule 14? Is it more complicated, having an extra rule? Quite the contrary, this dialect elides *all* final voiced plosives after homorganic nasals, and since this is a more general process, it is simpler and more regular. As expected, all three elisions in this dialect can be expressed by one rule, one that is simpler than rule 17:

18.

$$\begin{bmatrix} -\text{cont} \\ -\text{stri} \\ +\text{voice} \end{bmatrix} \longrightarrow \emptyset \left/ [+\text{nas}] \underline{\hspace{2cm}} \# \right.$$

We could go on ad infinitum giving examples of phonological analyses of numerous substitutions and elisions. For further examples, see the Annotated Bibliography.

## 14-4.1 Phonological Rules and Speech Analysis

In section 14-4, examples have been given of the way in which phonological rules not only *express* what is nonstandard in a certain speech sample but also—because of their formalized nature—help one to *discover* what is nonstandard. These rules also help in the planning of strategies to correct the problem, since they show what substitutions and omissions are the results of the same process and which are unrelated. Finally, we have seen that the formalized system can even give one a clue as to the kinds of substitutions one can expect.

In summary, then, phonological rules are used to express and discover **regularity** in nonstandard speech. This is the strength of this system and its benefit to the practical phonetician. An analysis of speech is always a precursor to its correction, since it is pointless to go about correcting something when you do not know precisely what is wrong or in what systematic ways.

We have seen a few examples of the rules describing the nonstandard phonology of the language-delayed child, the foreign speaker, and nonstandard dialects, as well as processes in standard English. In a similar way, this powerful system finds use in describing many other types of speech. It is used to describe the phonological development of linguistically normal children. It is used to describe the regularities in the speech of the deaf. It is used by linguists to describe standard languages, dialect variations, and the change of languages over time.

Since it has been developed first for standard languages, the system is perhaps better suited to their description than to the description of pathological speech conditions or aberrations of speech. Several authors have worked on bridging this gap, and we can look forward to advances in the phonological analysis of nonnormal speech, making it an even more useful tool in the pursuit of speech remediation.

## Exercise

1. Find samples of speech that is in some way nonstandard, and describe them using phonological rules.

## Annotated Bibliography

A discussion of the phonological features may be found in Jakobson, Fant, and Halle [1969], Chomsky and Halle [1968], and Fant [1973].

Introductions to phonological theory may be found in Schane [1973], Hyman [1975], Liles [1971], and Harms [1968]. More detailed arguments may be found in Chomsky and Halle [1968]. References to specific discussions on aspects of the theory may be found in the Bibliographies of these works.

Phonology as applied to nonnormal speech is discussed in Compton [1970], Ingram [1976], Oller [1973], and West and Weber [1973]. Look for recent articles in such journals as the *Journal of Speech and Hearing Disorders*.

Phonological analyses of normal first-language acquisition are discussed in McNeill [1970], Dale [1972], and Smith and Miller [1966], among others.

Phonological studies of sound change in language may be found in King [1969] and Anderson [1973].

# References

Abercrombie, D. *Elements of General Phonetics*. Chicago: Aldine, 1967.

Algeo, J. *Problems in the Origins and Development of the English Language* (2nd ed.). New York: Harcourt Brace Jovanovich, 1972.

Allen, H. B., and Underwood, G. N. *Readings in American Dialectology*. New York: Appleton-Century-Crofts, 1971.

Anderson, J. M. *Structural Aspects of Language Change*. London: Longman, 1973.

Barzun, J. The Retort Circumstantial. *American Scholar*, 20(3), 1951, pp. 289–293. Reprinted in G. Wilson, *A Linguistics Reader*. New York: Harper & Row, 1967, pp. 107–110.

Bau, S. First Message from the Planet of the Apes. *New York*, February 24, 1975, pp. 30–37.

Baugh, A. *A History of the English Language*. New York: Appleton-Century-Crofts, 1957.

Bloomfield, L. *Language* (2nd ed.). New York: Holt, Rinehart & Winston, 1961.

Bronowski, J., and Bellugi, U. Language, Name and Concept. *Science*, May 8, 1970, pp. 669–673.

Brosnahan, L. F., and Malmberg, B. *Introduction to Phonetics*. Cambridge, England: W. Heffer and Sons, 1970.

Brown, R. The First Sentences of Child and Chimpanzee. In *Psycholinguistics: Selected Papers by Roger Brown*. New York: Free Press, 1972, pp. 203–231.

Brown, R. *A First Language: The Early Stages*. Cambridge: Harvard University Press, 1973.

Chomsky, N., and Halle, M. *The Sound Pattern of English*. New York: Harper & Row, 1968.

Compton, A. J. Generative studies of children's phonological disorders. *Journal of Speech and Hearing Disorders*, 35(4), 1970, pp. 315–339.

Dale, P. S. *Language Development: Structure and Function*. Hinsdale, Ill.: Dryden, 1972.

D'Aulaire, E., and D'Aulaire, O. The Ape That "Talks" with People. *Reader's Digest*, October, 1975, pp. 94–98.

Delattre, P. C., Liberman, A. M., and Cooper, F. S. Acoustic Loci and Transitional Cues for Consonants. *Journal of the Acoustical Society of America*, 27, 1955, pp. 769–773.

Denes, P. B., and Pinson, E. N.   *The Speech Chain.* Bell Telephone Laboratories, 1963, 1967. Garden City, N.Y.: Anchor Books, 1973.

*Drills and Exercises in English Pronunciation: Stress and Intonation.* Prepared by English Language Services. New York: Macmillan, 1967.

Fant, G.   *Speech Sounds and Features.* Cambridge: M.I.T. Press, 1973.

Flanagan, J.   *Speech Analysis, Synthesis and Perception.* Berlin: Springer, 1972.

Fowler, H.   *A Dictionary of Modern English Usage* (2nd ed., revised by Sir Ernest Gowers). New York, London: Oxford University Press, 1965.

Fromkin, V. A.   The Non-anomalous Nature of Anomalous Utterances. *Language,* 47(1), 1971, pp. 27–52.

Fromkin, V., and Rodman, R.   *An Introduction to Language.* New York: Holt, Rinehart & Winston, 1974.

Gerber, S. E. (Ed.)   *Introductory Hearing Science: Physical and Psychological Concepts.* Philadelphia: Saunders, 1974.

Gerber, S. E.   The intelligibility of speech. In S. E. Gerber (Ed.), *Introductory Hearing Science: Physical and Psychological Concepts.* Philadelphia: Saunders, 1974.

Gleason, H. A., Jr.   *Workbook in Descriptive Linguistics.* New York: Holt, Rinehart & Winston, 1955.

Gordon, M. J.   *Speech Improvement.* Englewood Cliffs, N.J.: Prentice-Hall, 1974.

Gray, G. W., and Wise, C. M.   *The Bases of Speech* (3rd ed.). New York: Harper & Brothers, 1959.

Haggard, M. P.   The perception of speech. In S. E. Gerber (Ed.), *Introductory Hearing Science: Physical and Psychological Concepts.* Philadelphia: Saunders, 1974.

Harms, R. T.   *Introduction to Phonological Theory.* Englewood Cliffs, N.J.: Prentice-Hall, 1968.

Hill, A.   *Introduction to Linguistic Structures.* New York: Harcourt, Brace & World, 1958.

Hill, A.   Correctness and Style in English Composition. *College English* 12(5), 1951, pp. 280–285. Reprinted in G. Wilson, *A Linguistics Reader.* New York: Harper & Row, 1967, pp. 49–56.

Hook, J. N., and Mathews, E. G.   "Right" versus "Wrong" in Language and Levels of Usage. In J. N. Hook and E. G. Mathews, *Modern American Grammar and Usage.* New York: Ronald, 1956. Reprinted in D. Lee, *English Language Reader.* New York: Dodd, Mead, 1968, pp. 319–328.

Howell, R., and Vetter, H.   *Language in Behavior.* New York: Human Sciences Press, 1976.

Hyman, L. M.   *Phonology: Theory and Analysis.* New York: Holt, Rinehart & Winston, 1975.

Ingram, D.   *Phonological Disability in Children.* London: Edward Arnold, 1976.

Jakobson, R., Fant, G., and Halle, M.   *Preliminaries to Speech Analysis: The Distinctive Features and Their Correlates.* Cambridge: M.I.T. Press, 1969.

Jespersen, O.   *A Modern English Grammar on Historical Principles,* 7 vols. Phototyped Edition. Copenhagen: Munksgaard, 1949.

Jones, D.   *The Phoneme: Its Nature and Use* (3rd ed.). Cambridge, England: W. Heffer & Sons, 1967.

Jones, D.   *An Outline of English Phonetics* (9th ed.). New York: Dutton, 1972.

Joos, M.   Acoustic Phonetics. Language Monograph No. 23. *Language* 24(2) Supplement, April-June, 1948.

King, R. D.   *Historical Linguistics and Generative Grammar.* Englewood Cliffs, N.J.: Prentice-Hall, 1969.

Ladefoged, P.   *Elements of Acoustic Phonetics.* Chicago: University of Chicago Press, 1962.

Ladefoged, P.   *Three Areas of Experimental Phonetics.* London: Oxford University Press, 1967.

Ladefoged, P. *A Phonetic Study of West African Languages* (2nd ed.). London: Cambridge University Press, 1968.

Ladefoged, P. *A Course in Phonetics*. New York: Harcourt Brace Jovanovich, 1975.

Lado, R., and Fries, C. C. *English Pronunciation: Exercises in Sound Segments, Intonation, and Rhythm*. Ann Arbor: University of Michigan Press, 1954.

Laird, C. *Language in America*. New York: World, 1970.

Langacker, R. *Language and Its Structure: Some Fundamental Linguistic Concepts*. New York: Harcourt, Brace & World, 1968.

Lehiste, I. (Ed.). *Readings in Acoustic Phonetics*. Cambridge: M.I.T. Press, 1967.

Lehiste, I. *Suprasegmentals*. Cambridge: M.I.T. Press, 1970.

Lieberman, P. *Intonation, Perception, and Language*. Research Monograph No. 38. Cambridge: M.I.T. Press, 1967.

Lieberman, P. *On the Origins of Language: An Introduction to the Evolution of Human Speech*. New York: Macmillan, 1975.

Liles, B. L. *An Introductory Transformational Grammar*. Englewood Cliffs, N.J.: Prentice-Hall, 1971.

Linden, E. *Apes, Men and Language*. New York: Dutton, 1975, and Penguin Books, 1976.

Lloyd, D. Snobs, Slobs and the English Language. *American Scholar*, 20(3), 1951, pp. 279–288. Reprinted in G. Wilson, *A Linguistics Reader*. New York: Harper & Row, 1967, pp. 99–106.

Lloyd, D. Our National Mania for Correctness. *American Scholar*, 21(3), 1952, pp. 283–289. Reprinted in G. Wilson, *A Linguistics Reader*. New York: Harper & Row, 1967, pp. 57–62.

Lyons, J. *Introduction to Theoretical Linguistics*. London: Cambridge University Press, 1968.

McDavid, R. I. Dialect geography and social science problems. In H. B. Allen and G. N. Underwood (Eds.), *Readings in American Dialectology*. New York: Appleton-Century-Crofts, 1971.

MacKay, I. R. A. Tenseness in Vowels: An Ultrasonic Study. *Phonetica*, 34(5), 1977, pp. 325–351.

McNeill, D. *The Acquisition of Language: The Study of Developmental Psycholinguistics*. New York: Harper & Row, 1970.

Marckwardt, A. *American English*. New York: Oxford University Press, 1958.

Marshall, R. C. Conversion from Asai to Esophageal Speech. *Journal of Speech and Hearing Disorders*, 37(2), May 1972, pp. 262–266.

Mathews, M. *Americanisms: A Dictionary of Selected Americanisms or Historical Principles*. Chicago: University of Chicago Press, 1966.

Mencken, H. *The American Language* (4th ed.). New York: Knopf, 1936.

Miller, G. (Ed.). *Communication, Language, and Meaning: Psychological Perspectives*. New York: Basic Books, 1973.

Moore, G. P. *Organic Voice Disorders*. Englewood Cliffs, N.J.: Prentice-Hall, 1971.

Moorhouse, A. *The Triumph of the Alphabet: A History of Writing*. New York: Henry Schuman, 1953.

O'Connor, J. D. *Phonetics*. Baltimore: Penguin Books, 1973.

Oller, D. K. Regularities in Abnormal Child Phonology. *Journal of Speech and Hearing Disorders*, 38(1), Feb. 1973, p. 36.

Orkin, M. *Speaking Canadian English: An Informal Account of the English Language in Canada*. Toronto: General Publishing, 1970.

Palmer, J. M. Clinical Expectations in Esophageal Speech. *Journal of Speech and Hearing Disorders*, 35(2), May 1970, pp. 160–169.

Pedersen, H. *The Discovery of Language: Linguistic Science in the Nineteenth Century*. Translated by John Webster Spargo. Bloomington: Indiana University Press, 1967.

Perkell, J. S.  *Physiology of Speech Production: Results and Implications of a Quantitative Cineradiographic Study.* Cambridge: M.I.T. Press, 1969.

Peterson, H. A.  A Case Report of Speech and Language Training for a Two-Year-Old Laryngectomized Child. *Journal of Speech and Hearing Disorders,* 38(2), May 1973, pp. 275–278.

Pike, K. L.  *The Intonation of American English.* Ann Arbor: University of Michigan Press, 1945.

Pike, K. L.  *Phonemics: A Technique for Reducing Languages to Writing.* Ann Arbor: University of Michigan Press, 1947.

Pooley, R.  What Is Correct English Usage? *National Education Association Journal,* December 1960. Reprinted in D. Lee, *English Language Reader.* New York: Dodd, Mead, 1968, pp. 298–306.

Prator, C. H., Jr.  *Manual of American English Pronunciation* (rev. ed.). New York: Holt, Rinehart & Winston, 1957.

Premack, D.  Language in Chimpanzee? *Science,* May 21, 1971, pp. 808–822.

Rozin, P., Poritsky, S., and Sotsky, R.  American children with reading problems can easily learn to read English represented by Chinese characters. *Science,* 171, 1971, pp. 1264–1267.

Sapir, E.  *Language: An Introduction to the Study of Speech.* New York: Harcourt, Brace & World, 1949.

Schane, S. A.  *Generative Phonology.* Englewood Cliffs, N.J.: Prentice-Hall, 1973.

Scholes, R. J.  *Phonotactic Grammaticality.* The Hague: Mouton, 1966.

Schumsky, D. A.  Personal communication, 1977.

Shearer, W. W.  *Illustrated Speech Anatomy.* Springfield, Ill.: Thomas, 1963.

Smalley, W. A.  *Manual of Articulatory Phonetics* (rev. ed.). New York: Practical Anthropology, 1963.

Smith, F., and Miller, G. A. (Eds.).  *The Genesis of Language: A Psycholinguistic Approach.* Cambridge: M.I.T. Press, 1966.

Stewart, J. M.  Tongue Root Position in Akan Vowel Harmony. *Phonetica,* 16, 1967, pp. 185–204.

Twaddell, W. F.  *On Defining the Phoneme.* Language Monograph No. 16, March 1935, Linguistic Society of America. Reprinted, New York: Kraus Reprint Corporation, 1966.

Van den Berg, J.  Myoelastic-Aerodynamic Theory of Voice Production. *Journal of Speech and Hearing Research,* 1(3), Sept. 1958, pp. 227–243.

Van Riper, C.  *Speech Correction: Principles and Methods* (5th ed.). Englewood Cliffs, N.J.: Prentice-Hall, 1972.

Wakita, H.  The acoustics of speech. In S. E. Gerber (Ed.), *Introductory Hearing Science: Physical and Psychological Concepts.* Philadelphia: Saunders, 1974.

Wardhaugh, R.  *Introduction to Linguistics.* New York: McGraw-Hill, 1972.

Weinberg, B., and Westerhouse, J.  A Study of Pharyngeal Speech. *Journal of Speech and Hearing Disorders,* 38(1), February 1973, pp. 111–118.

West, J. J., and Weber, J. L.  A Phonological Analysis of the Spontaneous Language of a Four-Year-Old, Hard-of-Hearing Child. *Journal of Speech and Hearing Disorders,* 38(1), Feb. 1973, p. 25.

Wise, C.  *Applied Phonetics.* Englewood Cliffs, N.J.: Prentice-Hall, 1957.

Zemlin, W. R.  *Speech and Hearing Science: Anatomy and Physiology.* Englewood Cliffs, N.J.: Prentice-Hall, 1968.

Zwitman, D. H., and Calcaterra, T. C.  Phonation Using the Tracheo-Esophageal Shunt After Total Laryngectomy. *Journal of Speech and Hearing Disorders,* 38(3), August 1973, pp. 369–373.

# Appendix

## Phonetic Transcription Exercises

The following exercises are designed to give you practice in phonetic transcription. They may be supplemented with other materials or a laboratory manual.

Phonetic transcription provides the best method, outside of audio recording, of making a record of a speech event. Practice in using the phonetic alphabet will give you an opportunity to learn the conventions that are in use. Further, it will help you to get away from spelling and concentrate on the *sounds* of English speech.

It would be useful to review a few of the points brought up in Chapter 1 concerning phonetic transcription. Transcription is by no means an exact science. The transcription of speech is based on mutual agreement that two sounds are sufficiently similar in auditory impression that they can be represented with the same symbol. This is a matter of human judgment, which is subject to variation and certainly is tempered by the system of contrasts (phonemics) of one's own native language. Since this judgment is influenced by various factors, and since there is frequently ambiguity in the speech signal requiring interpretation using nonphonetic information (e.g., meaning), transcription is not something that—with present technology—could be accomplished by machine. It is based in large part on nonmeasurable phenomena.

In a practical sense, what this means is that you may sometimes record what does not exist acoustically and ignore acoustic information that is present. You will make errors based on what you know about English spelling and on what you know about correctness (Chapter 3). You will find that words spoken out of context have a low degree of intelligibility. Practice is the only method of reducing the errors one makes in transcription.

Since there is considerable diversity in the transcription systems in use, no answer key is given for these exercises (reasons for this diversity are discussed in Chapter 4). The instructor will indicate the appropriate transcriptions. The exercises have been roughly grouped according to sounds, but note that as a result of dialect differences, these groupings may not always be appropriate.

**Exercise 1**

The Front Vowels: /i, ɪ, e, ɛ, æ/

Text reference: Section 7-3 and preceding.

Transcribe the following words; that is, write them using phonetic symbols. The vowel symbols are listed above; the consonants in these words are all transcribed with symbols that will look familiar to you: /p/ as in pin; /t/ as in top; /k/ as in cough; /b/ as in bad; /d/ as in dog; /g/ as in good; /f/ as in food; /s/ as in sip; /v/ as in vat; /z/ as in zip; /r/ as in run; /l/ as in low; /m/ as in man; /n/ as in no; /h/ as in hat; and /w/ as in wave.

| | | | | | |
|---|---|---|---|---|---|
| 1. | heat | /hit/ | 21. | weep | ———— |
| 2. | stack | /stæk/ | 22. | wept | ———— |
| 3. | feast | ———— | 23. | sin | ———— |
| 4. | hate | ———— | 24. | fat | ———— |
| 5. | face | ———— | 25. | creep | ———— |
| 6. | sap | ———— | 26. | left | ———— |
| 7. | help | ———— | 27. | crate | ———— |
| 8. | hit | ———— | 28. | hilt | ———— |
| 9. | steak | ———— | 29. | feed | ———— |
| 10. | fist | ———— | 30. | west | ———— |
| 11. | trap | ———— | 31. | weeds | ———— |
| 12. | kept | ———— | 32. | still | ———— |
| 13. | trade | ———— | 33. | went | ———— |
| 14. | bend | ———— | 34. | fame | ———— |
| 15. | fast | ———— | 35. | mate | ———— |
| 16. | lip | ———— | 36. | fake | ———— |
| 17. | fade | ———— | 37. | fits | ———— |
| 18. | treat | ———— | 38. | men | ———— |
| 19. | mill | ———— | 39. | fell | ———— |
| 20. | pals | ———— | 40. | pin | ———— |

**Exercise 2**

The Back and Central Vowels: /u, ʊ, o, ʌ, ɔ, ɑ, ə, ɝ/

Text reference: Section 7-3.

These exercises continue to use only familiar consonants; some words contain front vowels as well.

| | | | | | | |
|---|---|---|---|---|---|---|
| 1. | puts | /pʊts/ | 21. | epic | ———— |
| 2. | bought | ———— | 22. | could | ———— |
| 3. | foster | ———— | 23. | rude | ———— |
| 4. | bus | ———— | 24. | faster | ———— |
| 5. | love | ———— | 25. | lovers | ———— |
| 6. | mull | ———— | 26. | water | ———— |
| 7. | hopes | ———— | 27. | cut | ———— |
| 8. | caught | ———— | 28. | bird | ———— |
| 9. | float | ———— | 29. | noon | ———— |
| 10. | cook | ———— | 30. | burn | ———— |
| 11. | putts | ———— | 31. | boater | ———— |
| 12. | sew | ———— | 32. | would | ———— |
| 13. | mood | ———— | 33. | upper | ———— |
| 14. | kook | ———— | 34. | boots | ———— |
| 15. | cot | ———— | 35. | haughty | ———— |
| 16. | fool | ———— | 36. | skipper | ———— |
| 17. | foot | ———— | 37. | crude | ———— |
| 18. | fasten | ———— | 38. | fuzz | ———— |
| 19. | mutter | ———— | 39. | winter | ———— |
| 20. | pots | ———— | 40. | curse | ———— |

**Exercise 3**
The Diphthongs and /ju/: /ai, au, ɔi, ju/
        Text reference: Section 7-5.

/ju/ is not a diphthong, but it is often grouped with the diphthongs because this sequence of sounds is so common that we often mistake it for one sound. There is a great deal of variation in the sound of the diphthongs depending on the dialect area and the surrounding consonants (see section 7-5); rather than arguing each case, we accept a standard phonemic representation. Also, there is a great variation in the representation of diphthongs; your instructor may prefer a different form. Here are some common transcriptions:

$$a\underset{\smile}{i} \quad aɪ \quad ay \quad aj \quad a^i$$

$$a\underset{\smile}{u} \quad aʊ \quad æw \quad aw \quad a^u$$

$$ɔ\underset{\smile}{i} \quad ɔɪ \quad ɔy \quad ɔj \quad ɔ^i$$

While it is common practice to omit the ligature in writing diphthongs (for example, /ai/ rather than /a͜i/), its use is recommended. For example, compare the word "naive" with the word "knives." The first word has a sequence of vowels in *two* syllables (/nɑiv/), whereas the latter has a diphthong in *one* syllable (/nɑ͜ivz/). Consistent use of the ligature thus makes the transcriptions clearer.

| | | | | |
|---|---|---|---|---|
| 1. | hives | /hɑ͜ivz/ | 21. | ewe | _____ |
| 2. | foils | _____ | 22. | mighty | _____ |
| 3. | buyer | _____ | 23. | eyes | _____ |
| 4. | fountain | _____ | 24. | trounce | _____ |
| 5. | house | _____ | 25. | write | _____ |
| 6. | miners | _____ | 26. | boiler | _____ |
| 7. | foist | _____ | 27. | dune | _____ |
| 8. | fighter | _____ | 28. | fryer | _____ |
| 9. | bounty | _____ | 29. | friar | _____ |
| 10. | about | _____ | 30. | bind | _____ |
| 11. | island | _____ | 31. | use | _____ or _____ |
| 12. | height | _____ | 32. | indict | _____ |
| 13. | oust | _____ | 33. | guide | _____ |
| 14. | glides | _____ | 34. | boys | _____ |
| 15. | sounder | _____ | 35. | joyful | _____ |
| 16. | mount | _____ | 36. | Cuba | _____ |
| 17. | bauxite | _____ | 37. | dyes | _____ |
| 18. | crisis | _____ | 38. | pound | _____ |
| 19. | precise | _____ | 39. | few | _____ |
| 20. | quite | _____ | 40. | counter | _____ |

**Exercise 4**

The Consonants (and Vowel Review)

Text reference: Chapter 8.

In the previous exercises, we have used only those consonants whose phonetic symbols look familiar to us: /p, t, k, b, d, g, f, s, v, z, r, l, m, n, h, w/. In this exercise, you will have practice in using those consonants whose symbols at first appear unfamiliar. These additional sounds and symbols are:

/θ/ as in thin, thought, ether, Beth
/ð/ as in the, though, either, bathe
/š/ as in ship, issue, sugar, nation (also written /ʃ/)
/ž/ as in vision, leisure (also written /ʒ/)
/ŋ/ as in sing, finger, think
/j/ as in yes, Europe
/ʍ/ as in which, when (only for those dialects that maintain this sound)*
/č/ as in church, chip, batch (also written /tʃ/ or /tš/)
/ǰ/ as in judge, jam (also written /dʒ/ or /dž/)

| | | | | | |
|---|---|---|---|---|---|
| 1. | judging | /ǰʌ́ǰɪŋ/ | 21. | vision | ———— |
| 2. | issue | ———— | 22. | chopper | ———— |
| 3. | yellow | ———— | 23. | charger | ———— |
| 4. | thin | ———— | 24. | chamber | ———— |
| 5. | ether | ———— | 25. | garage | ———— |
| 6. | batches | ———— | 26. | away | ———— |
| 7. | charging | ———— | 27. | pleasure | ———— |
| 8. | push | ———— | 28. | thought | ———— |
| 9. | jamb | ———— | 29. | bashing | ———— |
| 10. | yes | ———— | 30. | leisure | ———— |
| 11. | shipper | ———— | 31. | virgin | ———— |
| 12. | lane | ———— | 32. | finger | ———— |
| 13. | hutch | ———— | 33. | thorough | ———— |
| 14. | think | ———— | 34. | rasping | ———— |
| 15. | badger | ———— | 35. | hatchet | ———— |
| 16. | whine | ———— | 36. | sinker | ———— |
| 17. | weather | ———— | 37. | runner | ———— |
| 18. | whether | ———— | 38. | trade | ———— |
| 19. | watch | ———— | 39. | mashing | ———— |
| 20. | Beth | ———— | 40. | manning | ———— |

* Note: In handwritten work, the symbol /ʰʷ/, or the combination /hw/, is less open to misinterpretation than the symbol /ʍ/, which can be mistaken for an m.

**Exercise 5**

Practice with Vowels and Consonants

This is a continuation of exercise 4, giving you practice transcribing English speech sounds.

| | | | | | |
|---|---|---|---|---|---|
| 1. | shoving | ———— | 21. | witches | ———— |
| 2. | zany | ———— | 22. | pneumatic | ———— |
| 3. | sinned | ———— | 23. | wither | ———— |
| 4. | sang | ———— | 24. | only | ———— |
| 5. | fiend | ———— | 25. | jelly | ———— |
| 6. | bother | ———— | 26. | chafing | ———— |
| 7. | tough | ———— | 27. | lanky | ———— |
| 8. | colonel | ———— | 28. | cherries | ———— |
| 9. | hiccough | ———— | 29. | perception | ———— |
| 10. | posh | ———— | 30. | chalet | ———— |
| 11. | jaguar | ———— | 31. | lathe | ———— |
| 12. | feather | ———— | 32. | Cairo | ———— |
| 13. | bath | ———— | 33. | George | ———— |
| 14. | chomps | ———— | 34. | omission | ———— |
| 15. | ethyl | ———— | 35. | shuffle | ———— |
| 16. | hanger | ———— | 36. | raging | ———— |
| 17. | dizzy | ———— | 37. | shroud | ———— |
| 18. | flutter | ———— | 38. | warfare | ———— |
| 19. | languid | ———— | 39. | lithe | ———— |
| 20. | plumber | ———— | 40. | wanted | ———— |

**Exercise 6**

Stress

Transcribe these words, and mark the stress as indicated in Chapter 9.

| | | | | | |
|---|---|---|---|---|---|
| 1. | omission | /omíʃən/ | 16. | thirty | ———— |
| 2. | deception | ———— | 17. | thirteen | ———— |
| 3. | perforate | ———— | 18. | engineer | ———— |
| 4. | perimeter | ———— | 19. | redundant | ———— |
| 5. | periscope | ———— | 20. | transpose | ———— |
| 6. | heyday | ———— | 21. | obscene | ———— |
| 7. | watchdog | ———— | 22. | obscenity | ———— |
| 8. | renegade | ———— | 23. | oceanography | ———— |
| 9. | windshield | ———— | 24. | trajectory | ———— |
| 10. | Olympic | ———— | 25. | photoelectric | ———— |
| 11. | Iceland | ———— | 26. | personnel | ———— |
| 12. | Icelandic | ———— | 27. | repetition | ———— |
| 13. | mobile home | ———— | 28. | repetitive | ———— |
| 14. | Roman | ———— | 29. | scarecrow | ———— |
| 15. | romantic | ———— | 30. | festivity | ———— |

**Exercise 7**

Broad and Narrow Transcription

Text reference: Chapter 11.

After studying Chapters 10 and 11, particularly section 11-8, transcribe each of the following words twice. First, make a **broad,** or **phonemic,** transcription of each word (including stress), as has been done in the previous exercises. Then, make a **narrow** transcription of the same words, including as much phonetic detail as possible. There is no one correct answer to the narrow transcriptions, since more or less detail could be included, and there is much dialect variation in the pronunciation of these words.

**Samples:**

| | | |
|---|---|---|
| pool | /pul/ | [pʰuəɬ] |
| biting | /báitìŋ/ | [bɑ́ərìŋ], [bə́ɨtìŋ], etc. (many varieties of diphthong, intervocalic /t/, and word-final -ing, depending on dialect) |
| heard | /hərd/ | [hɚ·d˺] |

1. phonetics ——————— ———————
2. button ——————— ———————
3. knots ——————— ———————
4. trader ——————— ———————
5. loudness ——————— ———————
6. dress shop ——————— ———————
7. interesting ——————— ———————
8. whatnot ——————— ———————
9. battleground ——————— ———————
10. police ——————— ———————
11. supposing ——————— ———————
12. vulture ——————— ———————
13. discus ——————— ———————
14. cows ——————— ———————
15. house ——————— ———————
16. training ——————— ———————
17. united ——————— ———————
18. lowly ——————— ———————
19. soldier ——————— ———————
20. kept ——————— ———————

21. coped    _____    _____

22. incapable    _____    _____

23. children    _____    _____

24. renting    _____    _____

25. svelte    _____    _____

26. company    _____    _____

27. electrician    _____    _____

28. hinting    _____    _____

29. parade    _____    _____

30. during    _____    _____

# Glossary

Most of the important terms used in this book, including some words outside phonetic science, are given brief definitions here. Many of these terms are defined more fully in the text; you may find the index useful in locating those definitions. The italicized words are given their own definition within the glossary.

**affricate** (n): A single speech sound that can be analyzed as the sequence of a *plosive* followed immediately by a *homorganic fricative*.

**allophone** (n): A variant form of a *phoneme*; a *conditioned* variant.

**alveolar ridge** (n): The ridge just behind the upper front teeth, in front of the *palate*. Adj: alveolar.

**AmerIndian** (adj): Referring to (the languages of) the native peoples of the New World.

**amplitude** (n): With respect to sound waves, the amount of energy present; perceived as loudness. Indicated pictorially by the extent of deflection from the baseline.

**anomaly** (n): Something that is abnormal, peculiar, or irregular. Adj: anomalous.

**aphasia** (n): Loss of the ability to use (spoken) language; *dysphasia*. Adj: aphasic.

**apical** (adj): Referring to the apex (tip) (of the tongue).

**approximant** (n): A class of speech sounds characterized by close proximity, but usually not contact, of the *articulators*.

**approximate** (vb): To bring close together; to contact lightly.

**apraxia** (n): Paralysis (of the speech mechanism).

**arresting** (adj): The final consonant in a *closed* syllable is the arresting consonant.

**articulate** (vb): To move or position the speech organs so as to produce a speech sound.

**articulator** (n): An organ of speech, usually above the larynx, that is moved or *approximated* in speech.

**arytenoid cartilages** (n): The cartilages to which the back ends of the *vocal folds* are attached. They are mobile like levers, and they tense and position the vocal folds.

**aspirated** (adj): Said of a *plosive;* pronounced with greater pressure so that its *release* is accompanied by a mild explosion of air.

**aspiration** (n): The explosion of air that may accompany *plosive release.*

**assimilation** (n): A general process in articulation by which individual speech sounds become in some way more like those around them.

**audiology** (n): The study of hearing; evaluation of hearing is one of its areas.

**bilabial** (adj): Involving both lips.

**bronchi** (n): The tubes connecting the lungs with the *trachea.*

**cardinal vowels** (n): A set of vowels at the extremities of the vowel quadrangle that are used as reference points in classifying other vowels; usually /i, e, ɛ, æ, u, o, ɔ, ɑ/, but more extreme in their articulation than their English counterparts.

**cleft lip** (n): A congenital cleft or split in the upper lip; harelip.

**cleft palate** (n): A congenital cleft or split in the palate.

**close** (adj): Said of vowels; articulation above the mid vowel height; high.

**closed** (adj): Said of a syllable; terminating with a consonant sound.

**cluster** (n): A group of consonants in the same syllable without a vowel between.

**coarticulation** (n): A form of *assimilation* that affects the secondary rather than the primary *place of articulation.*

**cognate sounds** (n): Not a technical term; used here to indicate a sound that shares most features of the sound under discussion; for example, /p/ is the voiceless cognate of /b/, which is voiced.

**communication disorder** (n): A broad term for various pathological conditions of speech or language, including *aphasia, apraxia,* articulation disorders, *cleft palate*, *cleft lip*, delayed speech or language, *laryngectomy*, stuttering, voice (laryngeal) disorders, or severe foreign accent.

**conditioned** (adj): Said of speech sounds or *allophones*; produced or modified as a result of other sounds in the *environment*.

**cycle** (n): A dimensionless unit indicating one full sound wave.

**dental** (adj): Referring to an articulation involving the teeth.

**dental** (n): A speech sound whose articulation involves the teeth.

**descriptive phonetics** (n): That branch of phonetics dealing with a detailed specification of speech sounds and their patterning.

**diacritic** (n): A mark used in conjunction with a letter or syllabic character to indicate the quality of the sound represented; an "accent mark."

**dialect** (n): An identifiable regional or social variant form of a language, characterized by its vocabulary, grammar, and pronunciation.

**diaphragm** (n): The muscular band separating the chest cavity from the abdominal cavity; it plays a role in respiration and therefore in speech.

**diphthong** (n): A single vowel nucleus that changes quality within a single syllable.

**dysphasia** (n): A partial loss of the ability to use (spoken) language. Adj: dysphasic.

**dyspraxia** (n): Partial paralysis (of the speech mechanism).

**egressive** (adj): In reference to the direction of airflow from the mouth or nose, outgoing.

**elision** (n): The dropping of one or more phones in the pronunciation of a word. Vb: elide.

**environment, phonetic** (n): Refers to the *phones* and *suprasegmentals* in the immediate vicinity of the phone under discussion.

**epenthesis** (n): The addition of a sound, usually to allow easier transition from the preceding sound to the one following.

**epiglottis** (n): A structure in the *larynx* that covers the entrance to the larynx during swallowing; it has no role in speech.

**esophageal speech** (n): Speech produced using air that has been swallowed or "injected" into the *esophagus*; used by *laryngectomees*.

**esophagus** (n): The tube originating just below the pharynx, through which food and fluids descend to the stomach.

**flap** (n): A consonant produced with a very brief occlusion, normally apicoalveolar. May have an /r/-like quality, as in /ř/, or not, as in /ɾ/. Adj: flapped.

Note: In the IPA, the symbol /r/ represents a flap, but since we use this symbol for the American English /r/, the symbol /ř/ is used to unambiguously represent the flapped r-sound.

**formant** (n): A band of resonant energy that, in combination with several others, acoustically characterizes a particular vowel sound.

**fortis** (adj): Of plosive consonants, produced with a high degree of air pressure in the oral cavity, usually released with *aspiration*.

**frequency** (n): The number of times per second a sound wave (*cycle*) is repeated; measured in *hertz* (Hz).

**fricative** (n): A class of consonants in which air is forced through a constriction, producing a noisy turbulence.

**fundamental frequency** (n): In speech, the frequency of vocal fold vibration (as opposed to the resonant frequencies); also, the basic frequency of a vibrating object or a sound, as opposed to the *harmonics*.

**glide** (n): A class of speech sounds that are vowel-like in nature but must precede or follow a vowel to make a syllable; characterized by approximation of the articulators (not sufficient for friction) followed by movement of the articulators.

**glossectomee** (n): An individual who has undergone *glossectomy*.

**glossectomy** (n): Surgical removal of the tongue.

**glottalization** (n): Of a consonant; produced simultaneously with a glottal stop. Vb: glottalize.

**glottis** (n): The space between the *vocal folds*.

**grammar** (n): The *rules* of a language taken all together.

**haplology** (n): The dropping of one of two identical or similar syllables in sequence.

**harmonics** (n): Multiples of a *fundamental frequency*; called overtones in music.

**hertz** (n): A unit of frequency; one hertz is one cycle per second. Abbrev: Hz.

**homophone** (n): A word whose pronunciation is coincidentally like another; not dependent on spelling. Such words are said to be *homophonous* (adj); the phenomenon is called *homophony* (n).

**homorganic** (adj): Said of a speech sound; having the same *place of articulation*.

**idiolect** (n): The *dialect* or variety of language peculiar to an individual person.

**ingressive** (adj): In reference to the direction of airflow from the mouth or nose, ingoing.

**intercostal muscles** (n): The muscles controlling the rib cage; they play a role in respiration and speech.

**intonation** (n): Patterns of changes in the fundamental frequency of the voice, related to the grammatical structure of the sentence or discourse, that convey meaning.

**labial** (adj): Having to do with the lips.

**labial** (n): A class of speech sounds articulated with the lips.

**labialization** (n): The introduction of lip-rounding or lip-protrusion as a secondary articulation; rounding. Vb: labialize.

**laminal** (adj): Having to do with the blade of the tongue.

**laryngectomee** (n): A person who has undergone *laryngectomy*.

**laryngectomy** (n): Surgical removal of the larynx.

**larynx** (n): A cartilaginous structure at the top of the *trachea*, below the *pharynx*, that contains the *vocal folds*.

**lateral** (adj): Referring to the sides.

**lateral** (n): A class of speech sounds in which the mouth is blocked centrally by the tongue and air is allowed to pass out over the sides.

**length** (n): In reference to speech sounds, the duration, not the *quality*.

**lenis** (adj): Said of plosive consonants; produced with a low degree of air pressure in the oral cavity; usually released without *aspiration*.

**liaison** (n): A type of *sandhi* occurring in French in which word-final consonants are pronounced only when the following word begins with a vowel and is part of the same phrase.

**lingual** (adj): Referring to the tongue.

**linguistics** (n): A discipline that studies all aspects of human language.

**liquid** (n): A class of speech sounds, including /l/ and /r/, that are characterized by approximation of the articulators and a vowel-like quality.

**locus** (n): The extrapolated starting point of the formant transitions that acoustically characterize plosive consonants. Pl: loci.

**long** (adj): Said of a speech sound; a description of its duration, not its *quality*.

**manner of articulation** (n): In the classification of consonants, the type of articulation; for example, *plosive, fricative, nasal*.

**metathesis** (n): The inversion of two adjacent phones, either as a historical change or as an error.

**monophthong** (n): A vowel whose quality does not change; a "pure" vowel.

**morpheme** (n): In linguistic classification, the smallest unit that can be said to have a meaning; for example, walked contains two morphemes, walk and -ed (indicating past tense).

**mutually intelligible** (adj): Two languages or dialects are mutually intelligible if the speakers of one can understand the speakers of the other, and vice versa.

**nasal** (adj): Referring to the nose.

**nasal** (n): A class of consonants in which the oral cavity is blocked and air is diverted through the nose.

**nasalization** (n): A secondary articulation of a vowel resulting from *articulation* with a lowered *velum*. Vb: nasalize.

**normative phonetics** (n): A discipline devoted to correction of phonetic aspects of speech.

**nucleus** (n): The vowel or *vocalic* sound found in every syllable.

**onomatopoeic** (adj): Said of a word; imitating the sound it represents; for example, bow-wow, cuckoo.

**open** (adj): Said of a syllable; ending with a vowel sound. Said of a vowel; produced with low tongue and jaw height; low.

**palatal** (n): Any speech sound articulated with the tongue arched in the region of the palate.

**palatalization** (n): The addition of a secondary articulation in the palatal region; also, a change in the primary *place of articulation* to the palatal region. Vb: palatalize.

**palate** (n): That part of the roof of the mouth that extends from the *alveolar ridge* to the *velum*, with bony support. Adj: palatal.

**period** (n): The length of time required to complete one full *cycle* of a (sound) wave.

**pharyngealization** (n): The addition of a secondary articulation in the pharyngeal region. Vb: pharyngealize.

**pharynx** (n): The cavity behind the root of the tongue and above the larynx that serves as a passageway for food and air, and is a resonator in speech. Adj: pharyngeal.

**phonate** (vb): To vibrate the *vocal folds*, usually in speech. N: phonation.

**phone** (n): Any speech sound, without reference to its distinctive role in a particular language.

**phoneme** (n): A group of *phones* having the same contrastive or distinctive function in a particular language, and usually perceived by speakers of that language as the "same" sound when produced in expected *environments*.

**phonotactics** (n): The study of the ways in which *phonemes* are combined and ordered in the syllables and words of a particular language or *dialect*.

**place of articulation** (n): In the traditional classification of consonants, the position of the primary articulator (usually ignoring the tongue); for example, if the tongue touches the palate, the place of articulation is *palatal*.

**plosion** (n): The *release* of a *plosive*.

**plosive** (n): A consonant articulated with the oral cavity blocked at some point, resulting in a build-up of intraoral pressure and explosive *release* of that pressure.

**polysyllabic** (adj): Said of a word or phrase; having more than two syllables.

**postvocalic** (adj): Following a vowel.

**pulmonic** (adj): Referring to the lungs.

**pure vowel** (n): A *monophthong*.

**quality** (n): In reference to a vowel, the particular vowel sound (as opposed to its *length*).

**rarefy** (n): To reduce the pressure of a gas, to make the same number of molecules fill a greater space. N: rarefaction.

**reduced vowel** (n): A vowel that, under the influence of a lesser degree of word stress, tends toward an indistinct *quality* and a mid-central articulation.

**release** (n): With reference to a *plosive*, the moment at which the *articulators* are parted and air pressure can escape. Vb: release.

**releasing** (adj): The first consonant of a syllable is the releasing consonant.

**remedial phonetics** (n): *Normative phonetics*.

**rhotacized vowel:** A vowel having an r̲-like quality.

**rule** (n): A formal statement of the operation of some aspect of language; the rules taken all together form the *grammar* of a language.

**sandhi** (n): An assimilation or combinatory process that crosses a word boundary.

**segment** (n): A single speech sound, or *phone*.

**semantic** (adj): With reference to meaning of words.

**semivowel** (n): A voiced *glide*.

**short** (adj): Said of a speech sound; a description of its duration, not its *quality*.

**signs** (n): The manual gestures in the language of the deaf.

**spectrograph** (n): An instrument that analyzes a complex sound into its component frequencies and displays them graphically; such a display is a spectrogram.

**speech community** (n): A group of people speaking the same language and interacting verbally with one another.

**speech pathology** (n): The study of aberrations in speech production and of methods to correct these aberrations.

**speed of propagation** (n): Of a wave, the speed with which the wavefront advances through a medium.

**stoma** (n): A surgically produced opening in the body; *laryngectomees* breathe through a stoma in the front of the throat connected directly to the trachea.

**stress** (n): An emphasis given to a syllable or word, manifested as increased distinctiveness or loudness, and reduced *assimilation*.

**supraglottal organs** (n): The speech organs above the larynx.

**suprasegmental** (n): Those aspects of the phonetic quality of speech that cannot be divided into *phones* or *segments*, such as *intonation* and *stress*.

**surd** (adj): Voiceless.

**syllabary** (n): A group of symbols representing syllables of a spoken language and used to write that language; e.g., the Japanese Katakana and Hiragana.

**synonym** (n): A word having the same (or similar) meaning as another.

**tone** (n): Phonemic use of the pitch of the voice to distinguish words; do not confuse with *intonation*.

**trachea** (n): The windpipe; the tube connecting the *bronchi* to the *larynx*.

**umlaut** (n): A form of vowel harmony peculiar to the Germanic family of languages, including English; a *diacritic* used in German to indicate vowel *quality*.

**velum** (n): The muscular part of the roof of the mouth, behind the palate, that acts as a valve to the nasal passages. Adj: velar (in reference to tongue position in relation to the velum); velic (in reference to movement of the velum).

**vocal folds** (n): A pair of muscle bands in the *larynx* that may be made to vibrate in speech.

**vocalic** (adj): Referring to a vowel; vowel-like.

**vocalization** (n): A sound produced with the vocal organs, including speech, cries, moans, and the calls of animals having a superficially similar vocal apparatus as man.

**voiced** (adj): Said of a speech sound; produced with simultaneous *vocal fold* vibration.

**voiceless** (adj): Said of a speech sound; produced without simultaneous *vocal fold* vibration.

# Index

# Index

In this index, "n" following a page number indicates a footnote; "fig" indicates a figure; and "tab" indicates a table.

velar, 122
voiceless, 121
nasal (distinctive feature), 230
nasal cavity, 54 fig, 55, 81
nasal plosion, 166–167
nasal twang, 163
nasalization, 163
nasalized vowels, 107–108
neutralization, 184, 187
noise, 77, 134
noncontinuant, 170
Norwegian, 16
nucleus, 198
null sign, 237

octave, 72
Old English. See English, Old
onomatopoeic, 39, 39 n, 40
open o, 97
open syllable, 169, 199
opposition, 228
oral airstream, 59, 61 tab
oral cavity, 54 fig, 55, 81
organs of speech, 53–60, 54 fig
  subglottal, 58–60
  supraglottal, 54–56
overtone, 75

pair, minimal, 181
palatal, 55
palate, 54 fig, 55
  cleft, 60–61, 118, 163
palatalization, 162
Passy, Paul, 46
pathological conditions, 18. See also
    communication disorders
pauses, 213–214
period, 68
periodicity, 68
pharyngeal, 55
  airstream, 59, 61 tab, 62 fig
  cavity, 81, 84
  speech, 60, 60 n
pharyngealization, 163–164
pharynx, 54 fig, 55
  in vowel production, 91, 93
phase, 75, 79
phenomena, combinatory, 173–175. See
    also assimilation
phonation, 57, 57 fig
phone, 90
phoneme, 90 n, 177–194
  combinations of, 197
  contrastiveness of, 180–182
  phones and, 187–188
  practical implications of, 189–191
  predictability of, 180–181, 182–183
  and stress, 185–186

phonemic transcription, 191–192
phonetic alphabet. See International
    Phonetic Alphabet
phonetic context, 160
phonetic element, 37
phonetic environment, 160
phonetic similarity, 180
phonetic transcription, 191, 192
phonetician, 11, 22, 33, 36, 47, 90
phonetics, 12, 27–29
  and phonemics, 188–189
  practical, 29. See also
      communication disorders
phonetization, 40
phonological rules, 235–243
phonology, 227–243
  and nonnormal speech, 237–242
phonotactic restrictions
  and phoneme, 181
  and phonological rules, 236
phonotactics, 197–206
  practical implications of, 204–206
phrase stress, 210
physical exertion, 57
physics of sound, 65–87
physiologist, 22
pictograph, 31
pictographic writing, 31
pig latin, 200
pitch, 74 n, 75, 216
place of articulation, 115
  acoustics and, 131–132
plosion
  lateral, 167
  nasal, 166–167
plosive, 116–119, 125
  acoustics of, 131–134
  alveolar, 116–117
  aspiration of, 166
  bilabial, 116
  dental, 117
  glottal, 117
    acoustics of, 135
  release of, 118–119, 165–166
  released/unreleased, 118, 165–166
  velar, 117
Portuguese, 15, 43, 83, 107
practical phonetics, 29. See also
    communication disorders
predictability (of phoneme), 180–181,
    182–183
pressure, 71, 72, 73 fig
  intraoral, 118
  of plosives, 188
primary articulation, 162
primary stress, 143
propagation, speed of, 68
prosodeme, 185
psychology, clinical, 21, 22

pulmonic airstream, 59, 61 tab, 62 fig
punctuation, 216
*Pygmalion*, 21

quadrangle, vowel, 91–92, 96 fig, 109
   and stress, 144
quality, vowel, 98
quantity, vowel, 98
question intonation, 216

r-coloring, 95
r-less dialects, 96
race, 16
radical, 37
rarefaction, 71
rate, 213
realization, 14
rebus writing, 33, 36–37, 41
reduction, vowel, 143–147
redundancy rule, 232–233, 236
release of plosives, 118–119, 165–166
releasing consonant, 199
religion, 16
resonance, 76–78
resonant frequency, 76
resonator, 76–78
   hard-walled, 83
   material of, 83
   shape of, 83
   size of, 83
   soft-walled, 83
retroflex, 129–130, 129 fig
rhotacization, 95–96, 98
   and phonemics, 189
rhythm, 214–215
   stress-timed, 215, 221
   syllable-timed, 215, 221
Roman alphabet, 42–43
Roman numerals, 235 n
Romanian, 15
root of tongue. *See* tongue, root
rule
   descriptive, 11
   linguistic, 11, 14
   optional, 235
   phonological, 235–243
   prescriptive, 12
   redundancy, 232–233, 236
rule-system, 13, 16. *See also* grammar
Russian, 40, 42

sandhi, 174–175
   of stress, 213
   of tones, 220
sarcasm, 218
schwa, 96, 97
   and stress, 142, 143
schwar, 97
   in diphthongs, 100

second-language learner. *See* foreign
   speaker
second-language teaching, 22
secondary articulation, 162
secondary stress, 143
segment, 90
semantics, 14
semivowels, 123
sentence stress, 210–211
Sequoya, 39
Shaw, G. B., 21, 43
signs, 14
similarity, phonetic, 180
sinusoid, 79
slash marks, 191, 193, 194
Slinky, 69, 70, 70 fig
sonorant (distinctive feature), 232
sound
   physics of, 65–86
   speed of, 65
   wave motion of, 69
sound wave. *See* wave
Spanish, 15, 40, 101, 117, 118, 122, 149,
   185, 186
special education, 22
spectrogram
   of consonants, 136–139
   of formant transitions, 132–133
   frequency scale, 113
   of sentence, 139
   of soft-drink bottle resonator, 78
   of stress, 155–156
   and striations on, 113
   time scale, 113
   of vowels, 109–112
speech, 9–11, 13–14
   artificial, 85
   esophageal, 60, 61 tab
   sounds, 89–90
speech community, 14
speech organs, 53–60
speech pathology, 6–7, 21–22
speech scientist, 22
speed of propagation, 68
spelling pronunciation, 24–26, 44
spike, 134
spoonerism, 174
standard dialect, 23, 26
statement intonation, 216
stop, 118 n, 166
   glottal, 117
      acoustics of, 135
stress
   acoustics of, 154–156
   and assimilation, 164–165
   contrastive, 152
   contrastive and emphatic, 211–212
   in diphthongs, 148
   distinguishing function of, 151–152